Realistic Hope

Realistic Hope

Facing Global Challenges

Edited by
Angela Wilkinson and Betty Sue Flowers

Amsterdam University Press

Cover design: David Fartek
Lay-out: Crius Group, Hulshout

ISBN	978 94 6298 724 1
e-ISBN	978 90 4853 874 4 (pdf)
DOI	10.5117/9789462987241
NUR	740

To our children, for their future

Ruairi McNicholas
Emer McNicholas
John Michael Flowers

Contents

Foreword: Realising Hope

Ged R. Davis

Thinking about realistic hope

Hope and fear are universal in human nature, embedded as they are in the structure of the brain. Fear is situated in the ancient amygdala, the source of the 'flight or fight' response, and hope in the more recently evolved frontal cortex. This capacity to envision the future also relies partly on the hippocampus, a brain structure that is crucial to memory.[1] Recent studies indicate that directing our thoughts of the future towards the positive – hope – is a result of our frontal cortex communicating with sub-cortical regions deep in our brain.[2] The human tendency to hope is a consequence of this evolution of our brains.

But hope and fear are not just about the functioning of the brain. Philosophers have for millennia been reflecting on hope.[3] The contemporary debate about hope takes as its starting point what has been called the 'standard account', which analyses hope in terms of a wish or desire for an outcome and a belief concerning the outcome's possibility.[4]

Those things we hope for and those things we fear are very much shaped by the prevailing social context and dominant beliefs. For example, hope for a life after death was one of the major topics in medieval philosophy, as is still true for many today. The modern secular world view of hope conceives of the future as a space for potential fundamental change and, as such, hope is integral to the notion of social progress. But social progress can evoke new hopes and fears, whether as a result of new technologies – for example, the constructive solutions addressing pandemics or the destructive threat of

---

1   'Patients with damage to their hippocampus are unable to recollect the past, but they are also unable to construct detailed images of future scenarios. They appear to be stuck in time. The rest of us constantly move back and forth in time' (Sharot, 'The Optimism Bias').
2   *Ibid.*
3   Bloeser and Stahl.
4   Section 3 on 'The Standard Account and the Rationality of Hope' in Bloeser and Stahl.

Wilkinson, Angela, and Betty Sue Flowers (eds.), *Realistic Hope: Facing Global Challenges.* Amsterdam, Amsterdam University Press, 2018.
DOI: 10.5117/9789462987241_FORE

nuclear or biological weapons – or of impacts on the environment, besides many other possible changes.

Modern sociologists see hope as relational and social.[5] They recognise hope as a public good, highlighting the benefits of growing up in a society within which one can hope, rather than face despair. But hope is also a private good and part of life. One never knows what surprises may lie ahead, so one needs to be alert and hard-headed about how best to create a better future.

So how might we define 'realistic hope' for the pragmatic practitioner, such as the authors of this book, seeking to enable positive change that endures?

First, the outcome of the process must reflect the interests of all concerned and what we collectively believe to be good. Second, the process must examine the widest set of possibilities and consequences regarding the future and ensure that they are the product of analytically open and honest actions. And third, the process must be active in nature, inspirational, and capable of implementing actions that 'make a difference'.

But the ability to make a difference depends on how the powerful use power to effect change, and whether they create a space where collective actions can be implemented. Much depends on whether our view of human nature is that of democratic ideals, as espoused by Rousseau, who believed that people are 'naturally good', or more like Hobbes, who believed in the authoritarian use of power because people are 'naturally wicked'.

So there are boundaries to realistic hope. Some are shaped by our individual beliefs and others by our collective beliefs. These boundaries depend on how we answer questions such as, 'Are people naturally good or wicked?' 'Is our stance in approaching challenges naturally passive or active?' 'Are we prone to unfounded utopian wishful thinking or lean towards evidence-based realism?' 'Do we understand what can and cannot be changed?' or 'Does this lead us to being open to new possibilities?'

Acting with realistic hope

We are in the midst of a grand transition rife with extraordinary challenges of vast scale and with changes that needs to be managed over decades. Some of these challenges are covered in this book – international security, climate change, global poverty, water, digital technologies, and the future of work, to name a few. And many of these have been described as 'wicked problems'.[6]

---

5   Miyazaki and Swedberg.
6   See, for example, Camillus; Rittel and Webber.

A wicked problem has innumerable causes, is tough to describe, and doesn't have a right answer. It is one in which a purely scientific or rational approach cannot be applied because of the lack of a clear problem definition and the differing perspectives of stakeholders. How are we to best address them? Too often most approaches seem ideological, rooted in the present, narrow in scope, limited in perspective, and lacking in imagination. Most current governments are proving to be incapable of addressing these challenges. We are facing problems without borders and governments without solutions!

But we can see the elements of a silent revolution underway that promises to offer us the realistic hope that apt solutions can be found. In many cases those involved in finding solutions are international entities, ad hoc groups, non-governmental organisations, cities and regions, enterprises, and, only occasionally, national governments.

Faced with a challenge of substance, how might we go about finding solutions that will last? What can we learn from the many approaches practitioners have developed in finding solutions? Below we highlight the five main steps, based on our experience, that we need to employ in any fully designed process for realising hope.[7]

These five steps are conception, framing, scenarios, vision and actions. Let us examine them in turn.

1   Conception

The starting point is to recognise a challenge or problem area, a purpose, and a time horizon for a future-oriented project. The agreement to proceed should carry with it a commitment to act, consequent on the process being completed. In many cases, the definition of a problem area is straightforward. For example, an energy company examines energy futures with the purpose of identifying new risks and opportunities and developing a strategy prior to new actions, or a government commits to a country review with the aim of identifying current challenges and new policies. But increasingly, global forces and a disruptive environment are leading us to address more complex problem areas. For example, today we cannot understand energy futures without understanding climate change and in some regions both food and water futures.

The start of a new project requires an initial framing of the problem, the identification of those stakeholders and experts who are to be involved, and a judgement about what budget is needed. Critical for any futures-oriented

7   For those interested in a summary description of this process, see Davis *et al.*, and for a fuller description see Meredith *et al.*

project is the selection of participants that allows for the broadest set of perspectives feasible, the adoption of rules of engagement among participants that encourage dialogue as the main mode of communication, and a bias towards learning.

2 Framing

The starting point is a review of the interviews of participants in the project and the opinions of experts as a catalyst for conversations on the relevant framing of the problem area. Empathy and dialogue are critical to building collective ownership of the framing. The outcome of the framing leads to a focused research programme, which contributes to the subsequent work on futures development.

3 Scenarios

A small number of alternative futures, that is, scenarios, are developed to explore the key dimensions of the framing of the problem area. Narratives are developed for each scenario. Predictive analytics and systems modelling over the chosen time horizon reinforce the storylines. The scenarios provide a context for developing a strategy, policies, and a desired vision of the future.

4 Vision

Values are central to the creation of vision. In some cases they may be a reflection of goals stated elsewhere – for example, the Universal Declaration of Human Rights or the 2015 Sustainable Development Goals. The vision must be not just inspirational, but also realistic, set in the context of the scenarios. Clarifying a vision of the future – in effect, stating our 'realistic hope' – is the catalyst for identifying those actions needed to create change.

5 Actions

The participants who have developed the vision have a leading role in identifying the actions that will bring about change; but many others will be brought into the process of implementing and legitimising change. The actions are not just about new strategy and policies, but may involve a wider range, including new investments, institutional development, and a reconfiguration of assets and the skill base.

If all of these steps are covered correctly, such a process can deliver genuine solutions. But there are pitfalls to be avoided: limited stakeholder representation; lack of dialogue and the inability to build co-ownership of the problem's framing; weak scenario narratives not backed-up by adequate analysis; a vision lacking clarity, detail, and inspiration; and a lack of courage in the implementation of needed change.

And for a wicked problem there is no solution that lasts forever. As our knowledge expands, as new stakeholders emerge, and as mind-sets change, the framing of the problems will also change, and relevant scenarios will need modification. At some point a re-examination of the problem will be needed, using the process above. This may include re-visioning and identifying new actions. Tough problems are, in effect, 'infinite games'[8] and need to be re-addressed from time to time. You do not solve a problem like climate change or global poverty in a single attempt, but rather commit to address the problem again and again until it has been re-solved or dis-solved over time.

In summary, we have processes and tools tested for tackling wicked problems. They use our knowledge and ability to imagine the future, catalyse new actions to realise our deepest hopes, and help us create the world we want.

In this book are applied examples covering many of the toughest problems we face. I hope they will inspire you to action!

Works Cited

Bloeser, Claudia, and Titus Stahl. 'Hope'. *The Stanford Encyclopedia of Philosophy* (Spring 2017 edition), ed. Edward N. Zalta. https://plato.stanford.edu/archives/spr2017/entries/hope/. Accessed 5 June 2018.

Camillus, John C. 'Strategy as a Wicked Problem'. *Harvard Business Review*, May 2008. https://hbr.org/2008/05/strategy-as-a-wicked-problem. Accessed 5 Jan. 2018.

Carse, James. *Finite and Infinite Games*. New York: Free Press, 1986.

Davis, Ged R., Patricia Meredith, and Steven A. Rosell. 'Catalytic Governance and the Information Age'. *Policy Options*, Oct. 2017. http://policyoptions.irpp.org/magazines/october-2017/catalytic-governance-and-the-information-age/. Accessed 5 Jan. 2018.

Hobbes, Thomas. *Leviathan, or the Matter Forme and Power of a Commonwealth Ecclesiastical and Civil*. 1651.

Meredith, Patricia, Steven A. Rosell, and Ged R. Davis. *Catalytic Governance: Leading Change in the Information Age*. Toronto: University of Toronto Press, 2016.

8 Carse.

Miyazaki, Hirokazu, and Richard Swedberg. *The Economy of Hope*. Philadelphia: University of Pennsylvania Press, 2016.

Rittel, H., and M. Webber. 'Dilemmas in a General Theory of Planning'. *Policy Sciences* 4 (1973), pp. 155-69.

Rousseau, Jean-Jacques. *On the Social Contract, or Principles of Political Law*. 1762.

Sharot, Tali. 'The Optimism Bias: Human Brain May Be Hard-Wired for Hope'. *Time Magazine*, 28 May 2011.

Sharot, Tali. *The Optimism Bias: Why We're Wired to Look on the Bright Side*. London: Constable & Robinson Ltd., 2012.

About the Author

Ged R. Davis is Executive Chair, Scenarios, World Energy Council, former Managing Director, World Economic Forum, former Head of Scenario Planning at Royal Dutch Shell, and co-author of *Catalytic Governance: Leading Change in the Information Age*.

Introduction: Building Better Futures

Angela Wilkinson and Betty Sue Flowers

Why we created this book

In the classical Greek myth, when Pandora opened the jar, releasing death and all the other challenges of human life, she closed it again as quickly as she could, trapping inside it one remaining human attribute – hope.

The world today is full of so many large, complex, socially messy, and interconnected challenges that solving them often seems hopeless. News reports are full of fear of the future – a return to nuclear war; the unravelling of Europe; a crisis within democracy; global warming; water wars; a 'globesity' pandemic in some parts of the world, and food and water shortages in others; the rise of robots and the demise of decently paid jobs.

Contemporary life is objectively risky and unpredictable – but life has always been risky and unpredictable. What's new is the 'deep problem' of uncertainty. Uncertainty used to be thought of as a problem that could be solved with more data. But even with exponentially more data, we now have new issues of emergence, ambiguity, and interconnectedness so that we cannot easily reduce global challenges into quantifiable and manageable global risks.

But uncertainty can be a social resource – it can animate new ways of knowing and being, and it can be used to negotiate insecurity and to create new relationships. Uncertainty and hope are part of the evolutionary advantage of our entire species. Progress emerges not just from our ability to observe the world around us but from our capacity to organize imagination and create new and better future possibilities.

To face global challenges many of us – not just official leaders – must work together. Even though we can arm ourselves with more and better data, without hope, we cannot begin to address these challenges. If we abandon hope in the face of uncertainty, we risk the future of humanity.

Wilkinson, Angela, and Betty Sue Flowers (eds.), *Realistic Hope: Facing Global Challenges*. Amsterdam, Amsterdam University Press, 2018.
DOI: 10.5117/9789462987241_INTRO

We created this book to offer hope in relation to many of the major challenges facing societies. We weren't interested in offering theoretical fixes or idealistic, ungrounded, wishful thinking. We wanted hope to arise from people who were actively working with these challenges – *realistic* hope.

In this book we set out to achieve three things:

1   Demonstrate realistic hope in action;
2   Highlight the opportunities to make use of the future before it happens;
3   Provide a set of key principles that arise from these real examples, which anyone can use to leverage our greatest evolutionary trait – our ability to imagine and work together to create a future that is better for individuals and whole societies.

This book offers realistic hope for fourteen of today's pressing and most difficult global challenges, which will affect the future of us all.

Who we are

One of us is a poet, and the other is a physicist. Both of us are experienced in designing and facilitating processes that seek to enhance the futures preparedness and enable the futures-shaping potential of communities and organisations. We do not have a crystal ball, but we do possess a combined experience of 60 years of practice working with different storytelling traditions – images, narrative, and numbers – that enable people to experience and 'rehearse' the future using immersive and interactive learning methods. We have worked with leaders and their organisations across the public, private, civic, and academic sectors and in every region of the world – from the futures of the Arctic and space exploration, to the redesign of education and the rebuilding of whole societies. And both of us are mothers, working for a better future for our children, which, in this interconnected world, means a better future for all children.

Angela trained as a physicist and began her career trying to use science to reduce future uncertainties about climate change and energy futures. She soon discovered that opportunities to 'speak truth to power' were very limited and challenging in evidence-based policy settings because of the messiness of politics, the immaturity of team-based decision-making, and the constraints and barriers leaders have to overcome in order to make significant change happen. She found it was not easy to 'connect the dots' of the many-to-many perspectives and different interests and specialisms necessary to anticipate, appreciate, and address these complex and fast-moving challenges.

Betty Sue began her career as an academic, teaching and writing poetry and literary criticism – the analysis of stories. When she realised that the stories that most needed analysing were those that society was telling about itself and about what was real, she began to write and speak about the current global economic narrative, which is the story of the reality of our time. If the future is always and only a story, she argued, we can create better ones – and figure out how to get there. For the last 25 years, she has worked with politicians, government officials, lawyers, authors, architects, doctors, academics, security analysts, NGOs, the military, and corporations of many kinds to create and explore stories of the future as a way to transform the present.

What these chapters demonstrate

Each chapter approaches one global challenge and first explains what makes that challenge so difficult and why some feel that meeting that challenge is hopeless. Yet, as our authors show, there is reason for hope because we can find realistic examples of success in meeting that challenge. Scaling these solutions often takes imagination, resilience, and new approaches to acting with futures.

The chapters show that there is no best or right approach or one-size-fits-all solution. Instead, they present stories of groups of people who are motivated by a common concern, guided by a shared vision, empowered by collaborative action, and persistent in their openness to continuous learning. Some tackle seemingly impossible challenges (net-zero emissions and a better life for all). Some take on important disciplines. Others talk about how we can avoid new conflicts, whether at the level of cyberwar or water wars. How can leaders approach these big, messy, interconnected challenges, especially in the context of democracies where trust in government is eroding?

Realistic Hope deals with many global challenges – but not all. In the process of writing brief overviews of the most promising developments in relation to security, climate change, job loss, food and water challenges, globalisation, technology, poverty, healthcare, democratic leadership, trust in government, and other issues, our authors were asked to keep the focus on one challenge at a time – but we realise that *all* of these global challenges are interrelated. By the end of the book, many of these interconnections have emerged implicitly through many different voices and perspectives.

We conclude the book with a brief chapter describing the five principles of realistic hope that we have learned from working with the authors on all the chapters and offer an epilogue that calls on the power of the human will to turn our hope for a better future into reality.

Whom this book is for

The hopeful leader in us all.

1   Making Globalisation Work

Carl J. Dahlman

Abstract

Despite the many benefits it has brought, globalisation is under attack. It is being blamed for negative effects that are the result of other factors. Exploring alternative future scenarios for globalisation provides some perspective and insights on what must be done to harness the positive and reduce the negative effects. This requires a global governance system with better rules for interaction among nation states, better national systems that address inequality and disruption caused by new technologies, and support for less advanced countries. It is necessary to go beyond raising awareness of what is at stake to mobilising for concrete actions that can move main stakeholders and country policies in the right direction.

Keywords: globalisation, global governance, disruptive technology, inequality, job loss, scenarios

The threat of de-globalisation

Globalisation is usually defined as increased international trade in goods and services and international financial flows. But globalisation is also people flows (international migration), knowledge and information flows (through mass media and the internet), pandemics (which now spread much faster because of increased international travel), and environmental degradation, which goes across national boundaries (global warming in particular, which is a new element we were not aware of before).

The mass media, many governments, and large parts of the population are railing against globalisation. On the specific issue of international trade it is noteworthy that whereas 30 years ago most people in advanced countries had a positive view of trade, while many in developing countries

Wilkinson, Angela, and Betty Sue Flowers (eds.), *Realistic Hope: Facing Global Challenges.* Amsterdam, Amsterdam University Press, 2018.
DOI: 10.5117/9789462987241_CH01

had a negative view, the perceptions are now the opposite.[1] Most people in advanced countries think that trade has had negative effects on their well-being while most in developing countries think that it has been beneficial.[2] The reaction against trade in developed countries appears to be linked to a strong perception that trade has led to job losses.

There has also been a growing anti-immigrant sentiment in Europe, the US, and Australia. In Europe this sentiment has been exacerbated by the large inflow of refugees from countries being torn apart by war, such as Afghanistan, Iraq, Sudan, and Syria. But also, many economic migrants from Africa and the Middle East have come to Europe in the last five years. In the US anti-immigration sentiment has been increased by fear stoked by President Trump that terrorists as well as criminals may be imbedded in migrant inflows.

In addition to encouraging anti-immigration views, President Trump has also worked against globalisation by withdrawing the US from the Paris climate accord, claiming that it is an international plot to restrain the US. He has also withdrawn the US from the Trans-Pacific Partnership (TPP) trade agreement and threatened to withdraw it from the North American Free Trade Agreement (NAFTA) and to impose high tariffs on trade with China and other countries.

More generally there has been a concern that globalisation is also linked to increasing inequality. The greatest benefits of globalisation have gone to multinational companies that have relocated labour-intensive production to developing countries and to the owners of capital who have benefited from the profits of multinational corporations (MNCs) and from exploiting the opportunities of moving capital around the world. The greatest losers have been the workers in developed countries who have lost manufacturing jobs and have not been able to find new jobs or jobs in services that pay as well.[3]

The negative perception of globalisation has led to increasing threats of trade protectionism as governments have begun to raise tariffs and other barriers to trade, and, in the case of the US, to penalise MNCs that relocate jobs abroad.[4]

---

1   There is also a long literature that has focused on other downsides of globalisation, including slavery, colonialism, unfair trade practices, cultural imperialism, and other forms of international exploitation.

2   See, for example, Pew Research Center.

3   See Milanovich for an analysis of what has happened to the global income distribution between 1988 and 2008 (often called the elephant curve), Corak for a nice graphical illustration, and Freund for a further analysis showing the main losers have not been workers in Europe and the US, but workers in Japan and the former USSR.

4   See, for example, the biannual reports produced by an independent global trade-monitoring group at: http://www.globaltradealert.org/reports.

The slowdown in global GDP growth since the 2008-2009 recession in the developed world has been accompanied by a slowdown in global trade as well. Ford Foundation Professor of International Political Economy at the John F. Kennedy School of Government at Harvard University Dani Rodrik has claimed that democracy, national sovereignty, and deep global economic integration are incompatible – any two of them can be combined, but not all three. And it appears that the electorate in countries such as the US and the UK are making it clear that the one they want to give up is the deep economic integration of globalisation. As a result, de-globalisation has become an increasing threat.

The perception that globalisation is a threat is contradicted by the reality. Globalisation has had strong benefits. Increased specialisation and exchange through trade and the international movement of capital and people have raised incomes and increased welfare. The international dissemination of technology has narrowed productivity and development gaps and helped developing countries grow faster, fostering a move towards convergence. Increased information about other countries, cultures, and religions through mass media, the internet, and international travel has enriched the human experience and understanding across cultures. Increased awareness of planetary limits to environmental health has led to international efforts to address carbon dioxide (CO_2) emissions, however inadequately.

Part of the perception-vs-reality problem is that the anti-globalisation groups have just looked at the downside and blamed globalisation for negative effects that are really the result of other factors.[5] Job losses, for example, are largely the result of technological change (automation), not competition from imports.[6] In addition, problems such as the increase in inequality are often the result of the lack of appropriate policies to protect or compensate those suffering economic hardship from competition from imports and technological disruption. The same can be said for competition from immigrants. Policies to deal with these challenges include more active retraining and up-skilling programmes as well as more supportive social protection programmes.

5   Part of the problem of globalisation is how it has been mismanaged by some international institutions. See, for example, Stiglitz, who supports globalisation, but criticizes how the IMF and the World Bank have managed it.

6   For example, Hicks and Devaraj find that 88 per cent of job losses in US manufacturing employment between 2000 and 2010 was due to increases in productivity, while trade was responsible for only 13 per cent of the losses.

Globalisation and growing interdependence

A fruitful way to think about globalisation is to focus on interdependence. Globalisation implies interdependence in a world where geography is shrinking due to advances in transportation and communications. This interdependence is due largely to technology, but also to economic exchange, social/cultural issues, and global environmental constraints. Interdependence also involves the global geopolitical system, including the rules for interaction across states.

Matrix of Interdependence

Area	Key international elements of interdependence
1 Technological	– Increasingly global knowledge – Internet and digital economy – Global innovation system and disruptive technologies
2 Economic	– Economic growth and impact on trade – Trade and competitiveness across countries – International capital flows and foreign direct investment (FDI)
3 Social	– Information about other countries, events, cultures, and religions through television, media, and travel – International migration – Pandemics
4 Environmental	– Limited capacity of world to absorb greenhouse gases, resulting in global warming – Limited environmental resources – Pollution spilling across borders
5 Geopolitical	– Attitudes towards and stability and effectiveness of global governance system – Balance of geopolitical power, including economic and military alliances and military threats, including cold wars and actual wars – International terrorism and cybersecurity

Globalisation is also linked to geopolitics. Globalisation has been facilitated by technology, particularly falling costs of transportation and communication. Throughout history until the late 18th century there have been regional empires such as the Roman Empire, the Chinese Empire, the Italian city states, the Spanish, the French, and the Russian. There was some interaction through trade and travel such as Marco Polo and the Silk Road. The UK was the first global empire, thanks initially to its strong navy and then to the Industrial Revolution, which started in the UK and gave it a strong technological advantage over the rest of the world.[7]

The US replaced the UK as the global power in all relevant spheres (economic, military, social, political, cultural), thanks largely to technological leadership, large market size, and MNCs. After the devastation of WWII, the US launched the Marshall Plan for the reconstruction of Europe and set up the architecture of the global system through the creation of the United Nations, the International Monetary Fund, the World Bank, and the General Agreement on Tariffs and Trade (which was replaced by the World Trade Organization in 1995). This global architecture facilitated the rise of emerging countries such as Brazil, Russia, India, China, and South Africa (the BRICS).

Better transportation and communication technologies have facilitated globalisation and the opening of markets, but to avoid winner-take-all outcomes, markets must be regulated to control monopoly market power and other imperfections caused by asymmetric information and network effects.

Technology has been and will continue to be a game changer for better or for worse. New disruptive technologies – including digitalisation, the internet of things, 3D printing, automation, artificial intelligence, biotechnology, and nanotechnology – have tremendous potential to reduce costs, improve efficiency, substitute for limited resources, increase food availability, reduce negative emissions, produce alternative energy, reduce disease, replace faulty organs, prolong life, etc. But these technologies could also be used to produce weapons of mass destruction, super soldiers, designer babies, information about genetic make-up leading to companies refusing to insure high-risk persons, cyberterror, cybercrime, etc.

The rapid development and spread of digital technologies are already shrinking distance and disrupting businesses, changing regulation, and challenging the role of government. The global expansion of the internet economy is raising questions about the relevance of geographic definitions of community as people join virtual communities with others with whom they have more in common than with their neighbours. Even the boundaries of the nation state are challenged as data and transactions flow across national borders at the speed of light.[8] Digital technologies make some institutions

---

7   For a good multi-century overview of how international trade and technology have affected changing shares of global GDP, see Maddison.
8   But some countries, such as China, and, to some extent, the EU are trying to restrict the free flow of data and information.

and regulations obsolete as the boundaries between different actives are blurred, with implications for regulation (Is Uber a ride service platform where providers are individual contractors or a transportation company that needs to provide employment benefits to drivers and to be regulated by applicable laws regarding sexual harassment?); taxation (Should the tax on a digital service transaction be collected in the country of the seller or the buyer?); the role of banks (What is the impact of growing peer-to-peer lending, crowd funding, and other fintech trends? What is the extent of the threat to national currencies from digital money such as Bitcoin?); and even what is governance and what is to be governed (What is an individual's right to privacy? Who owns personal information collected digitally? Who can use it? Should access to the internet be a basic right?).[9] Moreover, the rapid advances in biotechnology (which already permit gene editing), the creation of new biological organs, and the creation of new life forms will raise complex ethical and moral issues, such as What is life? or What is permissible when the technology permits the creation of babies with made-to-order characteristics, or super soldiers, or even more powerful biological weapons of mass destruction?[10]

Realistic hope

If we look at the last 200 years, which coincide with a large increase in globalisation (albeit with some ebb and flow), we see that there has been massive progress in many aspects of development. Some striking figures based on a study of long-term trends since 1820 in global well-being covering 80 per cent of the world's population and ten dimensions of well-being include the following[11]:

– Average per capita incomes increased by a factor of ten even as population increased seven-fold;
– Literacy increased from 20 per cent to nearly universal in most regions of the world except Sub-Saharan Africa and South Asia, where it only increased to two-thirds to three-quarters of the population;
– Life expectancy (as a broad measure of health) has doubled worldwide, even during periods when some countries and regions did not experience much increase in GDP per capita, thanks to advantages in medical knowledge and the diffusion of healthcare technologies.

9   For a good series of critical questions from who we are to the nature of military conflict raised by advances in the digital technologies, see Rothkopf.
10   See Doudna and Sternberg for more details about some of the moral and ethical questions raised by these technologies and the risks they entail.
11   For full details on the methodology and coverage of the multiple dimensions of development and findings of this study, see Van Zanden *et al.*

What is most remarkable is how much progress has been made in the last hundred years, even though the century included major global disruptions such as WWI (1914-18), the Great Depression (1929-41), WWII (1939-45), and the financial crisis of 2007-2008.

A lot of the progress in the last two centuries was the result of the global dissemination of technology, starting with the Industrial Revolution. The first phase was the age of steam, water, and mechanical production equipment, which started in 1784 in the UK and spread through Europe and then the rest of the world. The second phase was the age of the division of labour, electricity, and mass production, which started in 1870 and spread rapidly throughout the world. This phase led to the massive expansion of trade in the 19th century combined with large movements of capital and mass migration, especially from Europe to the Americas. While this globalisation receded during the world wars, the third phase saw a renewed wave of globalisation following the 1950s, pushed forward by electronics, information technology, and automated production, which continued strongly until the financial crisis of 2007-2008.[12]

The success of globalisation since the 1950s depended on an open multilateral system, with adequate rules for interaction across countries. These included trade, finance, and security provided by the global institutions largely set up after WWII. But we are now in period where large parts of the population in various countries, particularly in Western democracies, are turning against their governments and against globalisation and the institutions that have helped to govern it. In addition, we are amid a major geopolitical power shift, which is also raising questions about the legitimacy of some of the institutions where the rising powers do not have voting rights in proportion to their new economic weight.

After the devastation of WWII, the US created a relatively open world order, which included institutions that pushed for free movement of trade in manufactured goods and of portfolio capital and FDI. It also provided a security umbrella for the West against the USSR. There is now a fraying of the system due to the change in US policy from its support for a broad, open global system to a new nationalist 'America first' policy, which includes protectionism and withdrawal from the Trans-Pacific Partnership (TPP) and the Paris climate accord. These actions, which undermine relationships with traditional geopolitical allies in Europe and Asia, are compounded by

---

12   These three phases are taken from the characterisation of what the World Economic Forum calls the three industrial revolutions, which predate the fourth industrial revolution, which they call 'the age of cyber physical systems' (Schwab, p. 1).

the relative shifts of economic power from advanced countries to developing and emerging countries. As of 2007 the share of global GDP (in purchasing power parity terms[13]) of developing and emerging countries surpassed that of advanced countries, and in 2012 China's share surpassed that of the US.[14]

Currently, the main emerging countries, the BRICS (Brazil, Russia, India, China, and South Africa) are playing by the rules of the existing global system. However, as the BRICS have not been given the voice commensurate with their new economic power in international institutions such as the IMF and the World Bank, China has led the creation of alternative international institutions, such as the New Development Bank and the Asian Infrastructure Investment Bank.

Clearly, China is the largest and most important emerging power and is widely seen as the main competitor to the US. Ironically, it also appears to be assuming a role as the key supporter of globalisation, at least in pronouncements, if not in actions.[15] A key question is whether there will continue to be an open, multilateral, multipolar system, or, instead, a free-for-all, with each country or group of countries on their own, where the strongest will have an advantage.[16]

Future thinking and new ways of approaching the problem

Given the increasing complexity and interdependence of the global system, it is very difficult to know what will happen to globalisation. Thus, it is useful to explore various alternative future scenarios to see possible new solution spaces. Many future scenarios have been prepared by different organisations. Two examples are the 2014 scenarios developed by the Organisation for Economic Co-operation and Development (OECD) and 2017 scenarios by the National Intelligence Council (NIC) of the US. They provide enabling frameworks – a platform for discussion about the links between governance-globalisation-development across scales (global, regional, national, community) to get a better perspective on the anti-globalisation/

13   Purchasing power parity (ppp) exchange rates have been developed to adjust the exchange rates to better reflect the purchasing power of money in each country so that country comparisons are not biased by distorted market exchange rates.

14   To see the large changes that have occurred in the relative share of global GDP in ppp terms, use the datamapper function in the IMF's World Economic Outlook.

15   Notable was President Xi's speech at Davos on 17 Jan. 2017, when he came out in defense of globalisation.

16   The free-for-all scenario has been developed in a story written by Putin's key advisor, Vladislav Surkov, cited in Luce, p. 173.

pro-globalisation dilemma. They do not claim prediction, but try to enable strategic knowledge exchange about the longer-term perspective, which is vital for navigating the medium-term period to 2030, and in turn, to developing new and better options for universal development.

The 2014 OECD scenarios explored the following three alternative world orders:

– *Quick Fixes*: a reformed multilateral order (China led/included, with digitally empowered citizens enabling faster bottom-up feedback loops, and an uneven digital productivity boom).
– *Multipolar*: a new world order, reordering pluralism, regionalism-enables-globalisation, smaller but more effective global agenda, different pathways in digital productivity boom.
– *City Power*: a more bottom-up order emerges and realigns top order; alignment of national-urban policy frameworks to avoid risk of growing divide of urban vs rural in push to localised, circular economies enabled in an era of digital globalisation.[17]

The 2016 NIC scenarios explored the following three alternative world orders:

– *Islands*: There has been strong push back against globalisation, and governments are challenged in meeting society's needs for economic and social security in the context of slow growth and disruptive technologies transforming work and trade; some governments are more successful than others.
– *Orbits:* A fragmented world order where competing powers seek their own spheres of influence in the context of rising nationalism, disruptive technologies, decreasing global cooperation, and interstate conflict.
– *Communities:* Rising expectations and diminished capacity of governments open space for local governments and private actors to provide some of the services typically provided by government; some governments resist, but others cede some power to the emerging networks.

There are signs of all the scenarios. For example, in the absence of national commitment to the Paris climate accord (Trump withdrawing the US), city mayors and local leaders are stepping up to the 'globalisation plate', pledging to fulfil national promises through work at the local level. In addition, some corporations are also pledging to help reduce carbon emissions or otherwise help to tackle the challenge of climate change.

17   OECD, 'Key Issues Paper'.

There are also many ad hoc coalitions taking on global challenges, which is a new part of the globalisation-governance story. For example, on health issues global NGO networks (such as Doctors without Borders, the Global Vaccine Alliance) as well as foundations (such as the Gates Foundation) have become active. On human rights there are also many global networks (such as Transparency International and Amnesty International) that monitor the actions of governments and bring public pressure on them. On the environment there are also many networks of concerned citizens and scientists that provide information on the risks to the environment and call for more environmentally friendly actions by citizens, companies, and governments. There have also been moves for exit of countries from regional groups (such as Britain from the EU), fragmentation of nation states (such as the former Yugoslavia and Czechoslovakia), and movements for secession of regions from nation states (such as Catalonians from Spain, or the Kurds from Iraq).

At the global political economy level, in addition to stepping up as the new champion of globalisation, China is also changing the balance of power in the geopolitical landscape through its One Belt One Road (OBOR) initiative involving over 40 countries from Asia to Europe and part of the Middle East and Africa. In addition, as an alternative to the US-led Trans-Pacific Partnership (TPP) trade agreement (which Trump withdrew the US from on his first day in office), a new Regional Comprehensive Economic Partnership (RCEP) free trade agreement is being negotiated by sixteen Asian countries (including China, India, Japan, Korea, Australia, and other members of ASEAN), representing 45 per cent of world population and 40 per cent of world trade. On the security front, the Shanghai Cooperation Organisation (SCO), a new Eurasian security organisation (which includes China, Russia, India, Pakistan, Kazakhstan, Kyrgyzstan, Tajikistan, and Uzbekistan), has been created to oppose foreign intervention in the internal affairs of the member states on the pretext of humanitarian or human rights.

It is likely that the future will contain some combination or permutation of all or some of these scenarios, as well as unexpected new challenges. However, it is useful to reflect on five elements that stand out from examining these two sets of scenarios.

The first is that both sets recognise various fundamental trends. These include:
- There is a strong push back against globalisation.
- The world has entered a period of slower growth and increased uncertainty.
- New technologies are transforming the relationships between citizens, communities, and states.

- There is a more complex relationship between individuals, groups, and governments, and governments are having trouble delivering on the expectations of digitally empowered individuals and groups or dealing with the economic and social restructuring caused by disruptive technologies and globalisation.
- There is an economic and political power shift from the West to the East.
- There are some serious global issues that require attention, such as global warming and security.

The second is that they construct the scenarios around the degree to which there is globalisation and the degree to which governments or groups or communities are the key actors in dealing with them. None of the scenarios assume globalisation will continue unabated.

The third is that scenarios also show that globalisation and technology can be disruptive or helpful, and that the outcome will depend on the actions of governments, groups, and individuals. In addition, the scenarios show that there can be different outcomes, not only across the scenarios but also for different parts of the world within each scenario, depending on the degree to which governments, communities, or people deal with the issues. Thus, there are very variegated outcomes.

The fourth is that in the different scenarios, governments are under pressure to provide better results. In some scenarios different national- or community-level coalitions bypass or substitute for the role of national governments. However, there are still many issues that require a response at the level of the nation state for the provision of basic public goods such as security, the rule of law, education, public infrastructure, health, and basic social protection; and to protect and represent the nation's interest on cross-border issues.

The fifth is that they are not very optimistic about the extent to which there will be enough coordination to deal with some of these cross-border issues such as climate change, terrorism, cybersecurity, or the potential impacts of biotechnology. Thus, there appears to be a need for more effective government or at least some sort of organisation that transcends national boundaries to reflect global public interests.

From considering some of the outcomes of these alternative future scenarios it appears that to harness the benefits of globalisation a three-tiered approach is required:

- A workable global governance system with rules for interaction among different nation states;

- Better national governance systems that address inequality and disruption caused by new technologies;
- An improved international system to support development of less advanced countries.

A workable global governance system

The relationships among major powers affect the global governance system, with history showing that that great power transitions have been difficult.[18] Clearly, a major overt confrontation among powers is to be avoided in the current age of nuclear bombs, cyberwar, and other weapons of mass destruction, including new ones being made possible by technological advances. The most likely arrangements are not convergence/divergence, but flexible coordination or cooperation of changing coalitions. The requirements for a reasonably stable world order would appear to be agreement on some basic issues and norms. These would need to include:

- Realistically dealing with the real threat of global warming and earth's limited capacity to absorb CO_2. This is likely to involve carbon pricing and improvements in energy efficiency and non-fossil fuel energy.
- Some effective rules for economic interactions among countries. There is not likely to be full free trade, but some sort of managed trade.[19]
- Some rules for dealing with the consequences of new technologies, cybersecurity, and some of the nefarious uses of biotechnology and new materials.
- Some agreements on helping the development of less advanced countries.

Better national governance with respect to the impact of globalisation

National governance must deal adequately with the inequalities and restructuring that accompany international trade competition and disruptive technologies. We need to recognise that this will be handled differently by different political systems. And we need to disabuse ourselves of the exuberant notion that the disintegration of the USSR marked the 'end of history' and the triumph of capitalist democracies,

18 See, for example, the new book by Harvard historian Graham Allison on the sobering history of power shifts between established and rising powers.
19 See, for example, Rodrik on the trilemma of globalisation where he argues that free trade, democracy, and national interests are incompatible such that it is necessary to consider managed trade as a practical solution.

as argued by Fukuyama. The return of an autocratic Russia to status as a major geopolitical player and the tremendous economic success of China's autocratic socialist regime make that clear. In fact, what we are currently witnessing is a crisis of democracy and capitalism. The latter was revealed by the global recession of 2009, which was not truly global, but rooted in the advanced capitalist democratic economies of the US, Western Europe, and Japan. China did not experience the crisis, but maintained high rates of growth. Moreover, the economic recovery in the advanced capitalist economies has been very slow, and inequality has increased in most of these countries.

There are also interaction effects between the crisis of capitalism and democracy. The pain of the economic crisis made it clear to many voters in the democratic, market-based countries that the system was not serving them well. Many suffered prolonged unemployment as well as loss of real purchasing power. In addition there was a clear realisation of an increase in inequality. It became clear that the rich were getting richer while the middle classes fell behind.

Therefore, in the sphere of geopolitical competition the democratic capitalist societies need to up their game. They need to respond to the angry electorate that feels it has been forgotten by the ruling elites and hurt by globalisation. Responding to them requires addressing the economic hardships they have endured. It requires putting in place effective programmes to cushion that pain. These include better unemployment insurance and affordable healthcare. It also requires better taxation and redistribution policies, but also more effective spending as well as improving the efficiency of public services such as health, education, and security. This is a tall order given all the vested interest groups and the oversized power of well-funded lobbies in democratic systems, as well as entrenched ideological party divides.

To break this logjam and avoid the continued decline of liberal democracy, which has been well articulated by Luce, it is necessary to put the issues of national governance in terms of the bigger picture of the ongoing competition among alternative economic political systems and the shifting of economic power to Asia. In addressing these issues it is worth looking at how some democratic countries, such as the Scandinavian nations, have managed to maintain social cohesion and growth despite increasing pressure from international competition. Also, given how rapidly technology is changing, and how it is affecting the very nature of community and the nation state, there needs to be more discussion and deliberation on these issues, including the role of the state and what individual rights are.

An improved international system to help less advanced countries develop

To preserve global stability, it is also necessary to have a better global system to give developing countries better opportunities to develop. Although some countries like China have made very impressive progress, many countries in the developing world have not. There is increasing inequality across countries as many still have average per capita incomes near the subsistence level, while average world per capita incomes have increased significantly.

The Sustainable Development Goals agreed to in December 2015 at the UN set ambitious multidimensional goals for all countries. Low-income countries will be the most challenged to meet the goals. While advances in technology can make it easier and less costly to meet the goals, virtually all can be met with current technology. Therefore, while technological advances focused on the needs of low-income populations are important, the most critical are political will, the allocation of appropriate resources, and effective institutions and capabilities.

We need an open international system to support equality of opportunity, and we need to think through what equality of opportunity means in the current context. For example, given the importance of the internet as a fundamental new infrastructure, access to the internet should perhaps be considered a new basic right, with more being done to extend coverage to people in developing countries who are currently not covered. The same goes for electricity and access to clean water. It is also necessary to see what is the moral responsibility of high-income countries that have emitted huge amounts of CO_2 without having had to pay for such use of the environment. Many poor developing countries are the ones most likely to face the highest costs of global warming, even though they have not contributed much to the problem since they have had very low per capita CO_2 emissions.

It is also worth noting that there are important interdependencies between different dimensions of globalisation and development and the three different elements raised above. For example, international policies towards trade may affect migration flows and development, and the latter may affect migration. And the successful East Asian development strategy of labour-intensive manufactured exports to developed countries is being challenged by increasing protectionism, pre-emption of exporting manufactured goods by the very competitive exports from China, and the rapid development and spread of automation, which is making the comparative advantage of low-cost labour irrelevant. Thus, there is a need for new development strategies, including the expansion of services, especially digital services, as well as the expansion of non-traded goods such as infrastructure, health, housing, and better public services. This will require careful thinking, including what developing countries need to do to take advantage not only of existing technologies but also of the new disruptive technologies that are being created mostly in advanced countries and in some large developing countries such as the BRICS.

Furthermore, many developing countries will need more technical and financial assistance from developed countries to avoid falling behind. Despite global commitments from OECD countries to spend 0.7 per cent of gross national income (GNI) on development aid, their spending between 2005 and 2015 has only averaged around 0.3 per cent of GNI. In addition, many members are diverting resources to pay for their in-country refugee costs. These have risen from 4.9 per cent of ODA in 2014 to 9.2 per cent in 2015.[20]

The issue of migration

Most migration is from developing countries to developed countries. It is driven by the search for better welfare (not just economic, but social, such as security and opportunity for children). Therefore, it is driven by inequality across countries, as well as by civil strife, terrorism, and failed states. In terms of international governance, unlike the virtually free flow of capital and manufactured goods, there is no free flow of people because of immigration barriers.

In the context of slow population growth in most developed countries versus high population growth in most developing countries, particularly in Sub-Saharan Africa and South Asia, there is obviously scope to have more migration from high-population-growth countries to low-population-growth countries. However, the potential supply is likely to be greater than the potential demand, particularly now that automation means that there may be a reduced demand for workers, even in countries with shrinking labour forces. If advanced countries erected barriers to the immigration of people from developing countries, the welfare of developing countries could still be improved if they could increase their exports and receive greater volumes of foreign investment to help relieve their capital constraints. However, exports of agricultural products, where many developing countries have the strongest comparative advantage, are constrained by barriers to agricultural imports in developed counties. Furthermore, most foreign

---

20   OECD, *Development Co-operation Report 2016*, p. 152.

investment does not go to the poorest developing countries because of poor investment climate. All these factors tend to increase pressures to migrate.

Not helping developing countries develop will increase migration pressures from people from developing countries seeking to migrate to developed countries. The influx of illegal migrants is part of what is fuelling the anti-globalisation sentiment in developed countries. In the long run, only broad economic and social development is going to solve the problem of excess supply of migrants to advanced countries.

The future is ours for the making

Given the challenges covered above, it is important to focus on concrete actions to help harness the benefits of globalisation. Globalisation has contributed a lot to the impressive progress that has been achieved in the world over the last 200 years. However, such progress has been neither automatic nor linear. It has been the result of trial and error, vision and leadership, and the creation of institutions and governance systems that have helped to harness the benefits while controlling the risks. Harnessing progress and making globalisation work is one of the key areas that need attention. We are perhaps the first species that has the power to annihilate itself quickly through nuclear war or more slowly through mismanagement of the global environment. We have the responsibility to make globalisation work.

The future is ours for the making. We must weigh in to help make globalisation work for increased global welfare or risk that the challenges to globalisation will undermine the benefits it can bring. While the world is subject to exogenous shocks, including not just from natural disasters, but also from the actions of players in the geopolitical system, we must be active agents to overcome whatever shocks occur and to harness the benefits of globalisation for the improvement of global welfare.

We need to raise awareness of common issues and global constraints as is done in this book and by other books, groups, NGOs, and social media. This awareness and understanding need to be built into the education systems in all countries. It requires more education in science and technology and in how technology is changing what is needed in terms of institutions and governance. It requires courses and teach-ins for adults who have left the formal educational system. It also requires massive dissemination campaigns using traditional mass media as well as the new social media.

But it is necessary to go beyond just raising awareness to active mobilisation for concrete action that can move main stakeholders and country policies in the right direction. This means putting pressure on critical agents such as governments, international institutions, MNCs, and social organisations to address these issues and to put in place institutions and mechanisms to harness the benefits of globalisation. As argued, this involves improving the global governance system as well as improving national governance to deal with the disruptions of globalisation, technological change, the effects of competing systems on global governance, and global efforts to deal with growing global inequality. Given the stakes and how fast the whole system is moving, there is no time to lose. There is a lot to be done, and the active participation of all concerned is critical.

Works Cited

Allison, Graham. *Destined for War: Can America and China Escape Thucydides's Trap?* New York: Houghton Mifflin Harcourt, 2017.

Corak, Miles. 'The Winners and Losers of Globalization: Branko Milanovic's New Book on Inequality Answers Two Important Questions'. Economics for Public Policy (blog), 2016. https://milescorak.com/2016/05/18/the-winners-and-losers-of-globalization-branko-milanovics-new-book-on-inequality-answers-two-important-questions/. Accessed 6 July 2017.

Doudna, Jennifer A., and Samuel H. Sternberg. *A Crack in Creation: Gene Editing and the Unthinkable Power to Control Evolution.* New York: Houghton Mifflin Harcourt, 2017.

Freund, Caroline. 'Deconstructing Branko Milanovic's "Elephant Chart": Does It Show What Everyone Thinks?' Real Time Economic Issues Watch (blog of the Peterson Institute for International Economics), 30 Nov. 2016. https://piie.com/blogs/realtime-economic-issues-watch/deconstructing-branko-milanovics-elephant-chart-does-it-show. Accessed 9 July 2017.

Fukuyama, Francis. *The End of History and the Last Man.* New York: Free Press, 1992.

Hicks, M.J., and Srikant Devaraj. 'The Myth and Reality of Manufacturing in America'. Ball State University Center for Business and Economic Research, 2017. https://conexus.cberdata.org/files/MfgReality.pdf. Accessed 5 June 2018.

IMF Datamapper. http://www.imf.org/external/datamapper/NGDP_RPCH@WEO/OEMDC/ADVEC/WEOWORLD. Accessed 30 June 2017.

Luce, Edward. *The Retreat of Western Liberalism.* New York: Atlantic Monthly Press, 2017.

Maddison, Angus. *The World Economy: Historical Statistics.* Paris: Organisation for Economic Co-operation and Development, 2004.

Milanovich, Branko. *Global Inequality: A New Approach for the Age of Globalization.* Cambridge, MA: The Belknap Press of Harvard University Press, 2016.

National Intelligence Council. 'Global Trends: Paradox of Progress'. Washington, DC: Office of the Director of National Intelligence, 2017. www.dni.gov/nic/globaltrends. Accessed 29 June 2017.

OECD. *Development Co-operation Report 2016 – The Sustainable Development Goals as Business Opportunities.* Paris: Organisation for Economic Co-operation and Development, 2016.

OECD. 'Key Issues Paper'. Meeting of the OECD Ministerial Council, Paris, 3-4 June 2015, pp. 5-6. Paris: Organisation for Economic Co-operation and Development, 2015. http://www.oecd.org/mcm/documents/Unlocking-Investment-for-Sustainable-Growth-and%20Jobs-Key-Issues-Paper-CMIN2015-3.pdf. Accessed 7 July 2018.

OECD. *Perspectives on Global Development 2017: International Migration in a Shifting World.* Paris: Organisation for Economic Co-operation and Development, 2016.

Pew Research Center. 'Faith and Skepticism about Trade, Foreign Investment', 16 Sept. 2014. http://www.pewglobal.org/2014/09/16/faith-and-skepticism-about-trade-foreign-investment/. Accessed 5 July 2017.

Rodrik, Dani. The *Globalization Paradox: Democracy and the Future of the World Economy.* New York: W.W. Norton, 2011.

Rothkopf, David. *The Great Questions of Tomorrow.* New York: TED Books, Simon and Schuster, 2017.

Schwab, Klaus. 'The Fourth Industrial Revolution: What It Means, How to Respond'. World Economic Forum website, 16 Jan. 2016. https://www.weforum.org/agenda/2016/01/the-fourth-industrial-revolution-what-it-means-and-how-to-respond/. Accessed 29 June 2017.

Stiglitz, Joseph. *Globalization and Its Discontents.* New York: W.W. Norton, 2002.

Van Zanden, J., *et al.*, eds. *How Was Life? Global Well-Being since 1820.* Paris: Organisation for Economic Co-operation and Development, 2014.

About the Author

Carl Dahlman is former Head of Research, Development Centre, OECD, and is currently Senior Policy Advisor for The Growth Dialogue.

2 Energy: A Better Life with a Healthy Planet

Jeremy Bentham

Abstract

If we are to avoid the worst effects of climate change while at the same time providing a better life for all, the global economy and its underlying energy system must go through a major transition. This will require government carbon pricing, changes in land use, and the transformation of four major energy sectors: power generation, buildings, transport, and industry. Even though such a transition is a huge undertaking, which will deeply challenge our socio-political capacity for cooperation, this chapter offers realistic hope that net-zero emissions can be achieved.

Keywords: net-zero emissions, climate change, energy system transition, carbon pricing, renewables, Paris Agreement

Two great challenges

The world today faces two great challenges. The first is reducing poverty – spreading the benefits of a decent quality of life from the minority towards the majority of people in the world. But alleviating poverty will require a significant increase of energy to fuel the necessary productive activity, which raises the second challenge – addressing the increasing accumulation of greenhouse gases in the environment. This rise of greenhouse gases is putting pressure not only on the climate and the atmosphere, but also on the oceans, with ocean acidification and temperature changes, and on food production. In many ways, vulnerable people, including those in poverty, are likely to suffer the most.

Over 80 per cent of primary energy currently comes from fossil fuels, whose use produces emissions that affect the heat balance of our planet. If we are to avoid the worst effects of climate change while at the same time

Wilkinson, Angela, and Betty Sue Flowers (eds.), *Realistic Hope: Facing Global Challenges*. Amsterdam, Amsterdam University Press, 2018.
DOI: 10.5117/9789462987241_CH02

providing a better life for all, the global economy and its underlying energy system must go through a major transition – a very major one. Everything is up for grabs: how we use energy, how we produce energy, how we distribute it, and how we pay for it.

The size of the energy transition

The energy transition is already underway. This is an exciting opportunity for the world, with many 'winners' as the energy system transforms: new industries, new business models, fresh investment, and new jobs. And this transformation is within humanity's grasp. Making a transition to a low-carbon energy future while meeting rising global demand is an achievable ambition for society. Even though it is a huge undertaking that will deeply challenge our socio-political capacity for cooperation, with the right policies, the right decisions, and enough willpower, it can succeed.

How big does this transition really need to be? How many people will we need to supply with energy? And how much energy are they going to need? There are currently over seven billion people on the planet. That number will probably increase to at least ten billion by the end of the century. Some estimates suggest it will grow significantly more. All these people will continue to strive, as they do today, for a better standard of living for themselves and their families. Similarly, efforts by governments and the global community to address the challenge of poverty will continue. Over time, this will help spread the benefits of a decent standard of living from the minority of people in the world towards the majority– *a better life* for all.

That is not to say everyone will necessarily enjoy a TV in every room in the house, a new smartphone every year, or the 'use once and throw away' practices that have become common in much of the rich world in the last 50 years. Instead, this 'better life' means a world in which the basic material needs associated with housing, healthcare, adequate sanitation, effective transport, and productive employment extend to everyone on the planet.

These developments require energy. Everything we do needs energy, from fuelling our vehicles to heating or cooling our homes to cooking our dinners. And it also takes even more energy to make the raw materials in that vehicle, to build that domestic boiler, and to deliver clean water with which to cook.

As the world's energy system stands at the moment, more energy means more greenhouse gas emissions, and more emissions mean a more severe climate challenge. The lifestyle of the average person in the US, for example, is currently underpinned by the use of 300 gigajoules of energy per person each year. To understand what that means, consider that over the course of a year, a human labourer will deliver work equivalent to about a gigajoule of energy. So to use 300 gigajoules of energy per person per year means the equivalent of every man, woman, and child in the country having 300 physical labourers working for them. That's a lot of sweat. Even the energy use of people in more energy-efficient economies, such as those of Japan and Europe, is about 150 gigajoules per head. That's 150 labourers – and that is still a lot of sweat.

If we assume very significant energy efficiency improvements in the world's economies, an average person could require about 100 gigajoules of primary energy to fuel a decent quality of life. If we multiply that level of energy consumption by a projected future population of 10 billion, we reach a rough figure for global primary energy need: 1000 billion gigajoules, or 1000 exajoules, a year.[1]

By that reckoning the people of this planet are going to need around double the amount of energy that we use today. Such an estimate is consistent with much more detailed modelling exercises that take into account both the large scope for efficiency improvements, demand reduction in many already industrialised economies, and the growing need for energy in developing economies.

The rise in emissions from a growing energy system also brings us hard up against another reality: money. People and governments naturally choose the most affordable way to meet their needs. This creates a tension between the *better life* we all want, and the *healthy planet* we all need. As things stand now, the cheapest way for many governments to buy much of that energy – burning coal – is bad for the planet's health.

The great challenge of the energy transition that lies before us is how to supply this rising energy demand while at the same time slowing and finally halting the accumulation of carbon dioxide (CO_2) in the atmosphere – helping to ensure a *healthy planet*.

---

1 Shell, 'A Better Life with a Healthy Planet', p. 8. Shell Scenarios are a part of an ongoing process used in Shell for almost 50 years to challenge executives' perspectives on the future business environment. We base them on plausible assumptions and quantifications, and they are designed to stretch management to consider even events that may be only remotely possible. Scenarios, therefore, are not intended to be predictions of likely future events or outcomes, and investors should not rely on them when making an investment decision with regard to Royal Dutch Shell plc securities. It is important to note that Shell's existing portfolio has been decades in development. While we believe our portfolio is resilient under a wide range of outlooks, including the IEA's 450 scenario, it includes assets across a spectrum of energy intensities, including some with above-average intensity. While we seek to enhance our operations' average energy intensity through both the development of new projects and divestments, we have no immediate plans to move to a net-zero emissions portfolio over our investment horizon of 10 to 20 years.

A vision of a more hopeful future

Energy transitions have happened before. The nineteenth and twentieth centuries saw initially growth in the use of coal for industrialisation, and then oil as the modern combustion engine took hold, and then natural gas as its availability and benefits as a cleaner thermal fuel were recognised. More recently, the world is seeing the dawn of a new energy transition with the prospect of wind and solar power achieving large-scale deployment.

It is, in fact, possible to sketch out a future in which mankind manages to achieve a better life for itself while keeping the planet healthy. It requires taking an optimistic view on broad world trends in economics, politics, and society, and then combining this view with plausible further specific shifts in policy and technology development. What can be glimpsed in such a scenario is a world in which living standards are raised and, crucially, mankind has stopped adding to the total amount of CO_2 into the atmosphere: a state known as 'net-zero emissions'.

How such a vision could be made real

It is important to consider the whole pathway to net-zero emissions and not just the first steps. There is currently a very real danger that policymakers could focus only on the short-term, relatively easy options to reduce emissions that can be realised in the next decade or so. For example, electricity can already be generated with negligible emissions from wind, solar, and nuclear energy, so the transformation of this sector can progress relatively quickly. Because for many people the words 'energy' and 'electricity' appear interchangeable, in their minds, deploying such developments addresses the energy challenge in its entirety, whereas, in fact, less than one-fifth of our current end-use consumption of energy comes via electricity. So transforming the sources of electricity generation addresses only a fraction of the challenge.

Such a narrow and short-term focus would mean that soon enough, policymakers would find that progress has run into a wall because the more technically or socio-politically difficult sectors of the economy have been neglected.

A closer look at the long-term transition

Most man-made CO_2 emissions from the use of primary fossil fuel energy occur in four sectors: power generation, buildings, transport, and industry.

Changes in land use also make a substantial contribution to greenhouse gas emissions. Each sector presents different technical challenges, and each has specific characteristics that will determine its potential to decarbonise. Some areas will not be able to decarbonise completely, but not all areas need to decarbonise to achieve a net-zero scenario – it is only important that remaining emissions are offset by other parts of the system.

Some of the less obvious, longer-term actions that need to be taken become clearer if we look through the prism of a future in which net-zero emissions has already been achieved.

A transformed power sector

In a net-zero world, the power sector has made much progress. Quite apart from technical advances and lower costs in renewable technologies, society has also come to accept onshore wind, nuclear, and carbon capture and storage (CCS). This revolutionised power sector has also seen zero-emission technologies – primarily renewables – progressively displace coal to take the largest share of workload. While not all countries and regions are equally sunny or windy, evidence suggests that potential solar and wind resources would be adequate to meet current and future power needs, even in densely populated regions, as long as transmission over a few hundred kilometres is feasible and acceptable and there is adequate storage to manage daily and seasonal intermittency. (The storage challenge is one of the most significant the world faces. Batteries will have to undergo a technological leap forward if they are to offer storage at sufficient scale.)

The fact that electricity is emission-free at its point of use means the decarbonisation of the power sector enables decarbonisation elsewhere throughout the economy. So it is critical that the power sector decarbonises, and it is equally critical that much of the world's energy consumption moves to electricity. Today, electricity provides less than 20 per cent of global final energy consumption. The net-zero world is one in which that share has grown to well over half of total demand.

As we have already seen, a growing world population with a decent quality of life is likely to entail a doubling of total energy demand. But the amount of electricity in that system needs to increase by far more than this in a net-zero world that consumes half its energy in the form of electrons. Electricity is to take a far bigger slice – 50 per cent instead of 20 per cent – of a far bigger pie, one that has doubled in size. The result is that the world needs about five times the amount of electricity generated today.

A transformed building sector

In our net-zero world, building design and operation are subject to high energy-efficiency standards with full electrification being now standard. Older housing stock is retrofitted where possible to ensure that heating, cooling, lighting, and cooking are all powered by electricity. For high-rise buildings and in densely populated cities there is an increased use of district heating networks that pipe recycled or waste heat in the form of steam from nearby industrial and power facilities. A move towards more compact urban living has allowed energy savings from efficient public transport systems, a reduced need to travel long distances, and better integration of utilities.

A transformed transport sector

In the transport sector, passenger road travel is also largely electrified for short and medium-distance travel in urban environments and densely populated regions. To minimise the risk of batteries running out of power mid-journey, recharging points are easily found in these environments. The growth of vehicles with batteries also provides one of the solutions to the intermittency of renewable energy sources: smart IT technology and algorithms enable an individual car owner to trade the power storage capacity of a car battery sitting in a garage to help balance the power grid. Car owners levy a fee from utilities to store excess or provide power from their vehicle batteries to match supply and demand.

The weight and size of batteries means that the movement of heavy freight over longer distances in ships and trucks continues to require portable energy-dense fuels. Here, the use of hydrogen, which emits no CO_2 when burnt, and liquefied natural gas (LNG) – both portable, energy-dense liquid fuels – has displaced a proportion of conventional fuels. For the longest journeys by air and sea, where the limitations of batteries will probably remain too challenging for the foreseeable future, liquid hydrocarbons and biofuels continue to dominate.

A transformed industrial sector

In the net-zero world the industrial sector, much like transport, is split between those areas that can decarbonise relatively quickly through elec-trification and those areas, especially in heavy industry, where either cost or the lack of viable options ensures emissions continue. Whether a specific industrial sector is decarbonised depends on whether its fundamental processes require very high temperatures and whether certain emission-generating chemical reactions are involved.

Some light-industry sectors, such as the manufacture of clothes, wood, paper, and food, require either no process heat or relatively modest temperatures of less than 250 °C. Sewing machines, saw mills, steam-heated paper-pulping machines, and food pasteurisation vats, for example, can all run on electricity, and so these industries are powered in a zero-emissions way in a net-zero world.

Heavy industry, on the other hand, is different. The primary production of iron and steel relies on intense heat – above 1200 °C – in furnaces. Today's industrial process technologies depend on hydrocarbons as thermal fuels to produce these high temperatures. A particular challenge for the iron and steel industry is that iron reduction also requires a source of carbon to convert the iron ore to the elemental metal, and CO_2 is released as a result. Similarly, the production of Portland cement – the most commonly used cement in the world – also involves both high temperatures and the release of CO_2 as part of the chemical process that occurs. On its own, cement accounts for around 5 per cent of global man-made CO_2 emissions today with almost 0.9kg of CO_2 released for every 1kg of cement produced. In the net-zero world, substitute materials, process changes, and the use of less carbon-intensive fuels than coal, such as gas, biomass, or hydrogen, mitigate some of the emissions, but half the CO_2 released in cement production is a result of the basic chemical process involved. Furthermore, the various processes involved in the production of chemicals from petroleum products – used in solvents, detergents, adhesives, plastics, resins, man-made fibres, lubricants, and much more – also require high temperatures.

While there is ongoing research, it is difficult to see any near-term technology breakthroughs that will radically reduce or eliminate the need for thermal fuels and some carbon in such fundamental industrial processes. Yet society can't easily do without these material products. These are the basic building blocks that enable a decent quality of life to be constructed for a growing population. In a net-zero world, carbon intensity is reduced through efficiency measures, and the increased use of electric arc furnaces to recycle scrap metal has reduced the amount of new metal needed, but, for the emissions that remain, CCS is the only viable solution.

In summary, while a large proportion of industry appears capable of being electrified at moderate cost, mitigating CO_2 emissions across large swathes of industrial activity will be more challenging and costly to achieve. Yet adding CCS to any power generation or industrial facility increases capital and operational costs. The deployment of CCS in our net-zero world is likely to have come about via the introduction of a financial framework that supports it. This is likely to be a price on carbon.

Transition to a new energy mix

Overall, in this new world, there is a significantly reduced relative share for hydrocarbons, including gas and biomass. Nevertheless, these will continue to play a role within heavy-duty transport and heavy industry as already outlined, as well as being a chemical feedstock and a back-up to manage the intermittent nature of renewables as long as there is insufficient or unaffordable storage available. Where hydrocarbons are still used, they are combined with CCS when practical to prevent most of the CO_2 from entering the atmosphere. There is also biomass power generation combined with CCS to enable 'negative emissions'. In effect, sustainably farmed vegetation sucks CO_2 from the atmosphere and then, when burnt as biomass, that CO_2 is trapped and prevented from ever entering the atmosphere, creating a net reduction in the world's atmospheric CO_2. Such negative emissions are needed to offset those sectors that cannot decarbonise and those areas in the world that are slow to decarbonise.

In summary, in this world, the primary energy mix looks very different from today. Perhaps 40 per cent of energy comes from wind and solar. About 20 per cent comes from nuclear and hydroelectricity, with potentially some growth in geothermal projects. About 15 per cent comes from the bio domain, whether as biofuels for transport or biomass with CCS to achieve negative emissions. And that leaves about 20-25 per cent hydrocarbon fuels, primarily oil and gas, in the global energy mix in a net-zero emissions world. Much of the hydrocarbon slice of the mix is gas, which will have displaced coal as a significantly lower-emissions thermal fuel. But the world of the net-zero future is a complete turnaround from today, when hydrocarbons constitute more than 80 per cent of the energy system.

Transition in land use

Finally, tackling the quarter of anthropogenic greenhouse gas emissions that currently come from agriculture, forestry, and other land use means changes in the net-zero world. First, the conversion of natural forests, peat lands, and grassland to agricultural use no longer happens. Indeed, this is being reversed. Second, the 30-50 per cent of total food production that is wasted today through poor harvesting, processing, and distribution practices is much reduced. Third, the world has reduced emissions from rearing animals, with some shifting to alternate diets, helping to mitigate the rise in demand for meat from the growing population. Fourth, agricultural production has significantly reduced nitrous oxide emissions from the use of fertilisers. (Nitrous oxide is approximately 300 times more potent as a greenhouse gas than CO_2 and remains in the atmosphere for over a hundred years.)

The need for policies that support the transition

The pathway to this renewed approach to land use, as with all the other sectors outlined, involves clear, stable policies that set the framework for the right decisions to be made. In the power sector that means massive growth in generation from solar and wind, partnered with a switch from coal to gas for reliable base-load generation, and the widespread introduction of CCS. In the built environment, it means efficient homes and offices running on electricity, but it also means compact, integrated urban development. In transport, it means the electrification of much of the system and particularly road vehicles, better public transportation, the use of biofuels where available, and the roll-out of hydrogen infrastructure. In industry, it means electrification of light industry and the deployment of CCS in those sectors unable to decarbonise. In agriculture sustainable intensification of land use is needed, particularly in underdeveloped economies.

There is a lot to do. If the world is to reach a state of net zero quickly enough to prevent the most extreme effects of climate change, then deep, long-term, action needs to be taken now to lay the foundations for the future. Fortunately, some of that work has already started, and much of the work that needs to be done is within reach.

Action is already being taken

You don't have to look hard to see that action is already being taken. Renewables are on the march, primarily for electric power generation. Costs for solar PV and wind are coming down all the time, and the amount they contribute to the grid is rising year after year. Hybrid cars are now commonplace in the developed world, while battery-electric cars are becoming more popular in urban settings, with new companies like Tesla now making battery-electric cars alongside more established manufacturers like BMW and Nissan. Momentum is building behind hydrogen-powered fuel cell cars, with common standards for infrastructure being agreed and a nationwide refuelling network being introduced in Germany, for example. There is research into ever-more innovative ways to access energy, including advanced biofuels processes that turn waste into liquid fuels, and technical solutions to balance power networks, such as advanced batteries and smart grids. Efficiency regulations are ensuring homes and appliances require less and less energy to operate. Gas-fired power, with its lower emissions profile compared to coal, is gaining market share at the expense of older, dirtier stations, with gas production also growing and becoming more widespread thanks to developments in drilling, liquefaction, and transport. Carbon-pricing systems are spreading, with at least 40 countries, along with more than 20 cities, states, and regions in other nations, now involved. And CCS has a slowly increasing number of projects in operation, demonstrating that the technology can capture and safely store away CO_2 produced during power generation or industrial processes.

And then there is the Paris climate accord. Reached at the United Nations Climate Change Conference (COP 21) in December 2015, the accord was an important and constructive milestone on the journey towards net zero. At this conference, 196 countries adopted the Paris climate accord, which sets out a global action plan intending to put the world on track to avoid dangerous climate change by limiting global warming to well below 2 °C.

The framework of this agreement has been described as a 'motorway' to address climate challenges in which there are different lanes, with different economies going along these lanes at different speeds and using different vehicles. But they will all be moving in the same direction on the same motorway – and this movement, over the course of the century, will bring us transitions in the way energy is used and move the world towards the increasing decarbonisation of its economies. Through adopting the Paris climate accord, countries have signalled their intention to enter the motorway, from which, in principle, it is hard to exit.

All of this is very promising. But there is more to do. Current steps are neither big enough nor fast enough to achieve net-zero emissions by around 2070, which is the timescale required to constrain global warming within the 2°C aspiration.[2]

Priority actions needed

As demand shifts across the key areas of the economy, such as power, buildings, transport, and industry, the energy system will witness an extended period of disruption and co-evolution between established and emerging

2   Shell, 'Shell Scenarios: Sky'.

technologies. When the sector-by-sector analyses are considered together, a logical order-of-priority of actions to decarbonise the system over time emerges:

- Redoubling efficiency measures and extending electrification across the economy wherever and whenever possible;
- Sustaining momentum of renewables production growth, particularly solar PV and wind, and maximising the ability of the grid to handle their intermittency;
- Accelerating the switch from coal to gas to swiftly reduce power sector emissions while ensuring supply to meet demand – a way of keeping cumulative emissions to a minimum during the transition;
- Improving buildings, urban planning, and city infrastructure to significantly lower energy service demand;
- Accelerating government-directed efforts to promote low-carbon technologies and infrastructures, including nuclear, CCS, hydrogen transport, bio-energy, and sustainable forestry, agriculture, and land-use practices.

By 2035-50, the first three of these priority actions could bring the world to the halfway point in the transition to net-zero emissions, when much of the global growth in energy demand will have been realised, and the relatively easy decarbonisation steps will have been taken.[3] But decarbonisation efforts could run out of steam at this point unless work also gets underway in earnest today on the fourth and fifth points.

It is important to recognise that every person on the planet has an important role in the energy transition. Consumers must also play their part in adopting attractive opportunities to make great advances in efficiency and in supporting relevant political action. Without such efforts, total energy consumption will not just be double today's level, but could grow to three times greater or more, making the quest for net-zero emissions essentially impossible because the capacity to include biomass in the energy system would be exceeded. Enough land and resources are available to produce the biomass needed to offset a doubling of energy demand – but not a tripling.

Consumers will need to choose lighter, more efficient, cars. They will need to instal heat pumps, LED lighting, and other energy-efficient appliances in their homes as well as increase their recycling and improve their insulation. Collectively, they can insist on structural efficiencies in their cities with good public transport, integrated waste, water, power, and heat management, efficient construction, and good building standards. Once built, such major

3   Shell, 'A Better Life with a Healthy Planet', p. 37.

infrastructures stay in place – and shape our energy needs – for decades. So it is critical they are designed and implemented as efficiently as possible from the outset. And by choosing to live in compact cities, consumers can lower demand for energy because they don't need to travel as far, and public transport can be much more effective.

The need for government-led carbon pricing

Progress requires some additional concrete actions as soon as possible, both to encourage the business investments needed and to motivate consumers in the right direction. The first of these actions is carbon pricing. Governments need to place a value on avoiding emissions, and allow this value to incentivise economy-wide restructuring. Government-led carbon-pricing mechanisms can reduce CO_2 emissions by changing the financial basis of key decisions. They reduce incentives for the use and production of carbon-intensive products and fuels by raising their price to producers and consumers. They also increase the incentives for the use and production of low- or no-carbon fuels and energy sources by making them more cost competitive. Furthermore, in tilting the financial equation, carbon pricing incentivises the use of emission-reduction technologies like CCS and innovation in low-carbon technologies, production processes, products, and infrastructure investment.

Finally, by increasing the costs associated with energy use, a carbon price can trigger behaviour change in how energy is used across the economy and create a 'pull' for low-carbon technologies, products, and lifestyles. In other words, the government implementation of effective carbon-pricing mechanisms would create a new cost ranking of goods and services based on their carbon emissions. In turn, this cost would influence the purchasing decisions of consumers. Products with a high carbon footprint would become more expensive, leading to the stimulation of greater end-use efficiency or to decisions by manufacturers to invest in projects to lower their carbon footprint.

If the temptation today is to buy energy associated with emissions because that is the cheapest way to get it, a carbon price changes that calculation. If a carbon price increases the cost of that emissions-linked energy above the cost of the clean, renewable energy, then those who consume energy – that's everybody – will be highly incentivised to make environmentally sensitive decisions.

Politically, of course, introducing such changes requires addressing the potential resistance of voters in what has become a politically fraught and polarising arena in many countries, as well as the natural concerns of other interested parties that will face short-term challenges, such as carbon-intensive businesses. Governments could choose to return the collected carbon revenue to consumers in the form of reductions in other types of taxes or use it to support climate policy objectives such as funding low-carbon research and development. Policymakers might also use carbon revenue to provide income support to those negatively impacted by carbon pricing or to drive energy-efficiency improvements.

To be truly effective in reducing global emissions, carbon pricing needs to be implemented across as much of the global economy as possible. While national- or state-level schemes may succeed in reducing the production or consumption of fossil fuels in a given region, they may also result in these activities simply moving across national borders – so-called 'carbon leakage'. The Paris climate accord has provided useful language for the eventual development of a broad-based carbon-pricing system, but significant effort and policy development will be required to implement such a global structure. A global carbon price is likely to be achieved only by progressively interweaving systems through linkage as they are developed. The cap-and-trade systems in California and Quebec are linked, and Ontario is now joining this carbon club, creating a bottom-up linked version of the Emissions Trading Scheme implemented across Europe from 2005. Carbon-pricing policies are either in operation or expected by 2020 in the EU, China, parts of North America, Australia, New Zealand, several Latin American countries, South Africa, and Korea. But these policies are not the equivalent of a global approach with sufficient breadth, maturity, and robustness to deliver lasting change. Even after Paris, and with concerted efforts by governments, an effective global approach may take another decade; and even then, it will still require considerable calibration to actually deliver on the Paris ambition.

The need for technology investment

The second concrete action needed is investment in technology. New technologies become cheaper only as a result of ongoing demonstration and eventually mass production. While carbon pricing can jump-start emissions reductions in some parts of the economy, it won't be enough in the near term to support the much more expensive fundamental research and early demonstration stage of the next generation of low-CO_2 technologies, particularly beyond the power sector. Their development must get underway as early as possible to ensure that solutions are available and affordable for large-scale deployment. More direct government-backed funding is critical.

The need for CCS technology

The third step that needs to be taken now is funding specifically for CCS technology.

In its Fifth Assessment Report, the Intergovernmental Panel on Climate Change (IPCC) estimated that the average mitigation costs of keeping to a 2 °C pathway over the period 2015-2100 would be nearly 140 per cent higher without CCS. Notably, less than 50 per cent of the scenarios they investigated could even deliver a 2 °C outcome without CCS. But CCS is a capital-intensive technology. To date, the commercial viability of individual CCS projects has largely relied on a combination of major capital grants from government to underpin construction costs and the ability to sell the captured CO_2.

The very large scale of CCS deployment needed to achieve net-zero emissions, however, cannot be delivered on the back of such grants. Commercial viability for a CCS plant would currently require a mechanism (for example, a carbon price) to reward capture and storage of CO_2 at over $100 per tonne, but this cost could decline to around $70 per tonne in the early 2030s as more CCS plants are built, and the supply chains they rely upon mature. This would put the price of CCS-based power generation from natural gas on a par with offshore wind. (For ease of comparison, that level of carbon price would be equivalent to increasing the gasoline price I currently pay as a consumer in the Netherlands by around 10 per cent.)

Given the present lack of effective carbon pricing, financial support for low-carbon technologies (as is offered to renewables in many countries) could be extended to include CCS. Such a framework could encourage the continuation of CCS research, development, and deployment until carbon pricing reaches levels sufficient to support commercial rollout. This is particularly the case for developing countries, where the financial impact of carbon pricing on business and society is likely to delay the introduction of a high enough price to drive CCS. Mechanisms such as the Green Climate Fund, set up as part of the Paris climate accord to help developing countries counter climate change, could consider providing funds to support CCS projects.

The need for green building policies

Finally, the policy challenges that stand in the way of a revolution in the built environment must be faced and overcome. The commercial and residential sector is an area where there is a particularly strong case for additional action. Either directly or indirectly, buildings account for almost a third of global energy use and therefore a significant proportion of global emissions. Yet adding a carbon cost to the use of electricity in buildings may produce only some of the necessary impact due to the nature of the sector itself. One example is the relationship between landlords and tenants, where the latter pays the electricity bill, and the former controls the capital budget that ultimately establishes the efficiency of the building. The World Business Council for Sustainable Development has proposed a comprehensive series of efficiency-improvement measures – such as mandatory codes for new and existing buildings that tighten over time – that target regulators, investors, developers, and occupiers of buildings.

The need for new ways of thinking

Perhaps the biggest transformation that needs to take place if society is going to avoid being misled by our political and personal prejudices is actually between our ears. We are too easily seduced into seeing difficult challenges as zero-sum trade-offs or seeking spurious probabilistic optimisations.

But fortunately our instincts are also to avoid both costly downside outcomes or missing good opportunities. Either way, we look to avoid or minimise our potential regrets. That's why we buy house or car insurance, or expect diversification from our pension funds.

In addressing poverty and greenhouse-gas emissions, there has been much credible work on the relatively modest macroeconomic impact of investing in economy-wide energy transitions. This should be contrasted with the range of costs of inaction from environmental and social disruption estimated by the scientific community, and the radical uncertainties that remain in this.

It is pretty clear that the pathway to minimising potential regrets is the path of collective actions. If we don't, and the consequences are as large as many foresee, then our potential regret is huge. However, if we take action, and nothing dramatic happens in the environment, then our disappointment in possibly investing unnecessarily would be modest at most, and in fact probably invisible because we won't know what would have happened otherwise – and we would still be benefitting from better air quality, urban design, transport systems, and land use.

At some point, many more people and politicians will recognise that this is a more effective and sensible way to frame the challenges ahead, and to make meaningful choices accordingly.

A better life for all with a healthy planet

The fact that it is possible to envisage a net-zero future with a better life for all is, in itself, reassuring, even inspiring. Some of what needs to be done has already been achieved, but there is a great deal more that lies in front of us. The world will need huge and courageous progress in economic restructuring. It needs the emerging and established components of the global energy system to evolve and grow together. It needs the large-scale implementation of alternative technologies. Above all, it needs the active involvement of millions of consumers, policymakers, civil society leaders, and businesses across the planet.

It can all be done. But it is a big job. We have to get to work now. *We must not allow more decades to drift by again with only half-hearted progress.* The direction is clear, the tools and technologies are available or close at hand, but how long it will take will depend on our collective choices and will indelibly affect the quality of life on this planet.

Works Cited

IPCC (Intergovernmental Panel on Climate Change). Fifth Assessment Report. https://www.ipcc.ch/report/ar5/. Accessed 5 July 2018.

Shell. 'A Better Life with a Healthy Planet: Pathways to Net-Zero Emissions'. Supplement to Shell *New Lens Scenarios* (NLS), 2013. https://www.shell.com/energy-and-innovation/the-energy-future/scenarios/a-better-life-with-a-healthy-planet/_jcr_content/par/relatedtopics.stream/1475857466913/a1aa5660d50ab79942f7e4a629fcb37ab93d021afb308b92c1b77696ce6b2ba6/scenarios-nze-brochure-interactive-afwv9-interactive.pdf. Accessed 22 Nov. 2017.

Shell. 'Shell Scenarios: Sky – Meetings the Goals of the Paris Agreement'. 2018. www.shell.com/skyscenario. Accessed 5 July 2018.

About the Author

Jeremy Bentham is Vice President, Global Business Environment and Head of Shell Scenarios, Royal Dutch Shell.

3 Are Major Wars More Likely in the Future?

Joëlle Jenny and Alyssa Stalsberg Canelli

Abstract

In the contemporary volatile global context where the balance of geopolitical power is in flux, the international system stands at an inflection point. Increased connectivity and the fast pace of change, largely driven by technological innovations, are straining the ability of norms, laws, and governance institutions to manage shocks and disruptions. Yet connectivity and innovation also make the international system more resilient. The conditions for hope rest in a simple fact: we are better equipped than ever to understand, and work with, systems effects.

Keywords: global security, international governance, dynamic resilience, asymmetric warfare, deterrence mechanisms, social narratives

For its 27 January 2018 edition, *The Economist* dedicated its cover to 'The Next War' with a special report on the new battlegrounds of geopolitical competition.[1] Days earlier, the World Economic Forum issued its annual *Global Risks Report 2018*, which assessed that the risk of political and economic confrontations between major powers, including outright military conflicts, had risen sharply. This risk is accompanied by a rise in 'charismatic strongman politics' and exacerbated by a decline in support for rules-based multilateralism.[2] Shortly after these two publications, the *American Bulletin of Atomic Scientists* issued a warning that growing nuclear threats, climate

---

1 *The Economist.*
2 The survey of nearly 1,000 experts from government, business, academia, and non-governmental organisations showed 93 per cent expect a worsening of political or economic confrontations between major powers in 2018, including 40 per cent who believe those risks have increased significantly.

Wilkinson, Angela, and Betty Sue Flowers (eds.), *Realistic Hope: Facing Global Challenges.* Amsterdam, Amsterdam University Press, 2018.
DOI: 10.5117/9789462987241_CH03

change, and a lack of trust in political institutions are bringing the world ever closer to 'apocalypse'.[3] To make their message explicit, they moved forward their symbolic Doomsday Clock, bringing it the closest to midnight that it has been since 1953 at the height of the Cold War.

These risk assessments are in stark contrast to the optimism that followed the end of the Cold War. In the 1990s, the prospect of state-on-state conflict had retreated considerably. There were still violent conflicts, but they were mostly within, rather than between countries. Even after the Second Iraq War, optimism prevailed. Science writer Stephen Pinker has been one of the most prominent voices making the case that, historically, violence has significantly declined. He argues that a careful examination of long-term trends shows how violence has steadily gone down across a wide variety of indicators, including in the numbers and intensity of wars, genocides, and other mass killings.[4]

Indeed, many historians agree that global violence over the past few decades is lesser in scale as compared to humanity's experience of war over the last several millennia. But it is an open question as to whether this benign trend will continue, or systemic global shifts will make large wars more likely. As noted in a recent joint UN-World Bank report, the number of major violent conflicts has tripled since 2010. In 2016, more countries experienced violent conflict than at any time in nearly 30 years. This increase is taking place in a volatile global context where the balance of geopolitical power is in flux, and transnational factors like advances in information and communication technology, population movements, and climate change create new risks.[5] At the same time, the report notes that several of these same factors have the current and future potential to drive trends of prosperity and stability.

Within this confluence of double-sided factors that can influence both global instability and stability, three key trends stand out as particularly critical to determining the future landscape of global security:

1   In the information age, characterised by the growing ubiquity of digital technology, there has been a significant increase in global connectivity between people, corporations, organisations, and economic, political, and information systems.

2   Global connectivity has made the international system more complex, in large part because the number of state and non-state actors with agency has rapidly increased.

3   Science and Security Board.
4   Pinker.
5   World Bank Group and UN.

3   The global security effects of increased connectivity and complexity are exacerbated by the insufficient adaptability of international mechanisms to prevent and de-escalate crises.

In a more connected and complex world, single events can have global repercussions. In systems analysis, such 'ripple' effects are a well-known phenomenon. When several systems interact, as is the case in international politics, these effects become almost impossible to predict. A street vendor immolating himself in Tunisia triggered the Arab Spring. The policy choices in response to the 9/11 attacks irremediably changed international security. The decision to invade Iraq led to the unravelling of the Middle East.[6] As historian Christopher Clark puts it, '9/11 exemplifies how a single, symbolic event can change politics irrevocably, rendering old options obsolete and endowing new ones with an unforeseen urgency'.[7]

In a complex and fast-evolving system, there are greater risks that an accident or a political miscalculation between big powers could escalate into a major war. This is particularly true in a context of hybrid or asymmetric warfare, in which a weaker party wages disruptive hostile actions that often fall below the threshold of open warfare. Collusion between states and criminal or terrorist groups adds to this 'fog of asymmetric war'. For instance, the WannaCry ransomware attack in 2017 was first attributed to Russia, even if security experts fairly rapidly concluded that it had originated in North Korea. The 2015 cyberattack on France's TV5Monde was claimed by ISIS, but investigations found the source to be located in Russia. Even once intelligence services correctly attribute the source of an attack, there is a high risk of miscalculation in decision-making and responses to events because misinformation, multiple conflicting aims, and public expectations can severely narrow down options.

Post-WWII security rests on an architecture of treaties, agreements, and organisations best exemplified in the UN system. Their primary purpose is to enable international cooperation and dispute resolution. A wide diversity of regional cooperative arrangements, such as the EU, complement this global architecture. Whether we subscribe to the thesis that post-WWII global institutions were once capable but became gridlocked, or rather, as

---

6   'Discourse does more than merely reflect events that take place in the world; discourse interprets those events, formulates understandings, and constitutes their socio-political reality. [...] Language is used to create meanings; and the process of meaning making is inherently political in that it is imbued with relations of power that come together to manoeuvre, contest and negotiate the meaning at stake' (Hodges and Nilep, p. 2).

7   Clark, p. xxvii.

we would contend, that global institutions were never sufficiently developed to deal with the complexities of an interconnected world, the result is the same: multilateral cooperation is under severe pressure. The formal process by which laws and treaties are formed is slow, burdensome, and increasingly blocked.[8] In a more complex and more connected world, the fast pace of technological innovation is straining the capacity of governance mechanisms to provide agile rules for the game. As cyber technologies, 3D printing, bioweapons, drones, hypersonic weapons, and many other disruptive innovations broaden the range, scope, and complexity of threats, we lack the mechanisms to agree what is and what is not an acceptable use of technology.

Discussions about the risks of an artificial intelligence arms race illustrate the extent to which the international system stands at an inflection point, with innovations outpacing evolution in norms, protocols, and governance mechanisms.[9] This challenges the effectiveness of the organisations vested with the power of arbitration – in effect, straining the resilience of the international system to manage shocks and disruptions and to decrease the risk of escalation into warfare. Technology and the contested global landscape increasingly favour pre-emptive over defensive military postures, a shift reflected in the new military doctrines of all big powers.

Against the backdrop of these systemic trends, there has been a troubling return to 'strongman politics' and nationalist discourses, as the leaders of many countries have adopted increasingly antagonistic policies based on 'us-against-them' rhetoric. Information and communications technology (ICT) is a central plank of this battle. Web and mobile communication technologies are transforming who is an opinion shaper, and how policies are made. This phenomenon is in part driven by the internet's underlying business model, which is based on the 'attention economy': access to content is generally free for the public because profit is generated by advertising revenues and by collecting online behavioural data on those visiting the website. For this to work, people are enticed to stay as long as possible on the web pages they visit. Under this model, in which everyone from politicians to the media to corporations compete for attention, news has become increasingly sensationalistic, appealing to people's fears, hopes, and other emotions.

When used to feed exclusionary narratives, ICTs can lead to mass disruption of political institutions and outcomes. The phenomenon of disinformation

8   For an extensive discussion of these challenges, see Hadfield.
9   Kaspersen.

is nothing new. Denying even the most glaringly obvious facts, undermining the legitimacy of those who bring evidence of the truth, and generally sowing confusion in people's minds about whom to trust, are all time-honoured techniques in warfare and in political strife. But the rise of social media has increased the global reach of such operations, as shown by Russia's involvement in the 2016 US presidential election and in European elections. The reach and effects of 'hybrid warfare' – namely, the conduct of disruptive operations below the threshold of war aimed at destabilising another country – has been greatly amplified through the proliferation of ICTs.

Disinformation campaigns are effective because they tap into deep-seated narratives about group and national identity and leverage threat perceptions against those identities. When paired with the psychology of social media, disinformation campaigns amplify exclusionary messages, effectively creating echo chambers that build on positive feedback loops and amplify system perturbations. This makes social media a perfect medium for manipulating a group's feelings, fears, and ideas about their own collective identity. Ultimately, post-truth relativism erodes social consensus and undermines the credibility and legitimacy of the norms and institutions in which we have vested the powers of arbitration. The interconnectedness of people through digital media and technology has enabled the weaponisation of information and disinformation on an unprecedented scale.

Disinformation campaigns and ethno-nationalist rhetoric are also effective because people have grounds for resentment, fear, and uncertainty. What some have called the hyperglobalisation of the 1990s, during which market deregulation and an acceleration in global trade of goods and services had the adverse effect of deepening inequalities, created a fertile ground for public dissent. In his book on the retreat of Western liberalism, *Financial Times* columnist Edward Luce dissects the impact that stagnating growth has had on between one-half and two-thirds of people in the West, who have been treading water – at best – for a generation, and argues that the erosion of middle-class incomes has eaten away at liberal democratic consensus.[10] Not only have deep disparities between the richest and the poorest increased, but they have also become much more visible, feeding a sense of resentment and injustice felt by those left behind. The financial crisis of 2007-2008 brought this into sharp contrast. In a context in which citizens of many Western societies feel insecure about their jobs and economic prospects, it has become easier to manipulate and amplify those fears through the widespread use of ICT.

10   Luce.

The very notion of international cooperation faces significant challenges. Against the backdrop of greater complexity in a digitally connected world, the rise in antagonistic discourse between the big powers contributes to creating a more dangerous international order. While it may not be in any one country's interest to escalate geopolitical tensions into war, the risk of political miscalculation and of accidental escalation into open conflict is not insignificant. Deep inequalities are on the rise. A world in which the richest 1 per cent own more wealth than the rest of the planet is not morally defensible.[11] Untethered liberalism has led to a global backlash against free trade; consumerism, which is seen as the engine of growth, plays a significant part in driving pollution. Stunning medical advances may never get within reach of large segments of the population, within both advanced and developing economies. These problems are real and important, but fixing them will not happen by pulling up the drawbridge of nationalism. Nor can it be done at the expense of the very global architecture of norms, laws, and institutions that have enabled cooperation and brought greater stability and prosperity.

The case for realistic hope: Dynamic resilience

Against the backdrop of greater complexity in a digitally connected world, the rise in antagonistic discourse between the big powers contributes to creating a more dangerous international order. While it may not be in any one country's interest to escalate geopolitical tensions into war, the risk of political miscalculation and of accidental escalation into open conflict is not insignificant. Navigating this fluid landscape requires new and more agile ways of handling disputes in order to limit the risks that crises will escalate out of control. It requires adapting the existing limits that international law places on the conduct of warfare to the reality of new and emerging technologies. The world of our grandchildren could be one of peace and prosperity, or it could be one riven with violent conflict and instability.

The good news is that there is no deterministic path from complexity to violent conflict. Single events can increase or decrease the risk of major conflict, but they are almost impossible to predict. Yet it is possible to examine some of the structural factors that will help strengthen global resilience to shocks and conflict. For example, the trend towards increasing complexity could also contribute to greater stability. Complex systems tend to be more resilient than linear ones because they offer better alternatives

11   See, for example, Oxfam.

when one element of the system fails. Corrective mechanisms gradually fix what is not working. Mutual dependency, known as entanglement, increases the incentives to avoid conflict and to cultivate resiliency to shocks.

Two influential US academics, Robert Keohane and Joseph Nye, noted that the future lies neither exclusively with the state nor with transnational relations: geographically based states will continue to structure politics in an information age, but they will rely less on material resources and more on their ability to remain credible to a public with increasingly diverse sources of information.[12] The new 'glocal' – the merging of global and local – of the digital age creates unprecedented opportunities to harness the benefits of science and technology for all and to distribute power more equally. This could help address many of the pressures that drive the risks of war. More actors with greater agency complicate decision-making, but also bring to the table more voices, with greater influence, that can contribute to mutually beneficial outcomes. The search for global solutions is no longer the prerogative of states alone: corporations, networks of cities or universities, venture capitalists, international coalitions of civil society organisations, and even single individuals, such as Bill Gates, all carry significant weight at various levels. Even though social media has demonstrated its power to divide, it can also help convey narratives that call for greater cooperation and support the search for multilateral solutions.

Shaping the norms and institutions that enable global cooperation is no longer the remit of governments alone; this, in itself, is a reason to be optimistic. The same system characteristics described above – greater complexity, increased connectivity, and the growing agency that individuals, groups, and corporations have gained to shape discourse – could also increase the adaptability and nimbleness of the international system, thus making it more resilient to crises and shocks. We call this 'dynamic resilience', and we illustrate our point through five key factors that can support the growth of these 'glocal' systems of cooperation.

Reasons to be optimistic

The factors that will determine future global peace and security will be a mixture of human decisions, unforeseen events, technological developments, and sheer luck (or absence thereof). We have little control over some of them. But we can choose to invest in the mechanisms that make cooperation more likely than confrontation; we can develop the collective norms, laws,

12   Keohane and Nye, p. 84.

and institutions that help de-escalate crises before they erupt into open confrontation; and we can improve our ability to recover and adapt after major disruptive events such as man-made and natural disasters, in ways that help address deep-seated inequalities. In a complex system – or rather, in a complex system of systems – small steps can go a long way towards building greater resilience to crises and shocks. In the words of Ron Lehman, former US Chief Negotiator on Strategic Offensive Arms (START):

> The key to preventing disasters is nearly always found in the successful management of lesser events that might otherwise encourage or enable dangerous outcomes we wish to avoid. Thus, the human factor is more important to maintaining strategic stability than is the technological factor. Nevertheless, technology influences both the context for human behaviour and decision-making itself. Of course, technology also provides tools to create strategic change or respond to it.[13]

Some of these investments in the infrastructure needed for international cooperation are already underway, and more can be done if we are prepared to adopt more agile governance mechanisms. Technology, which is fuelling accelerated competition between major powers, also offers tremendous avenues to enhance dynamic resilience. Not only has technology enabled spectacular leaps in human knowledge, it has also made knowledge accessible to a greater number of people than ever before. This alone means that single individuals have gained unprecedented ability to shape the norms and institutions that underpin societies' ability to cooperate.

1   *Governments, corporations, interest groups, and private citizens are working together to adapt laws and institutions.*
Higher-level cooperation requires bottom-up rule-making with multiple stakeholders. Citizens and the private sector have increasingly mobilised to push for new forms of global governance in response to the challenges associated with new technologies. For instance, Microsoft has called for a 'digital Geneva convention' to 'commit governments to protecting civilians from nation-state attacks in times of peace'.[14] For years, artificial intelligence scientists and innovators such as Stuart Russell and Elon Musk have been sounding the alarm about the risks of unregulated AI development,

---

13   Lehman, p. 148.
14   Smith.

particularly in terms of lethal autonomous weapons systems (LAWS).[15] These discussions have now started in earnest in the UN disarmament and arms control bodies in Geneva.[16] They are likely to be slow and may not solve all the problems, but they will help strengthen the safeguards. As Wendall Wallach, the renowned AI scientist, ethicist, and Yale scholar, points out, 'A ban will help slow, if not stop, an autonomous weapons arms race. But most importantly, banning LAWS will function as a moral signal that international humanitarian law (IHL) retains its normative force within the international community'.[17] Another example is the International Campaign to Abolish Nuclear Weapons (ICAN). Although it is unlikely to achieve its objectives in the current geopolitical context, it sends a powerful message, further amplified by having been awarded the 2017 Nobel Peace Prize.[18]

2   *Science and technology are helping improve decision-making.*
With billions of additional devices to become connected, combined with advances in sensors, geolocalisation, computing power, and digital technologies in general, the availability of data is expected to grow exponentially. This is already fuelling dramatic scientific advances. Feeding on this data, breakthroughs in artificial intelligence and machine learning are transforming our ability to analyse and learn. Advances in behavioural sciences and neurosciences are helping us better understand how humans make decisions, and what biases intervene. Increasingly, we have the tools to improve early warning of natural and man-made disasters, and thus to be better prepared to manage crises. AI is already helping improve diagnostics in the medical domain, and is used, for example, to sift through case law to facilitate sentencing in legal cases. Provided adequate safeguards are put in place, notably as regards the transparency of algorithms, AI could help make political decision-making more accurate and more predictable, thus decreasing the risks of strategic surprise that can lead to crisis escalation.

3   *Cooperative science and technology helps tackle global threats and promote common goods that would otherwise be ignored.*
Public health experts have long known that diseases do not respect borders, and that in order to combat epidemics, we need significant horizontal

---

15   Galeon.
16   For example, in the UN Office for Disarmament Affairs. For a commentary on UN CCW discussions on LAWS, see Ban Lethal Autonomous Weapons.
17   Ban Lethal Autonomous Weapons.
18   Norwegian Nobel Committee.

collaboration across sectors (government, NGOs, science, corporations, grass-roots educators, economic infrastructure). Climate change is perhaps the most significant long-term threat to our existence, and despite the ambivalence of the current US administration, the Paris climate accord represents international cooperation and cross-sector advances. In the same way, the global security landscape can be made more resilient through the collaborative mobilisation of these networks of scientists, governments, citizen-activists, communities, corporations, and private institutions.

4   *Technology can protect the integrity of our systems and ICT infrastructures and protect it against cheats; this, in turn, helps build the legitimacy of institutions.*

We are already seeing instances of how ICT crises can make the system more resilient by triggering adaptation. Companies such as Alphabet use algorithms not only to identify radicalising content but also to target potential recruits with messages aimed at countering violent extremism. The social media manipulations surrounding the 2016 US presidential election have acted as a wake-up call about the need to tackle fake news, incitements to violence, and the use of algorithms, bots, and trolls to distort public information. Navigating the delicate landscape between reliability of information and freedom of information will be a difficult task that technology alone cannot fix, but the vibrancy of the debate is in itself salutary. Fact-checking initiatives, many of them stemming from academia and from the public, are an example of networked approaches to fighting fake news. AI, machine-learning, and big data analytics can help identify outliers, bots, and other distortions. Blockchain, which makes it possible at any time to identify who created and disseminated content, offers a promising avenue to build trust in the integrity of the information.

5   *Individuals – you and I – have unprecedented ability to shape the world around us.*

In the age of social media one does not need to be a priest, a general, or a tribal leader in order to shape our communities' narratives. As historian Yuval Noah Harari points out, 'Any large-scale human cooperation – whether a modern state, a medieval church, an ancient city or an archaic tribe – is rooted in common myths that exist only in people's collective imagination'.[19] For millennia, the power to shape those myths rested with religious, political, or military leaders. Today, anyone with a connected device can be an

19   Harari, p. 27.

influencer. The problems that this creates – sharpening of moral differences, information overload, lowering trust – can be addressed through both technology and a renewed commitment to global education. Digital skills are now part of most school curricula. The next generations could be much more agile at recognising and ignoring the pernicious claims being made on their time, money, and information as digital consumers. Education prepares people for the future – it sets the conditions of mind, evaluation, critique, and careful risk-taking that are necessary to respond to the multilevel systemic shifts that are happening right now.

The conditions for hope

The conditions for hope rest on a simple fact: the same factors that increase the risks of major war can also make the international system more resilient to them. We are better equipped than ever to understand and work with networked effects.

The digital age is here to stay, and with it the trends towards greater complexity. This, in most likelihood, will manifest itself through continued shocks and crises. There is no putting the genie back in the bottle, but we can get better at working with systems-effects. Crises and international tensions can help us do that if we recognise their learning value. We can invest in correcting the deeply divisive effects of disinformation campaigns and their propagation through social media. We can promote discourse and investments that value cooperation over confrontation. We can hold our leaders to account when they encourage reckless escalatory rhetoric that could result in major state-on-state war. We can invest in increasing the agility of the global governance mechanisms that exist to manage and de-escalate international tensions.

Peace is not the absence of conflict: it is the absence of violence as a means of coercing others into one's system of values, interests, and power. Conflict is part of the natural process of change that enables societies to adapt, both on the micro-community and the macro-institutional levels. Without some degree of conflict, most communities could not interrogate old traditions and integrate new values or members. The challenge is how to develop norms, laws, and institutions that make possible the peaceful resolution of disputes and the search for mutually beneficial arrange-ments. By harnessing the power of technology to connect people, ideas, and resources, we can create the conditions for many independent initiatives and innovations which will, in turn, allow us to respond to crises and conflicts in nimble ways.

Works Cited

Ban Lethal Autonomous Weapons. 'Recaps of the UN CCW Meetings Nov 13-17'. http://autonomousweapons.org/recaps-of-the-un-ccw-meetings-nov-13-17/. Accessed 22 Jan. 2018.

Clark, Christopher. *The Sleepwalkers*. New York: Harper Perennial, 2012.

The Economist. 27 Jan.-2 Feb. 2018.

Galeon, Dom. 'Elon Musk Leads AI Experts with Letter Urging UN to Consider Threat of Autonomous Weapons'. *Futurism*, 21 Aug. 2017. https://futurism. com/elon-musk-leads-ai-experts-with-letter-urging-un-to-consider-threat-of-autonomous-weapons/. Accessed 22 Jan. 2018.

Hadfield, Gillian K. *Rules for a Flat World*. Oxford: Oxford University Press, 2017.

Harari, Yuval Noah. *Sapiens*. New York: HarperCollins, 2015.

Hodges, Adam, and Chad Nilep, eds. *Discourse, War and Terrorism*. Amsterdam: John Benjamins, 2007.

Kaspersen, Anja. 'We Are on the Brink of an Artificial Intelligence Arms Race. But We Can Curb It'. World Economic Forum, 15 June 2016. https://www.weforum. org/agenda/2016/06/should-we-embrace-the-rise-of-killer-robots. Accessed 30 Jan. 2018.

Keohane, Robert O., and Joseph S. Nye, Jr. 'Power and Interdependence in the Information Age'. *Foreign Affairs*, Sept.-Oct. 1998, pp. 81-94.

Lehman, Ronald F., II. 'Future Strategic Stability and Technology'. In *Strategic Stability: Contending Interpretations*, ed. Elbridge A. Colby and Michael S. Gerson. Carlisle Barracks: US Army War College Press, 2013.

Luce, Edward. *The Retreat of Western Liberalism*. New York: Grove Press, 2017.

Norwegian Nobel Committee. 'The Nobel Peace Prize for 2017'. Nobelprize.org, 6 Oct. 2017. https://www.nobelprize.org/nobel_prizes/peace/laureates/2017/press. html. Accessed 22 Jan. 2018.

Oxfam. 'An Economy for the 99%'. Jan. 2017. https://www.oxfam.org/sites/www. oxfam.org/files/file_attachments/bp-economy-for-99-percent-160117-en. pdf?cid=aff_affwd_donate_id78888&awc=5991_1516293457_9d50a6f2708e47 6fbaf0ab96331d67f9. Accessed 22 Jan. 2018.

Pinker, Steven. *The Better Angels of Our Nature*. New York: Penguin, 2011.

Science and Security Board. 'It Is 2 Minutes to Midnight: 2018 Doomsday Clock Statement', ed. John Mecklin. *Bulletin of the Atomic Scientists*. 25 Jan. 2018. https://thebulletin.org/sites/default/files/2018%20Doomsday%20Clock%20 Statement.pdf. Accessed 29 Jan. 2018.

Smith, Brad. 'The Need for a Digital Geneva Convention'. Microsoft on the Issues (blog), 14 Feb. 2017. https://blogs.microsoft.com/on-the-issues/2017/02/14/need-digital-geneva-convention/. Accessed 22 Jan. 2018.

World Bank Group and UN. *Pathways for Peace: Inclusive Approaches to Preventing Violent Conflict*. Washington, DC: International Bank for Reconstruction and Development/The World Bank, 2018.

World Economic Forum. *Global Risks Report 2018*. 13th ed. Geneva: World Economic Forum. http://www3.weforum.org/docs/WEF_GRR18_Report.pdf. Accessed 22 Jan. 2018.

About the Authors

Joëlle Jenny is an Associate at Harvard University's Weatherhead Center for International Affairs and a member of the World Economic Forum's Global Future Council on International Security. Until 2016, she was the Director for Security Policy and Conflict Prevention at the European Union's External Action Service.

Alyssa Stalsberg Canelli, PhD, is the Assistant Dean of Academic Affairs at the Graduate School of Arts and Sciences at Brandeis University. Her research expertise is in global Anglophone literatures, postcolonial theory, globalisation, and the narratives of nationalism.

4 The Future of Work

Peter Schwartz

Abstract

Rapid advances in artificial intelligence and robotics are leading to fears of massive job loss in many industries. There is little reason to fear the extreme scenarios of destructive AIs and robots taking over. But the concerns over jobs are quite real. The US created over 100 million new jobs between 1950 and 2015. We can already see how many new jobs in old industries and wholly new industries are coming into being, enabling humans to work alongside smart machines. There are at least four possible scenarios driven by how rapidly new jobs are created and how fast today's jobs disappear. The real issue is the transition and the ability to retrain and reskill today's work force most impacted.

Keywords: artificial intelligence, machine learning, future jobs, retraining, employment scenarios

Is the future of work, no work?

There is a growing fear that technology will displace workers, leaving vast numbers of unemployed, under-employed, and unemployable workers. The gaps between the top, the middle, and the bottom are widening, and the fear is that the middle and bottom will be left further and further behind as only the most skilled remain in employment.

Fear of technological displacement began when weaving machines were introduced in Scotland, and the Luddites opposed the displacement of the weavers. Fears of job loss have accompanied every major technological transition. And indeed, many jobs have disappeared along the way, often with their whole industries. Local dairies and their milkmen are a thing of the past. Draftsmen gave way to Autocad. Personal servants for the middle class gave way to modern appliances. Typing pools gave way to word processors and personal computers.

Wilkinson, Angela, and Betty Sue Flowers (eds.), *Realistic Hope: Facing Global Challenges*. Amsterdam, Amsterdam University Press, 2018.
DOI: 10.5117/9789462987241_CH04

Is something different this time?

Yes. In the past most technology replaced human physical functions like motion, lifting, hitting, and so on. The new technologies are cognitive technologies taking on human mental functions like speech, hearing, vision, and so on. Technology appears to be going right for what it means to be human. It is one thing for a bicycle rider to replace a runner or a car to replace a horse, but more challenging when an AI replaces an accountant or an editor. The fear is that as the capabilities of artificial intelligence grow, there will be little left that human beings can do better.

It is this fear that this chapter addresses. Will most human workers be replaced by smarter machines? Will retail clerks follow telephone operators into history as automated check-out and home delivery take over the retail experience? Will truck drivers go the way of pony express riders as self-driving trucks hit the road? It is these kinds of questions that are much on the minds of workers today. Do they face a future of technological obsolescence? Students face the question of how to make educational and career choices that are not a dead end.

A second question about the future of AI also commands a great deal of attention because it is so scary and has been the subject of many major films. It is that AIs will become so powerful that they threaten our very existence. Whether it is *The Terminator, The Matrix,* or *Colossus: The Forbin Project,* or the HAL 9000 killing off the astronauts one by one in the film *2001: A Space Odyssey,* smart machines are usually deadly machines. The fear is that a malevolent machine will take over from humanity. This vision of AI is shaped by the early concepts of artificial intelligence as a human brain substitute. The idea was to understand the brain sufficiently well that it becomes possible to take neural functions, like sight, memory, or speech, translate them into computing terms, and put them on a chip in order to create a self-aware, purposeful, robotic being. It would have consciousness, intent, judgement, and essentially every aspect of human nature, including potentially even emotion.

The early pioneers of AI, like Marvin Minsky, followed this route with little success. At least two waves of interest in and funding for AI gave way to AI winters when the funding dried up due to lack of progress. Understanding the brain sufficiently well that we could map it onto silicon has proven to be extremely difficult. Indeed, the more we learn about the brain, the harder the problem gets. In other words, the Terminator is not about to come through your door anytime soon. The US government has a multi-decade programme of neural research that may reach fruition by mid-century. So, it is possible that we might see a general-purpose artificial intelligence with human-like abilities in the second half of this century, but it is not certain. It just may prove too hard.

Another approach to AI, machine learning, has taken a very different path and does not represent the kind of threat that a runaway AI might. Machine learning involves running large volumes of data through interpretive algorithms that make sense of it and get better with each run. These algorithms focus on one cognitive function at a time, such as facial recognition or language translation. As the algorithms see more faces or translate more words, they get better at that specific task.

But we can add up all the neural algorithms we know without arriving at a general-purpose AI. Getting better at language translation does not lead towards a self-aware purposeful intelligence. The algorithms are simply comparing strings of letters with no awareness of their meaning. The algorithm determines that '*Haus*' in German equals '*casa*' in Spanish without knowing what a house is and what you do with it. There is no 'knower'. Machine learning is leading to very useful functions without raising the threat of runaway robotic intelligences. While someday the concerns about self-aware and purposeful but malevolent AIs might be worth paying attention to, these machines are many decades off in the future. So we will focus on the real issues of job displacement that motivate concerns today and in the next few decades.

The future of jobs

To address the future of jobs we need to recognise that jobs fulfil three functions. First, they get things done, the production function. Second, they provide income. But equally important, jobs provide a sense of meaning and purpose to the worker. So, in addressing the future we need to think about all three functions. For example, we might imagine a future where robots do all the work and make us so rich that we could provide incomes to everyone – but such a future might leave us adrift with no sense of purpose.

How will new technologies impact current employment? McKinsey has recently done a thorough analysis of which human skills are most vulnerable to the new automation and which are likely to remain uniquely human.[1] For example, predictable physical tasks, like moving goods around a warehouse, take 18 per cent of all time spent at work in the US. Of that time 81 per cent could be automated with a great impact. On the other hand, unpredictable

1   Manyika.

physical work (like plumbing repair) takes 12 per cent of the time, of which only a quarter could be automated, with much less impact. Managing only takes 7 per cent of the time, but only 9 per cent could be automated. Keep in mind that these are tasks and time, not jobs. A job usually involves multiple tasks. A manager may spend some of their time collecting data, a task easily vulnerable to automation, freeing time for interfacing with other people, a task much less vulnerable to automation. We now spend 16 per cent of our time interfacing with others – 20 per cent of that time might be vulnerable to automation. For example, coordination software, like Slack, facilitates team collaboration, allowing more to be done in less time.

McKinsey also considered which sectors of the economy are most vulnerable to automation. Not surprisingly, accommodation and food services (73 per cent), manufacturing (60 per cent), transport (60 per cent), agriculture (57 per cent), retail (53 per cent), and mining (51 per cent) are most vulnerable. At the other end of the spectrum, education (27 per cent), management (35 per cent), professional services (35 per cent), and healthcare (36 per cent) are much less vulnerable. So, some tasks in some industries – say, repeatable physical tasks in manufacturing – are very vulnerable. If that is your entire job, you are very vulnerable to job loss. On the other hand, managing doctors in a hospital means you are likely to keep your job.

Of course, just because a task or job could be automated from a technology point of view does not mean it will be. Several factors come into play to determine what will actually happen. How easy is it technically? Some technologies can be extremely challenging to make work. Sometimes the cost may outweigh any gains. Labour markets have a big impact. If labour is cheap and abundant, then automation may not make sense – for example, China 25 years ago. On the other hand, if labour is scarce and expensive, then the push for automation is almost inevitable – China today. Finally, regulation and social acceptability can have a big impact. Labour laws and trade regulation have been used for a long time to protect jobs. For example, regulations on hairdressers assure not only quality of service but protect the jobs as well.

In many instances machine learning and other forms of AI will be used to augment human capabilities rather than replace them. For example, rather than simply replacing their jobs, AI can enable predictive maintenance, making repair people much more productive by helping them focus on the high priority tasks. Indeed, repair and maintenance is likely to be one of those jobs that will grow in demand as more and more technology gets embedded in nearly every aspect of life. Many jobs in the future will have an augmented intelligence element to them as AI is applied to make them more productive, or safer, or more interesting.

What has happened to jobs since the end of WWII?

In 1950, of the US population of about 160 million, 60 per cent of the working-age population was employed. By 2015, with a population that had doubled to 330 million, nearly 80 per cent of the working-age population was employed. Within those gross numbers there was an enormous amount of change. In 1950 nearly 60 million people had jobs, while in 2015 almost 150 million people were employed.[2] The US economy created 90 million jobs in that half century. In that period, of course, many women came to work, taking up many of those jobs. But along the way many jobs disappeared or diminished dramatically, like telephone operators, typists, and milk men, while whole new categories of jobs were created, like software programmers, television producers, jet pilots, clean room operators, theme park actors, and many more.

Jobs decline for several reasons. The mechanisation of agriculture not only vastly expanded productivity and output, it drove employment on the farm from over half of the population in the 19th century to about 2 per cent today. The farms of the 19th century could not feed a population of 300 million people, let alone be a major exporter. Whole industries disappear with technological change. With the advent of industrial cooling and refrigerators, the ice industry, icehouses, and ice delivery all vanished. Modern plumbing ended the night soil industry. Social change combined with technological change leads to profound dislocation. In Europe and the US vast numbers of people were household servants. It was said that in the UK, before WWII, 'half the people were servants downstairs, and half the people were served upstairs'. Being middle class meant having a servant or two. Home appliances and social attitudes towards service eliminated servants except for the very wealthy. As the diesel engine took over from the steam locomotive, fireman who shovelled the coal slowly disappeared, lingering beyond their useful lifetime only because of a strong labour union. Technological displacement has been a driver since the beginning of the industrial revolution and is unlikely to stop any time soon.

The evolution of global trade has also led to massive declines in some industries, driven by labour and material costs. Textiles, clothing, and furniture all moved to low labour-cost countries over the course of the 1970s and 1980s. As foreign labour costs have risen and technology evolved, some of that manufacturing has returned to the US and Europe. The ability of China to produce steel much more cheaply led to a huge decline in the

2   Bureau of Labor Statistics.

US steel industry. Only protection saved the European steel industry, but now it is no longer European owned. Of course, new ways of producing steel, like the mini-mill recycling scrap steel, led to some recovery of the domestic industry in the US. The huge rise in oil prices in the 1970s led Americans to want smaller, more efficient cars. But Detroit's business and union leaders failed to adapt, and the market went to Japanese and European manufacturers. Today, of course, there is a huge foreign-owned domestic industry as nearly all the non-US carmakers produce huge numbers of cars in South Carolina, Kentucky, Tennessee, and Mississippi for the US and the global market. BMW is the largest exporter of cars from the US, and Chrysler is part of Fiat, an Italian company. Consumer electronics took off in the 1970s, but US makers, like RCA, Sylvania, and Motorola, all failed to adapt, while Japanese companies Sony, Panasonic, and Toshiba all took the market. My father worked for RCA and fought a losing battle to adapt as tubes (valves) gave way to solid-state electronics. Higher quality products from Korea are now taking the market from Japan. The evolution of global supply chains was another form of job displacement. Cars, furniture, appliances, and heavy equipment assembled in the US all rely on components sourced from all over the world.

The story of job losses, therefore, is not as simple as either technological obsolescence or predatory trade practices. It is the result of a complex array of very dynamic forces evolving and interacting over time. That reality is inevitable and is unlikely to stop anytime soon. Good policy choices can mitigate that dynamic and facilitate more benign trajectories but cannot stop it without an implausible freeze on change. European labour policies slowed the rate of adaption because they constrained labour mobility, leading to many fewer jobs being created. So, some jobs in some places will continue to decline.

The critical questions are how quickly do new jobs come along, where do they come from, who qualifies for them, and what are the income implications? One source of new jobs, of course, is simply growth. From the 1950s the vast expansion of the consumer society led to a huge increase in jobs that we already knew how to do: home and infrastructure construction, appliance and car manufacturing, retail and banking, healthcare and education. Nearly all the traditional categories of jobs grew with the great wave of economic growth from 1950 to 1970. A key factor in job growth, therefore, is how rapidly the economy grows. High growth leads to new jobs and higher wages as labour markets remain fairly tight. That is what produced the growth of the middle class in the US, Europe, and Japan in the 1950s and 1960s. The period from 1995 to 2000 was a great example as the internet boom led to high growth in jobs and higher wages. Part of the current tension over jobs is the result of slower growth since 2000. Lower growth in employment and wages was the result.

What will it take to return to higher, 3 per cent+, growth? Since most of the workers of the near future are already born, we can be sure that labour force growth will be fairly slow. In most nations the biggest variable is immigration, and that has huge political uncertainties. Productivity gains in existing industries appear to be slowing down, so the crucial questions are whether new technologies such as AI will restore productivity growth and whether they will lead to whole new industries and new categories of jobs. A return to higher growth will mean many more of today's jobs in the future. This includes everything from nurses, skilled crafts, and delivery drivers to entertainment producers and so on. Undoubtedly, some jobs will disappear or diminish in number, but high growth alone can absorb much of the labour force. If higher growth comes back with more jobs and higher incomes, then the questions become those of new industries and new categories of jobs.

Higher innovation-driven growth is self-amplifying. New technologies like modern pharmaceuticals can drive growth by creating and distributing wealth for growing investment and wages. It also creates demands for new kinds of jobs like molecular biologists and drug salesmen. High growth and high technology feed each other in a virtuous circle. In a high-growth scenario driven by innovative technology, jobs are being created in existing industries and new ones in traditional job categories, often in entirely new ones. It is also easier to launch new innovative products and services in a booming economy than in the midst of recession.

What are the key uncertainties?

The future of jobs is fundamentally uncertain because it takes imagination to see this future. Simply extrapolating the past will inevitably be wrong as technology and industries evolve. So, looking ahead requires identifying the potential and relevant scenarios. That begins with the key uncertainties and what drives them. To understand those drivers, it may be helpful to look at the birth of Silicon Valley as a very successful example of technology-driven economic transformation.

In 1972, Santa Clara County had tens of thousands of unemployed engineers made redundant in the aerospace industry by the end of the Vietnam War. Defence contractors like Lockheed, Sylvania, and GTE were shutting down in the region. At that moment two connected fortuitous events drove rapid evolution. First, Intel started producing its first commercial microchips, which became a universal engine of change. Second, two former engineers, Eugene Kleiner and Tom Perkins, launched the first venture fund. That combination of desperate unemployed engineers based around two great universities, Stanford and the University of California, a high-potential technology like microchips, and risk-oriented, technologically sophisticated capital drove a huge wave of start-ups that ultimately became companies like Apple, Cisco, and Google. The key point is that the success of Silicon Valley was both accidental and particular to that place and time. Any scenario of the future will also be particular to the technology and the geography.

The first key uncertainty is how quickly do current jobs diminish or disappear altogether? How quickly will cab drivers and truck drivers give way to automated vehicles? How quickly will junior accountants and lab technicians give way to AIs? How quickly will retail clerks give way to automated checkout? If the technology gets better and cheaper fast, and if consumer acceptance is high and regulatory barriers are low, then it is plausible in many places that there will be significant job losses in traditional categories fairly soon, say within a decade. However, it is equally plausible that self-driving vehicles may be very difficult to operate in large numbers in the city and therefore might replace human drivers far more slowly. Or accountants and lab technicians might find new ways of delivering creative value. Or retail clerks might find new ways of giving customers valuable experiences. It is not a foregone conclusion that the new technologies will kill a large number of jobs soon in most places. Some jobs in some places sometime soon … maybe.

The second major uncertainty is how quickly new jobs will develop both in traditional categories and in new industries. As technology gets embedded nearly everywhere, support and repair services will become a huge opportunity. When your smart front door won't let you in, you will want your remote service technician to unlock and repair the door fast. As life becomes more complex, more people will use combined human and virtual assistants to navigate and manage that complexity. Production of complex pharmaceutical molecules is likely to require new kinds of active chemical technicians. The growth of the commercial space industry will create a large number of jobs in launching those vehicles from a variety of space bases. The new jobs are likely to emerge first in the great centres of innovation, like the San Francisco Bay Area or New York or Munich or London or Shanghai, while other regions are likely to be laggards. At one extreme, therefore, we will have regions with rapid growth in new jobs while at the other end of the spectrum we will see few if any new jobs. There are very few microchip designers in West Virginia or Glasgow. Of course, most of these new jobs depend upon a growing economy. Economic stagnation would almost certainly slow the development of new industries and new jobs. And poor societies do not generate vast numbers of service jobs. Only relatively affluent societies support layers of service.

What are the resulting scenarios?

The combination of uncertainties leads to at least four possibilities.

False Alarm: If the current jobs persist and new ones take a very long time to emerge, then tomorrow may be very familiar. Perhaps the technologies prove more challenging to implement than anticipated, or regulation slows the rate of change. After all, AIs and robots were supposed to replace workers many years ago, but a second AI winter in the 1990s slowed the deployment. It is not hard to imagine regulation slowing the rate of diffusion of self-driving vehicles. Or slower economic growth might not justify either the capital costs or the R&D budgets to drive a rapid shift towards new technologies. We should recognise that this has happened several times in recent decades as waves of automation swept through the economy, raising similar alarms about job loss – but many more jobs were created than destroyed, so the concerns turned out to be enormously exaggerated. Prosperous, more slowly changing regions, like Scotland, could look like this.

Jobs Crisis: This is the scenario people are most worried about. Current jobs are displaced quickly, but new jobs emerge only slowly, leading to massive unemployment. New technology turns out to be cheap and powerful, customers love it, and regulators don't want to stand in the way of progress. Whole categories of jobs, like drivers, clerks, assemblers, auditors, etc., begin to disappear. But this time is different. The new technologies do not spawn new job-creating industries nor improve productivity enough to create vast new wealth, so few new jobs are coming along. Consumers benefit at the cost of worker – an equation that doesn't work. Unemployed workers are poor consumers. The industrial Midwest of the US could look like this. Manchester, Glasgow, Detroit have all gone down this path in the past.

The New Economy: If the current jobs give way to a rapid growth in new jobs, the economy will begin to feel very different. Rapid changes in manufacturing and service delivery lead to big changes in economic structure. 3D printing combined with rapid design and local delivery could lead to a highly distributed and localised manufacturing sector with very different skills required. The key issue in this future is training for the new jobs. Perhaps the only place on earth that really feels this way today is Singapore. This is the scenario that has the highest growth potential and is a big win for both workers and consumers.

Labour Shortage: This is the surprise scenario. Suppose we are adept at creating new jobs, but the old ones do not fade. Imagine that the demand for delivery drivers is so great that we keep the human ones and add automated vehicles, or that most applications turn out to need both humans and machines. The San Francisco Bay Area is like that today – a rapid creation of new jobs even though the old ones aren't gone yet. The Bay Area is actually facing a labour shortage.

What should we do?

The world economy is going through another major technology-led transformation as it does whenever fundamental new technologies like electricity, microchips, or artificial intelligence are invented. Such transformations create great opportunities but are also very disruptive. The goal of policy is to enable the transformation and smooth out some of the rough edges, to capture the upside in, for example, new industries, to help assure the widest participation, and to cushion against some of the downside consequences. Policies need to address three broad areas: raising the rate of economic growth, stimulating entrepreneurship, and supporting workers.

At the macroeconomic policy level the debate has been dominated by a focus on austerity to avoid both rising debt and the recurrence of high inflation. The focus is now shifting towards raising growth rates and thereby increasing demand for more goods and services and the jobs that deliver them. The policy levers include public sector spending, especially infrastructure, interest rates, research and development, international trade conditions, and regulation. Even countries like Japan, which have suffered nearly two decades of economic stagnation, are slowly raising their growth rates through an aligned set of macro policies. Nearly all the major economies of the world have the potential for an economic policy alignment that could raise national and global economic growth rates by a meaningful amount, say 1 or 2 per cent.

The second arena for intervention is stimulating entrepreneurship. Even societies that are notably entrepreneurial, like China or Egypt or the Netherlands, can put many barriers in the way of business formation and development. And ones that are less notably so, like Singapore, have undertaken to make their societies more entrepreneurial. They have used some combination of low-interest, high-risk investment loans, trade lending, eased licensing procedures, regulatory reform, and government as the biggest buyer in the country. All are aimed at making it easier to start a business and grow it while it is still small. While the vast number of new jobs will come from fairly large companies, most of them begin small.

Finally, there are all those policies that focus on the workers themselves. The most important actions have to do with education, from early days to apprenticeships to vocational training and retraining. This includes all the new models of education that make it far more accessible to many more people and more sophisticated in its pedagogy. The latter is important because many of the jobs of the future emphasise soft skills and emotional intelligence, enabling people to work closely together. A second set of policies is focused on making it easier for workers to change jobs, including affordable housing, mobile benefits, and unemployment benefits with incentives for training and a return to work. The workforce is becoming more liquid than solid as the demand for labour evolves quickly. Immigration policy can also be very important in many countries. A controversial area of policy is incomes. What is the impact of minimum wage policies? Will we need a universal basic income (UBI) because there won't be enough jobs? The goal should be to provide jobs that will fulfil all three purposes mentioned earlier in this chapter: provide income, get things done, and provide a sense of societal self-worth to the individual. But if job creation is weak, while a UBI might ease the issue of incomes, it might also undermine that sense of individual self-worth.

There is little downside in enabling smooth economic transitions. In three of the four scenarios above, the best response is the same – investment in training and education, and policies that support labour mobility. Only in the *False Alarm* scenario is the need modest. But the risks of the others are so great that on balance it is vital to take the steps today that will enable disruptive economic transformations without shattering social fabrics. If workers feel that change is not their enemy because they have the tools to adapt and the support they need, then the legitimacy of the system will remain unchallenged. But if change feels overwhelming, disruptive, and of benefit only to distant 'others', then the legitimacy of the market economy and the technological progress that drives it could be fundamentally undermined.

Works Cited

Bureau of Labor Statistics. 'Employment Status of the Civilian Noninstitutional Population, 1947 to Date'. US Department of Labor. https://www.bls.gov/cps/cpsaat01.htm. Accessed 4 Mar. 2018.

Manyika, James. 'Technology, Jobs, and the Future of Work'. McKinsey & Company, May 2017. https://www.mckinsey.com/global-themes/employment-and-growth/technology-jobs-and-the-future-of-work. Accessed 3 Nov. 2017.

About the Author

Peter Schwartz is an American futurist, innovator, author, and co-founder of the Global Business Network (GBN), a corporate strategy firm specializing in future-think and scenario planning. He currently serves as Senior Vice President Strategic Planning, Salesforce.com. Schwartz is author of several best-selling books, including *Inevitable Surprises* and *The Art of the Long View* and script consultant on such films as *WarGames* and *Minority Report*.

5 Digital Technologies: Every Cloud Has a Silver Lining

Claire Naughtin and Stefan Hajkowicz

Abstract

Digital technologies have blurred the line between the physical and the virtual, creating both opportunities and challenges for societies around the world. But the pace of change within our institutional structures and that of digital technologies is out of sync, giving rise to unintended consequences and exacerbating existing asymmetries in society. What lies ahead is a burning platform: the need to adapt our social, political, and economic systems to operate in a digital world so that we can unlock our full intellectual capacity to innovate, discover, and create.

Keywords: technology, innovation, social and institutional change, digital disruption, industrial revolution

> *We tend to overestimate the effect of a technology in the short run and underestimate the effect in the long run.*
> – Roy Amara, former President of the Institute for the Future

Blurred boundaries in an increasingly digital world

Digital technologies have become smaller, more sophisticated, and ubiquitous, impacting and shaping every facet of our lives.

The once clear divide between the 'real world' and the digital world is now blurred. Who we are online is no longer considered as separate from how we interact with people in person; instead, what we do online increasingly impacts what we do in the physical world, and vice versa. Our personal life has become intertwined with our professional life. Our work time has been muddled up with our leisure time. We now need to manage not only a physical

Wilkinson, Angela, and Betty Sue Flowers (eds.), *Realistic Hope: Facing Global Challenges*. Amsterdam, Amsterdam University Press, 2018.
DOI: 10.5117/9789462987241_CH05

identity, but a virtual one as well. This has led many to turn to 'digital detoxes' to gain any sense of separation from technology to remind themselves – or even to prove to themselves – that they can function without it.

Not only is the boundary between the digital and the physical becoming increasingly blurry, but so are the boundaries between technologies themselves. We have shifted from individual products and devices to a digital ecosystem. A smartphone is no longer used simply for calling and messaging; rather, it is the key device through which individuals can purchase products, interact with their financial institutions, access news and current affairs, and stream music and videos. People can now seamlessly interact with and transfer applications and services from one device to another. This convergence of technologies has given rise to the 'Internet of Things', which presents opportunities to make our lives more streamlined, easier, and simpler, and provide new market opportunities, but also challenges the traditional ways in which we view the world.

Threats to our social institutions

The diffusion of the digital world within the real world inevitably means the two are dependent upon each other; changes in the digital world are impacted by how well they are received in the physical world, and vice versa. Therefore, as technology changes and adapts, so, too, must our 'real world' social and institutional structures. Increasingly though, this does not always seem to be the case; the pace of change in the digital world seems to be accelerating, yet the pace of institutional change is lagging behind. The common distinction between the 'digital economy' and '*the* economy' in itself is evidence of the fact that the changes arising in digital domains are viewed separately from the broader institutional structure.

Technology continues to progress in line with Moore's law (the observation that the number of transistors in a dense integrated circuit doubles about every two years). This is seen in the explosion of computing power, data storage capacity, device connectivity, robotics, and artificial intelligence. In *The Age of Spiritual Machines*, the scientist and futurist Ray Kurzweil uses a chessboard analogy to illustrate the exponential growth trajectory observed for many digital technologies. As the story goes, the emperor plays a game of chess with its inventor and agrees to pay the inventor a grain of rice for the first square, two grains for the second square, four grains for the third square, and so on, doubling the number of grains with each subsequent square. By the 32nd square, the end of the first half of the chessboard, the emperor is in debt to the inventor almost four billion grains of rice – a large but manageable debt.

Things change dramatically as they cross over to the second half of the chessboard where the rate of rice increases exponentially and quickly places the emperor in trouble. This analogy explains why the current digital age can feel so dramatic all of a sudden. As we spill over to the second half of the digital chessboard, the level of impact can intensify quickly. The way traditional markets, industries, and societies operate can change dramatically.

But increasingly it seems that the systems that govern the impact of technology on society are not always keeping up. Political, social, economic, and legal frameworks – many of which have been developed for the physical world – can be slow to adapt and transform and are therefore ill-suited to operating in a digital form. Traditional regulatory frameworks, for instance, were established around clear boundaries for services, infrastructure, and property rights; they are not designed to handle the complexity and interoperability that can come with converging mobile, broadband, and cloud technologies.

The mismatch between the speed of technological advancement and changes in legacy frameworks is problematic for two reasons. First, it can lead to unintended consequences in the form of data and privacy breaches, cybercrime, and online scammers, to name just a few. And second, this mismatch can limit our capacity to exploit the value of new digital technologies. This has certainly been seen with driverless vehicles, where the legal frameworks, along with the public's perceptions around safety and security, have been slow to adapt, which acts as a barrier to the productivity, road safety, and mobility gains that these vehicles could bring.

This disparity between the pace of technological change and institutional change can also give digital a bad name, and has raised concerns about whether technology is causing society more harm than good. Is technology actually making us happier and more productive in our lives? Despite the fact that we are living in an advanced digital age, productivity levels among many developed countries have plateaued in recent years. Are digital technologies themselves causing these negative impacts, or are we, as a society, simply not adapting quickly enough to reap the benefits that digital technologies present? Here we argue that while there is much to be gained from digital technologies, these opportunities are only virtually here until they are supported by the institutional context.

A rising gap between the haves and the have-nots

Digital technologies can exacerbate existing asymmetries in society – the rich get richer, and the poor get poorer. The elite few reap the benefits of the latest gadgetry and software systems, while those in the lower percentiles continue to struggle to meet their basic human needs. It begs the question – who wins in the digital age?

Increasingly, we see the importance of digital inclusion and its relation to social inclusion. In order to participate in society, an individual, business, or community needs to have the necessary digital literacy skills and access to affordable internet. Unfortunately, though, the digital divide between the regional and metropolitan areas and between developed and developing countries still persists due to barriers in digital access, affordability, or skills.

In the digital age, data has become a highly sought-after resource. This becomes a risk when the lion's share of this resource is held by only a few entities. In recent times, we have seen the emergence of 'digital behemoths' – large technology-enabled companies, including the likes of Google, Amazon, and Apple, which dominate the global market and have the profits to match. This has led to a massive concentration of wealth, with only 10 per cent of the world's publicly held firms generating 80 per cent of global profits.[1] Even though digital technology is often positioned as breaking down traditional barriers and allowing new players to enter the market, do these new players really stand a chance against these corporate giants? So far, it seems unlikely.

Technology does not *create* these problems for society, of course. But it can exacerbate existing inequalities. The lack of skills, capital, or access to the resources required to embrace the opportunities of the digital age can increase the divide between the haves and the have-nots. While this divide might not be new, the digital age has brought bigger and more specific changes that, along with the increased pace of change, require more proactive attention.

The threat of job loss and underemployment

Historically, it is not uncommon for job loss to follow technological innovation, causing despair. This was certainly the case during the early stages of the Industrial Revolution, spanning from 1760 to 1860. This was a time of rapid technological advances that saw the introduction of the steam engine and railroads and innovations in the textile and iron industries, all of which improved productivity. While technology was booming, unfortunately, wages and living standards were not. The first half of this revolution saw incomes for most people remain relatively steady and no improvement in life expectancy. Many were left feeling pessimistic about the actual pay-off of technology and whether it was in fact doing more harm than good.

1   Dobbs *et al.*, p. 3.

We see a similar story playing out today. Traditional jobs are increasingly at risk of redundancy due to computer automation. Depending on where you look, anywhere from 9 per cent to 47 per cent of existing jobs will reportedly be completed by a robot or computer in the coming decades.[2] This variability creates a great deal of uncertainty around the impact of technology on future jobs and employment models. Worryingly, those most impacted by the automation are middle-skilled workers, leading to a hollowing out of the labour market, particularly in countries whose workforce is exposed to higher levels of routinisation.[3] These changes brought about by task automation could place some workers at increased risk of chronic unemployment if they find themselves displaced from work and unable to find a suitable replacement job.

On the other hand, digital optimists argue that the internet is creating new job opportunities for millions of people previously shut out of the world economy. Peer-to-peer economies and platform models are opening up new opportunities for work and employment and breaking down traditional barriers for new market entrants. Popular platforms such as Upwork, Kaggle, InnoCentive, and Freelancer have introduced new avenues for workers to earn an income and for employers to outsource jobs. Rather than relying on the traditional nine-to-five model, workers can now use teleworking and co-working facilities to work anytime, anywhere, for anyone.

In theory, these new platforms' employment models should provide greater flexibility for work and help to create a truly global workforce. But it's not clear whether these potential benefits will be materialised. With the perks of freelance work come issues of income instability, volatility in the job market, increased global competition, and difficulties accessing finance. A survey of sellers on Etsy – an online marketplace for independent retailers to sell unique handmade or vintage items – found the average seller income was US$44,900, which was 10.2 per cent lower than the average national US income.[4] While it is common for workers to use freelancing and platform businesses as supplementary sources of income, these non-traditional lines of work would likely not be viable as a full-time option even if potential workers needed them to be.

---

2   Carl Benedikt Frey and Michael Osborne from the University of Oxford were the first to estimate the impact of computerisation on the US workforce, estimating that around 47 per cent of jobs were at high risk of disappearing at the hands of computers (Frey and Osborne, p. 38). More recent research from Melanie Arntz, Terry Gregory, and Ulrich Zierahn from the University of Heidelberg use an alternative, task-based approach to modelling the impact of computerisation and found only 9 per cent of US jobs are at high risk of future automation (Arntz, Gregory, and Ulrich, p. 4).

3   IMF, p. 139.

4   Etsy, p. 2.

New employment models created by technology can come at a cost. Traditional and non-traditional employment models are subject to the broader institutional environment in which they operate and the conditions that come with this. And it is young workers who are most at risk from these potential consequences. They are likely to work in the 'gig economy' and are therefore more vulnerable to underemployment or income insecurity than those in more conventional, stable roles typical of previous generations.[5] Instead of creating jobs for future generations, peer-to-peer economies and automation may in fact do the opposite.

The rising threat of cybercrime

Cybercrime is a global issue, and the number of cyberattacks has continued to grow year by year, costing governments, businesses, and citizens around the world hundreds of billions of dollars annually. In 2016 alone, cybercrime cost the global economy approximately US$126 billion and impacted an estimated 689 million victims.[6] The potential scale and severity of cybercrime has seen it become a top priority for national security for many countries. Indeed, in 2016, the US deemed cybercrime its biggest threat, ahead of all other economic, environmental, societal, and geopolitical risks.[7] Digital is the new face of global warfare.

Heralded as a 'silent global digital epidemic',[8] cybercrime has left many internet users feeling fearful that their personal information will not be protected online. But this fear is not always enough to change their online behaviour. Indeed, recent research by Norton found that 76 per cent of respondents are relatively lax in how they protect themselves online, continuing to share passwords and engaging in other risky online behaviours.[9] This is yet another symptom of a failure to adapt how we manage our information in a virtual environment: consumers are operating online but acting as if locking their computer in their home is enough to protect their information from online thieves. As the number of connected devices increases, failing to enact appropriate protective measures against online risks could leave consumers as easy targets for hackers.

---

5   Pennycook *et al.*, p. 10.
6   Symantic, *Norton Cyber Security Insights Report*, p. 5.
7   World Economic Forum, p. 69.
8   Symantic, *Norton Cybercrime Report*, p. 3.
9   Symantic, *Norton Cyber Security Insights Report*, p. 1.

The social costs of living in a digital world

Platforms such as Facebook and Twitter have become key environments in which we can cultivate our virtual personas, maintain connections with colleagues and loved ones, and develop new social and professional networks. But the rise of mobile technologies and social media has brought with it the concern that we could lose our ability to socialise, empathise, and connect with other human beings. In this sense, technology and the increased connectivity it provides could actually be working to sever 'real' social ties rather than strengthen them.

Researchers from the University of Michigan have examined these social changes over time. An analysis of studies of American college-aged students from 1979 to 2009 found their level of empathetic concern declined 48 per cent over this period, along with a 34 per cent decline in their capacity to take another person's perspective.[10] These changes corresponded with the introduction of various social media platforms and likely contributed to these declines. Perhaps we are getting worse at navigating social situations and relating to others in the physical world due to the amount of time we spend interacting online; or perhaps the amount of time that we spend online means that we have less and less time to dedicate to our real-world relationships. Either way, technology seems to be having a less-than-desirable impact on our interpersonal relationships.

The loss of privacy

The line between what is public and private information is becoming less clear-cut. This raises questions about how much of our own personal information and data we own – or rather, what *should* we own – and who is able to access and use it. Data are increasingly being used to create unique customer experiences, with platforms such as Netflix and Spotify able to use algorithms to map consumers' previous behaviour and to tailor their selection of movies, television shows, and music to suit their predicted preferences. Other examples come from Uber, which uses customer information to determine its surcharge rates, or driver data to gamify the driver's experience.

Knowledge of these data tricks can sometimes cause outrage and apprehension among the general public. How dare *they* use *my* data to manipulate me? In a world where we have more data at our fingertips than we know what to do

---

10   Konrath *et al.*, p. 186.

with, there are ample opportunities to track and collect data on consumers. A popular sentiment is a fitting reminder to the current reality: 'If you're not paying for it, you're not the customer – you're the product being sold.'[11] Despite these concerns, convenience often gets the best of us, with consumers opting to share their personal details sourced from their other online accounts in exchange for a quick and easy pre-filling service. Our consumer behaviours are ill-suited for the new digital environment we are operating in.

The threat to democracy

Increased digital connectivity has brought with it other ills, including social media trolling, online stalking, identity theft, and fake news. Fake news, in particular, has been the subject of significant public attention. Thanks to online platforms, anyone can now create and publish information that may – or may not – be grounded in objective facts. As a result, internet users are regularly faced with information overload and find it challenging to distinguish fact from fiction. Traditional media outlets have been brought into question too, with public doubts around the trustworthiness of the information they report. This has been a particular challenge for communicating information about science to the public. A survey of the UK public in 2014 found that around 70 per cent of respondents felt the media sensationalises science and makes it difficult to know what to believe.[12]

If there is little faith left in traditional media, where will citizens turn for information on current affairs? Social media, perhaps? Research from the Pew Research Center has found that about six in ten adults in the US source at least part of their news from social media, with Reddit and Facebook among the top platforms people use.[13] But social media does not seem be immune to fake news either. The issue was emphasised in the 2016 US presidential election, which saw Donald Trump elected as the president of the United States. Polling of the US public during this time found fake news was more prevalent on social media than in traditional media outlets,[14] and that citizens were poor at distinguishing real news headlines from fictional ones.[15] This has led some to speculate about the extent to which fake news can skew public perceptions and its power to influence citizen decisions.

11   Lewis.
12   Castell *et al.*, p. 76.
13   Gottfried and Shearer, pp. 2 and 9.
14   Silverman.
15   Silverman and Singer-Vine.

Technology is an influencer not a determinant

A key theme that emerges across examples from the digital economy is that its impact is not inherent in the technology. The technology itself does not inevitably lead to positive or negative consequences. A new platform or device on its own is not sufficient to cause great havoc and disruption. By the same token, technology alone cannot create significant social change.

Evidence that technology alone is not sufficient to bring about social change comes from attempts to use the internet, social media, and e-petitions to drive positive collective action and large-scale grass-roots movements. We don't deny the value of these new forms of digital activism: they provide ways for like-minded individuals across the world to connect and to gain social momentum around a given social, environmental, or political issue. But while supporters recruited through social media campaigns might be willing to give the issue a 'thumbs up', relatively few actually make a financial donation or recruit fellow supporters.[16]

As American history professor Melvin Kranzberg put it, 'Technology is neither good nor bad; nor is it neutral.'[17] Kranzberg argues that the outcomes produced by technology are not inherent in the digital tools themselves, but arise in the context and conditions in which the technology is applied. In other words, it is the institutional structures within which the technologies are used that ultimately determine whether they have a positive or a negative impact on society. As Donald MacKenzie and Judy Wajcman further argue in *The Social Shaping of Technology*, all too often the focus is on how technology impacts society, rather than how society impacts technology.

Applications of technology are embedded in social and cultural institutions, and therefore their impact is shaped by this broader context. It is only when the pace of institutional and societal change trumps or at least keeps up with that of technology that we can see the true benefits of this digital revolution. Failing to keep pace is essentially like going backwards. The new digital age can unlock countless opportunities for technology to be used for good and have a profound transformative effect on what it means to be human.

But how then do we reap the benefits of the current digital age and unlock the transformative potential of digital technologies?

16   Lewis *et al.*, p. 2.
17   MacKenzie and Wajcman, pp. 4-5.

Avoiding empty hope

The first step is to correct the false assumption that technology will solve our biggest problems. Subscribing to this idea merely leads to empty hope and a lack of real action, distracting us from the core societal or political issues that warrant our attention. Instead, we, as a society need to focus on how we can use technology to create the necessary institutional change, rather than assuming that positive change will be a natural by-product of whatever techno-fix we choose to employ. We need to see technology as a tool for change, but not a solution in itself.

Automating routine work tasks will not produce a thriving labour market, but it will free workers up from mundane drudgery to engage in more interesting and satisfying work tasks that require creativity, problem-solving, and social intuition. Virtual reality will not eradicate discrimination and prejudice, but it can allow someone to experience the perspective of a minority group member and make them more conscious of ways in which they can engage in more inclusive behaviours. Electric cars will not be the sole fix that reduces the harmful effects that greenhouse gas emissions have on the environment, but they will promote greener lifestyle behaviours and foster a broader shift towards lower-carbon economies that are needed to address the climate crisis. And the list could go on.

Evidence for realistic hope

How do we know that it is possible to use technology to generate institutional change and transform societies? Because we have seen it happen before and because there are countless examples of this popping up around the world today. The second half of the Industrial Revolution saw a rapid increase in income, life expectancy, and educational attainment for the majority of humans. The national average life expectancy at birth in England and Wales rose from 40 years in the 1800s to 46 years in the 1890s.[18] Similarly, wages went also up, increasing from around 55 pence at the beginning of the century to 190 pence by the end.[19]

And life expectancy and living conditions are leaps and bounds better today than they were back in the 1990s. Thanks largely to technological innovation, the majority of us enjoy greater opportunity and better quality of life than our great grandparents. The digital technologies of the current

18   Szreter and Mooney, p. 104.
19   Clark, p. 1325.

era are on track to deliver the same benefits to humanity as the industrial technologies of the previous era. As with the Industrial Revolution, there will be a difficult adjustment period. But if we adjust well and make good decisions about how the digital technologies can be deployed for broad societal benefit, the transition will happen faster and more smoothly.

We only have to look to the field of science to see that the digital dividends are starting to pay off. Digital technologies have provided a multitude of ways for researchers from around the world to pool their collective brainpower and tackle some of the most challenging scientific problems. In 2015, researchers from the European Organization for Nuclear Research (CERN) set a new record for cross-border collaborations with their work on the Large Hadron Collider, which included 5154 scientists and engineers. Digital connectivity now also means that ground-breaking research, such as finding a cure for cancer, is no longer a product of individual research labs. It's a global 24/7 process. As researchers in one time zone finish up for the day, they can share their outputs with researchers in another to continue from where they left off.

'Big science' projects have become commonplace, too. The Human Connectome Project, for instance, is a collaborative effort that aims to map the functional and structural anatomy of the human brain in a way similar to what has previously been done for the human genome. The potential benefits that this could provide for personalised medicine and the diagnosis and treatment of health conditions are endless. Such efforts would not be feasible if it weren't for the internet and its ability to connect research labs from different parts of the world to share data, knowledge, and learnings.

Technology is also enabling science to push cultural boundaries and unite scientists from otherwise hostile nations. SESAME (the Synchrotron-Light for Experimental Science and Applications in the Middle East) is an international research cooperative that has united researchers and scientists across different disciplines in the Middle East and neighbouring countries, including arch-rivals Iran and Israel. This initiative uses technology and science as a bridge between otherwise diverse societies to encourage international cooperation and peace. Not only does this approach enrich the scientific process and the knowledge that can be gathered, but it also opens the door for more positive cultural relations and mutual understanding.

Digital technologies have also transformed the way we administer healthcare, dramatically improving the accuracy and ease with which doctors can diagnose and treat a patient's condition. An example comes from IBM Watson Health, which has transformed cancer diagnosis. Using artificial intelligence, IBM Watson Health is able to digest and synthesise an overwhelming amount of patient information and records in a fraction of the time it would take a human oncologist. When tested, IBM Watson Health selected the same course of treatment as the human oncologist in 99 per cent of cancer cases and found a better treatment that was missed by an oncologist in 30 per cent of cases.[20] The opportunities this technology unlocks for the treatment of life-threatening illnesses is astonishing – not to mention the untapped potential for developing countries that do not have access to specialised medical professionals.

Distributed ledger technology, or 'blockchain', as it is more commonly referred to, is another technology that is shaking up the status quo. Proclaimed by some of its biggest proponents as the 'Internet 2.0', blockchain provides a novel, more efficient, and tamper-proof way to transfer value between parties, whether that be currencies, ideas, information, or votes.[21] The bucket list of potential applications for blockchain is endless, ranging from banking and finance to food production and distribution to government management. While blockchain has the potential to save on time, costs, and the need for intermediary services, it can also help to restore trust and transparency in systems where they are currently lacking.

Among the great benefits of blockchain is its potential to overcome societal norm barriers, empowering financial independence in women in developing nations. In *The Age of Cryptocurrency*, Paul Vigna and Michael Casey detail the story of Parisa Ahmadi, an Afghani woman with a passion for film and writing.[22] Parisa earned a modest wage writing film reviews for a US-based arts group, Film Annexe. Because Afghani girls and women are not permitted to have a bank account, Parisa did not have direct access to any of her hard-earned wages; instead, they went directly into her father's or brother's account. Parisa is among the two billion people around the world who do not have a formal bank account (the 'unbanked') and who struggle to save money, gain credit, and effectively participate in the global economy.[23]

To circumvent this problem, Francesco Rulli, the founder of Film Annexe, came up with an innovative solution. He began paying his writers in Bitcoin – a form of digital currency that is governed by a blockchain system. Unlike regular currencies, this method of payment did not require employees to have a bank account, and workers' wages could be paid directly into their own digital 'wallet'. In the case of Parisa Ahmadi, the use of this digital

20 Lohr.
21 Tapscott and Tapscott, p. 20.
22 Vigna and Casey, pp. 204-7.
23 Demirguc-Kunt *et al.*, p. 14.

payment system effectively freed her from financial dependence on her male family members, empowering her to make her own financial decisions and participate in a global economy that had previously been unattainable.

Digital technologies and the use of big data are also transforming urban environments, enabling them to operate more efficiently. With two-thirds of the world expected to reside in cites by 2050,[24] cities will increasingly become a key hub for human activity. They present a goldmine of possibilities in administering critical services more efficiently and reducing the harmful impacts of wasted natural resources. Arguably, one of the most significant applications of big data has come from Singapore's Digital Twin project. 'Virtual Singapore' is a digital carbon copy of the city of Singapore, providing vast stocks of data derived from sensors to gain real-time insights into transport flows, pedestrian movement patterns, and water and energy usage, just to name a few. Digital twin applications present immense potential to transform the urban environment from static, reactive systems into efficient hubs for humanity.

Technology can also make our work safer and more fulfilling. Much of the analysis of the impact of automation on jobs focuses on the economic gains that can come of it, but a key benefit comes from the ability of technology to complete work tasks that are dangerous, tedious, or plain boring. An analysis of Australian jobs found that the number of days lost to workplace injury could be reduced by 11 per cent if the most risky physical work tasks were instead automated.[25] The benefits of this have been seen in the mining industry, where automated trucks replace the need for human drivers to put themselves at risk.

Technology may also help make work tasks more stimulating. Machines and robots are well-placed to complete routine, predictable tasks, which are typically the least enjoyable ones for workers to complete. If current trends in automation continue, low-skilled workers are predicted to find their work 62 per cent more satisfying by 2030, with positive benefits for middle-skilled (56 per cent) and high-skilled (30 per cent) workers, too.[26]

Technology is also providing new sources of economic growth. 3D printing, for example, may revolutionise the manufacturing industry, which, until recently, has been on a downward spiral in many industrialised nations. Such opportunities are seen in the realm of 'micro-manufacturing', which specialises in the production of customised, small-batch products for specific

24   UN, p. 2.
25   Alpha Beta, p. 21.
26   *Ibid.*, p. 23.

customer needs and niche markets. The birth of these new digitally enabled industries will be critical for countries desperately looking for the next wave of economic growth. 3D printing is also changing the nature of global trade, opening up new avenues for smaller players to participate in global value chains; rather than having production dispersed across countries, it can be localised closer to the customer.

These innovations only scratch the surface for what is possible with digital technology. The potential for technology to transform every facet of humanity for the greater good is boundless. The limits are only those we place on it. But as we have seen, there are many outstanding challenges in intertwining technology with our existing institutional structures to create a platform for change. And there are more challenges waiting for us around the corner. There is a very real need to transition our societal and political frameworks to function effectively in a digital age.

Emerging questions

Many ethical and moral dilemmas are emerging with digital technology. Should robots have moral rights? Should we tax robots that replace humans at work? Should we limit the extent to which children and citizens are exposed to digital content? The blurring of national boundaries that comes with digital technologies also presents issues in areas such as cybersecurity, taxation, intellectual property, and international trade regulations. How do we handle tax evasion in global digital companies? What impact will 3D printing have on global trade? It is also unclear how the digital world is meant to interact seamlessly with the real world. Should platform businesses be liable for their environmental footprints? Should Facebook have to pay for the electricity grid, or should Uber have to pay to use roads?

These questions illustrate just some of the key issues that are intensifying the need for broad institutional change in the digital age. Technology is created by people for people, and thus, we are in control of whether we flourish or flounder in the digital age. As Clay Shirky famously wrote in *Here Comes Everybody*, 'Revolution doesn't happen when society adopts new technologies – it happens when society adopts new behaviours'.[27] Technology alone is insufficient for change, but in conjunction with a truly digitally enabled society, we can unlock its latent potential for transformation.

Not only do we need to get better at recognising the need for institutional change, we also need to get better at responding to change. The earlier

27   Shirky, p. 160.

chessboard analogy illustrates how digital technologies have the potential to scale exponentially, rapidly changing business, political, and societal environments. Adapting the social and institutional frameworks to operate in a more digitally enabled world, therefore, requires a transformation not only of the frameworks themselves but of the processes through which we respond to future technological changes.

Digital technology is not the solution to problems but the enabler to find solutions. We need to adapt our social, political, and economic systems to operate in a digital world by keeping pace with the rate of digital innovation and mindfully choosing how we apply, regulate, and integrate digital technologies into modern society. Just as we continue to invest and develop the data, algorithms, and devices, so, too, must we develop the social and institutional structures in which these technologies are embedded.

In this new era lies a great potential to free ourselves from drudgery and toil and to use our full intellectual capacity to innovate, discover, and create. Our digital toolkits are well-stocked with useful aids, and we have never been in a better position to solve some of humanity's greatest challenges. The digital age presents a new frontier that is enabling more connected, efficient, data-rich, and virtual forms of social organisation and society. We are already seeing the fruits of the digital age – and this is just the beginning.

Works Cited

Aad, G., *et al.* 'Combined Measurement of the Higgs Boson Mass in *pp* Collisions at $\sqrt{s}$ = 7 and 8 TeV with the ATLAS and CMS Experiments'. *Physical Review Letters* 114.19 (2015), pp. 1-33.

Alpha Beta. *The Automation Advantage*. Sydney: Alpha Beta, 2017.

Arntz, Melanie, Terry Gregory, and Ulrich Zierahn. 'Revisiting the Risk of Automation'. *Economic Letters* 159 (2017), pp. 157-60.

Castell, S., *et al. Public Attitudes to Science 2014*. [London]: Ipsos MORI, 2014.

Clark, G. 'The Condition of the Working-Class in England, 1209-2004'. *Journal of Political Economy* 113.6 (2005), pp. 1307-40.

Demirguc-Kunt, A., L. Klapper, D. Singer, and P. Van Oudheusden. *The Global Findex Database 2014: Measuring Financial Inclusion Around the World*. Washington, DC: World Bank, 2014.

Dobbs, R., T. Koller, S. Ramaswamy, J. Woetzel, J. Manyika, R. Krishnan, and N. Andreula. *Playing to Win: The New Global Competition for Corporate Profits*. New York: McKinsey Global Institute, 2015.

Etsy. *Redefining Entrepreneurship: Etsy Sellers' Economic Impact*. New York: Etsy, 2013.

Frey, C.B., and M.A. Osborne. *The Future of Employment: How Susceptible Are Jobs to Computerisation?* Oxford: Oxford University Press, 2013.

Gottfried, J., and E. Shearer. *News Use across Social Media Platforms 2016*. Washington, DC: Pew Research Center, 2016.

IMF. *World Economic Outlook: Gaining Momentum?* Washington, DC: International Monetary Fund, 2017.

Konrath, S.H., E.H. O'Brien, and C. Hsing. 'Changes in Dispositional Empathy in American College Students over Time: A Meta-analysis'. *Personality and Social Psychology Review* 15.2 (2011), pp. 180-98.

Kranzberg, M. 'Technology and History: "Kranzberg's Laws"'. *Bulletin of Science, Technology & Society* 15.1 (1995), pp. 5-13.

Kurzweil, R. *The Age of Spiritual Machines: When Computers Exceed Human Intelligence*. London: Penguin, 2000.

Lewis, A. *User-Driven Discontent*. MetaFilter website. http://www.metafilter.com/95152/Userdriven-discontent#3256046. Accessed 8 Aug. 2017.

Lewis, K., K. Gray, and J. Meierhenrich. 'The Structure of Online Activism'. *Sociological Science* 1 (2014), pp. 1-9.

Lohr, S. 'IBM Is Counting on Its Bet on Watson, and Paying Big Money for It'. *New York Times*, 16 Aug. 2017. https://www.nytimes.com/2016/10/17/technology/ibm-is-counting-on-its-bet-on-watson-and-paying-big-money-for-it.html. Accessed 28 Nov. 2017.

MacKenzie, D., and J. Wajcman, eds. *The Social Shaping of Technology*. Milton Keynes: Open University Press, 1985.

Manyika, J., *et al*. *Global Flows in a Digital Age: How Trade, Finance, People, and Data Connect the World Economy*. New York: McKinsey Global Institute, 2014.

OECD. 'Global Economy Stuck in Low-Growth Trap: Policymakers Need to Act to Keep Promises'. Press release, Organisation for Economic Co-operation and Development, 7 March 2016.

Pennycook, M., G. Cory, and V. Alakeson. *A Matter of Time: The Rise of Zero-Hours Contracts*. London: Resolution Foundation, 2013.

Shirky, Clay. *Here Comes Everybody: The Power of Organising without Organizations*. London: Allen Lane, 2008.

Silverman, C. 'This Analysis Shows How Viral Fake Election News Stories Outperformed Real News on Facebook'. *BuzzFeed News*, 16 Nov. 2016. https://www.buzzfeed.com/craigsilverman/viral-fake-election-news-outperformed-real-news-on-facebook?utm_term=.pxx6v4Dmvo#.guOyXBwdX5. Accessed 28 Nov. 2017.

Silverman, C., and J. Singer-Vine. 'Most Americans Who See Fake News Believe It, New Survey Says'. *BuzzFeed News*, 7 Dec. 2016. https://www.buzzfeed.com/craigsilverman/fake-news-survey. Accessed 28 Nov. 2017.

Symantic. *Norton Cybercrime Report: The Human Impact.* Mountain View: Symantec, 2010.

Symantic. *Norton Cyber Security Insights Report.* Mountain View: Symantec, 2016.

Szreter, S., and G. Mooney. 'Urbanization, Mortality, and the Standard of Living Debate: New Estimates of the Expectation of Life at Birth in Nineteenth-Century British Cities'. *Economic History Review* 51.1 (1998), pp. 84-112.

Tapscott, D., and A. Tapscott. *Blockchain Revolution: How the Technology behind Bitcoin Is Changing Money, Business, and the World.* London: Penguin, 2016.

Taylor, M., G. Wells, G. Howell, and B. Raphael. 'The Role of Social Media as Psychological First Aid as a Support to Community Resilience Building'. *Australian Journal of Emergency Management* 27.1 (2012), pp. 20-26.

UN. *World Urbanization Prospects: 2014 Revision.* New York: UN Department of Economic and Social Affairs, 2014.

Vigna, P., and M. Casey. *The Age of Cryptocurrency.* New York: St. Martin's Press, 2016.

World Economic Forum. *The Global Risks Report 2016.* Geneva: World Economic Forum, 2016.

About the Authors

Claire Naughtin, PhD, is a Senior Research Consultant in strategic foresight at Data61 – an entity within Australia's national science agency, the Commonwealth Scientific and Industrial Research Organisation. As part of the Data61 Insight Team, she specialises in the application of strategic foresight to explore future trends and scenarios impacting government, business, and society. Naughtin works to bridge the gap between research and real-world application, using data to help people make informed, evidence-based decisions.

Stefan Hajkowicz, PhD, is a Principal Research Scientist in strategic foresight at Data61 – an entity within Australia's national science agency, the Commonwealth Scientific and Industrial Research Organisation. He leads the Data61 Insight Team, a group of researchers and consultants exploring future trends, risks, and scenarios related to the digital economy. During the past 20 years, Stefan has delivered over a hundred research and advisory projects to government, industry, and community clients in Australia and internationally.

6 Cities to the Rescue: A New Scale for Dealing with Climate Change

Keith Clarke, Viviana Jiménez, and Tim O'Riordan

Abstract

Cities have a significant impact on climate change but are also potential saviours of the planet. The city consumes vast amounts of fossil fuels and other resources in buildings, transport, and heating and cooling, and produces large quantities of waste and pollution. Yet the city is a continuing spark of ingenuity and innovation with an inspiring capacity to create lower carbon infrastructure and living patterns, offering hope for a sustainable future. Here we canvass the scope for transforming the character of urban design, mobility, and consumption in favour of healthy and planet-friendly activity that could provide benchmarks for cities across the planet, given encouraging governance. It is a tough call, but in offering hope, an exciting one to answer.

Keywords: urban vulnerability, resources grab, climate-resilient cities, urban agriculture, low-carbon mobility, sustainable infrastructure

The city: New challenges and global opportunities

The benefits of living in large human settlements have been recognised for over 6,000 years. Over millennia and through centuries of sea-based mercantilism and industrialisation, cities have been the cradle of culture, trade, learning, economic transformation, art, governance, and innovation.

In 2008, more than half of the world's seven billion people lived in cities.[1] Today, there are more than 500 cities containing over one million inhabitants.[2] By 2050 three-quarters of the estimated global population of nine

---

1   UN DESA.
2   JLL and the Business of Cities, p. 6.

Wilkinson, Angela, and Betty Sue Flowers (eds.), *Realistic Hope: Facing Global Challenges.* Amsterdam, Amsterdam University Press, 2018.
DOI: 10.5117/9789462987241_CH06

billion people will live in cities. This is the equivalent of building a new city of 1.4 million people every week.[3] About 95 per cent of that growth will occur in the developing world.[4] Millions of people migrate to cities every week. According to the German Advisory Council on Global Change (WGBU):

> In sub-Saharan Africa, two-thirds of all new city-dwellers currently move into informal settlements or slums, and half of them are expected to remain there in the long term. According to UN forecasts, Africa's population could rise to a total of 4.4 billion people by 2100. If the current urbanisation trends were to continue in Africa, and, for example, 80 per cent of the people in Africa were to live in cities by 2100 – and 60 per cent of these in slums – this would mean about 2 billion people having to live in degrading city districts.[5]

Cities are diverse in shape, size, geography, global connectivity, and culture. Yet urbanisation shares many common characteristics. Cities generate more than 80 per cent of the world's gross domestic product, and a notable component of urban wealth generation depends on sizeable transfers of energy and natural resources from well beyond city boundaries.[6] As cities grow, they tend to increase their demand for energy and resources, as well as their production of waste and pollution, at a much faster rate than per capita growth.

Cities provide huge opportunities for human development because of the way they concentrate people and assets in one place. But they are also increasingly vulnerable to new challenges, including water stress, urban and regional air quality, rising pressures for migration, public ill health generally, low levels of investment, and extreme weather risk.

And as complex and dynamic systems, cities evolve in unexpected ways. Poorly governed cities can lock themselves into a pattern of inefficient energy, food, and water use for decades to come. Well-governed cities give attention to global, as well as local, developments; avoid locking themselves into carbon-intensive futures via inappropriate infrastructure design in buildings and transport networks; and address the growing inequalities between the urban elites and others – including rural elites, urban middle classes, urban poor, and informal migrants.

3   Shell Global, p. 4.
4   EC, p. 79.
5   Krass *et al.*, p. 1.
6   Radjev.

Over the near future, new models of inclusive, resilient, and sustainable urbanisation could emerge, or a cascade of erroneous and possibly irreversible decisions could lock urbanised humanity into a deepening global crisis. How we design the city of the future and behave within it will substantially determine how we succeed or fail as a viable and morally sentient species.

Cities will determine the future of climate change

Currently, cities account for around 44 per cent of global greenhouse gas (GHG) emissions, over 70 per cent of carbon-based emissions, and nearly 75 per cent all global energy use.[7] These contributions are heavily influenced by population size and age distribution, by spatial scale and location, and by the state of economic development, mobility, and governance.

The global climate challenge is inexorably linked to the future of the city though there are large variations according to regional wealth. North American cities account for up to 80 per cent of national carbon-based emissions, while Chinese, South Asian, and Latin American megacities release only about 60 per cent of total national emissions.

One reason for these increasing contributions to GHG emissions from cities is that they are huge energy users. A 2008 International Energy Agency (IEA) report estimates that urban regions consume 250 exajoules per year of energy, amounting to over 70 per cent of primary energy production.[8] In 2016, the IEA projected that two-thirds of the growth in global energy demand to 2050 will come from cities in emerging and developing countries.

Reaching the nationally determined contribution (NDC) targets that form the UN Framework Convention on Climate Change (UNFCCC), the Paris climate accord goal of effective global decarbonisation by around 2075 will require an emissions pathway of over 80 per cent reduction from current levels in some 30 years.[9] Unless these NDCs are met by 2050, global temperature rises could reach three degrees by 2100. The latest report from the UN Environment Programme concludes that current emissions removals are only a third of what is needed to meet the required trajectory, and emphasises the importance of cities in taking a lead in necessary actions

---

7   Seto and Dhakal, p. 1.
8   The Fifth Assessment Report of the Intergovernmental Panel on Climate Change is a goldmine of information. The Panel's Working Groups 2 (see Revi and Satterthwaite) and 3 (see Seto and Dhakal), reporting on the impacts of and vulnerabilities to climate change, offer a very comprehensive review of the relationships between urban growth and the emissions of greenhouse gases. What they report is both sobering and frightening.
9   UNEP.

– the rolling out of tested technologies in renewables, vehicle propulsion, and efficient appliances.[10]

Vulnerability to climate change in expanding urban settlements

Cities are also victims of climate change and extreme weather events. In South Asia, more than 1200 people died during the 2017 monsoon season. Floods in Nepal, Bangladesh, and India heavily affected another 40 million people across large areas.[11] The impacts of these events are increasing year on year as a result of more frequent climate catastrophes and inadequate urban planning.

Flooding is a big problem and is exacerbated by poor or non-existent land-use planning, inadequate drainage or maintenance of drainage, steep slopes with weak protection against mudslides and soil erosion, and the location of dwellings, which is sometimes the manifestation of deep poverty and the inability to choose habitation safety in zones close to rivers or coastlines. The inability to be adequately warned, to have access to safe and nearby places of refuge, and to be offered any restorative support in the aftermath of damage all contribute to vulnerability.

In 2017, the US and the eastern Caribbean experienced one of the severest hurricane seasons to date. The estimated economic costs of Hurricanes Harvey and Irma for the mainland US are estimated to be around $290 billion.[12] A few weeks later, Hurricane Maria, packing 150mph winds, struck the same zones.[13] Puerto Rico and other islands still lacked potable water, energy, and food supplies after months of destruction. They are now tasked with rebuilding and reimagining their storm defences in the dire financial context of seriously depleted economies and in the meteorological context of even more powerful storms.

In coastal cities, which are uniquely vulnerable to sea level rise, over 350 million are at risk. But all cities are vulnerable to a range of climate change impacts because of their dense human settlement, dependency on fresh water, and sensitivity to power supplies, building design, and the many hazards of extreme weather events, especially the combination of excessive heat and humidity.[14] Cities with poor planning, corrupt building practices, and disorganised land use are excessively at risk.

---

10   *Ibid.*, p. 51.
11   Siddique.
12   Wile.
13   Hester and Echenique.
14   Thread.

Cities are increasingly vulnerable to the combination of air pollution and climate change

Most of the world's cities don't measure up to air quality standards set by the World Health Organization (WHO) for all or some of the time. The WHO estimates that urban air pollution is contributing to the early death of ten million people per year.[15] Increasingly, the main culprit is the poor emissions regulation of diesel vehicles, especially the particulate-dense idling of the diesel car engine. These combinations of gases and particles contribute to heart disease, lung ailments, asthma, diabetes, and many neurological failures associated with worsening mental health. Killer smogs in China and other Asian cities have also hit the headlines in recent years, triggered by a combination of local and long-range air pollution such as the burning of large swathes of forests in Indonesia for economic development.

The 2017 wildfires across northern California, Spain, and Portugal killed hundreds of people. In Europe, the strong southerly winds of Storm Ophelia and the ensuing heat wave intensified the impact of the fires. Air pollution from continental Europe rapidly reached the UK.[16] In California, it is estimated that wildfires caused as much pollution in a week as vehicles did in one year across the state.[17]

Climate change is expected to further increase the frequency and intensity of unintentional forest fires. Increasingly, there is a proven connection between global climate change and extended droughts, dust storms, prolonged periods of anti-cyclonic high pressure, and the diversion of gusty frontal systems. All of these increase the disposition and persistence of airborne toxicity in rapidly growing urban areas, reaching a point of regional persistence and forming citywide health hazards. This is even creating the beginning of urban exodus through health migration.

The urban food-water-energy nexus

For 6,000 years we have been moving people to cities (locations rich in water sources), and for the latter half of most of that, using engineering solutions to move water to people (Roman aquifers, for example) as urban populations swelled. Many large cities across the world are already defined as 'water

---

15   Seto and Dhakal, p. 33.
16   Light.
17   Santiago and Scutti.

stressed', including Tokyo, Los Angeles Mexico City, and Delhi – and water crisis hotspots include cities such as São Paulo and Khartoum.

Today's cities also rely on increasingly distant sources for other basic amenities. Food and oil are scarce or difficult to access in large urbanised spaces. The cost of and access to transportation can constrain the healthy growth of cities.

Many of the world's largest cities increase their water consumption by taking it away from irrigated agriculture. In Chennai, a thriving tank truck industry has emerged that buys water from farmers and sells it in the city to thirsty residents.[18] Beijing now draws water from the Yangtze River some 800 miles away.[19] In 2003, San Diego bought annual rights to 247 million tonnes of water from farmers in the Imperial Valley for 75 years. This scheme, increasingly popular in the American West, has now been coined 'buy and dry' as water rights are diverted from farmed fields to urban housing and industry.[20]

Food security in cities also depends increasingly on long-distance transport. For example, even though Tokyo gets its rice largely from Japan, its wheat comes from the Great Plains of North America, its corn from the US Midwest, and its soy from the Brazilian Cerrado.[21] The energy used for long-distance freight transport and the storage and distribution of food and other goods contributes one of the fastest-growing sources of GHG emissions. Associated land use changes and the intensification of agriculture to feed growing populations also contribute to global environmental stress, including the reduction of biodiversity and the undermining of ecosystems functioning.

Realistic hope for the future of cities

An increase in city-scale foresight initiatives and futures thinking in recent years has resulted in the exploration of many alternative pathways for the future of cities. City-centric futures, territorial scenario planning, and participatory vision-in-action initiatives enable a more holistic and systemic view and contribute new city-scale solutions.

For example, the Future of Cities Programme of Oxford University worked with a range of stakeholders to determine future visions for cities.[22] Three

---

18 Brown, p. 42.
19 Chinese Ministry of Water Resources, pp. 60-61.
20 Runyon.
21 Brown, p. 146.
22 Raford.

plausible scenarios emerged. In *Gulliver's World* there is business-as-usual continued progress and innovation for a reduced number of elites, surrounded by a large, fragmented fringe of developing power blocks. In *Massive Sociotechnical Revolution*, climate change impacts and energy and resources shocks impact cities across the world, catalysing the emergence of a new generation of young leaders who push work-life-ecology balance and enable a revolution in holistic systems governance. In *Triumph of the Triads* global systemic risks leads to failed states, economic stagnation, and predatory war-lordism.

The Economist Intelligence Unit explores the concept of the technologically smart city, where citizens provide real-time feedback to government, using technology as a catalyst for urban change and the private sector as a collaborator in advancing digital infrastructure.[23] The creation of smart cities offers the possibility that solutions to climate change challenges can be implemented more quickly than expected.

Designing people-centric sustainable cities

In addition to scenarios that show hope for the future of cities and their role in slowing down the rate of climate change, there are also many city-scale vision-to-action initiatives. An increasing number of city leaders understand the need for accountability and responsiveness to their citizens.[24]

The WGBU, a German think tank, has identified how a future city can become more resilient and more capable of mitigating its emissions. It notes that if present infrastructure investment trends continue, the projects that result will use up over two-thirds of the available carbon budget by 2050. To counter these consequences, it suggests that radical changes in building design, city formation, inclusive governance, and full incorporation of the UN sustainable development goals need to be included in city design and evolution.

The WGBU offers a holistic view of city-region ecosystems, including liveability, social infrastructure, and cost frameworks. It also suggests that a mixture of inspirational possibilities enabled by new technologies, social movements, and politically active citizens can put a stop to the concentration of the megalopolis and create all manner of new urban living and governing experiences in linked communities of sustainability. An interesting conclusion of the WGBU is that transformative governance of a city is rooted in

23   Economist Intelligence Unit, pp. 8-22.
24   Government Office for Science, p. 48.

the fundamental concept of 'character', called in German *'Eigenart'* – an emerging culture of togetherness based on history and aspiration and combined with a polycentric approach to governance.

These inviting and alternative futures make it clear that there is hope for change, and that given the networked effects of individual and global connections, cities are not just the nexus of problems but the fulcrum for solutions. New urban vision-to-action approaches offer citizens a way to adapt to a low-carbon future whilst addressing other challenges. Creative urban governance is the hallmark of the low-carbon and socially decent city complex of the latter half of this century.

Global leadership: The rise of city-scale solutions

When the US government decided to withdraw from the Paris climate accord, over 1200 US mayors, governors, businesses, and universities joined the 'We are still in' coalition and committed to continuing the steps outlined in the accord.[25] Over 350 mayors have signed the pledge to do their part.[26] Local governments acting together are supporting innovative technology across the board, including in advanced battery technology, cleaner transportation, more efficient infrastructure and buildings, and better appliances.

Globally, around 8000 actions are being taken, and projects worth US$52 billion are underway to build a new sustainable global economy. Cities are increasingly recognising sustainable investments as catalysts for job creation and urban attractiveness. Over 7,000 mayors are now part of the Global Covenant of Mayors for Climate and Energy, signposting their commitment to building tomorrow's green economy.[27] And the C40 Cities Climate Leadership Group network connects the world's megacities to find solutions to climate change.

Climate-resilient cities

Because of their geography, Dutch cities have put climate adaptation high on their agenda for a long time. Rotterdam, for example, has always been susceptible to floods because 80 per cent of it is below sea level. Even so, its port is the largest in Europe and a main driver of the Dutch economy. It has developed most of its port on land that is elevated between three to

25   McCarthy.
26   Creative Science Labs.
27   Appleby.

five metres above sea level, which is also protected by the Maeslantkering (a storm surge barrier). Protective dykes are designed as part of recreational areas, as cycle routes. The city has led the way in implementing climate adaptation measures. By 2025, Rotterdam aims to be 100 per cent climate proof and to have achieved a 50 per cent reduction in CO_2 emissions, compared to 1990 levels.[28]

Increasingly, other cities are taking note, learning from leaders such as Rotterdam, while also addressing their own particular challenges. In response to the recognition of the need for resilience, the 100 Resilient Cities network was created as a way of bringing together industry leaders to deliver solutions and create new tools and services at the city level.[29]

Building in demand-side energy solutions

Research shows that the proportion of global energy use in cities will rise from 66 per cent in 2010 to about 80 per cent by 2040.[30] Most of this energy use will be concentrated in buildings and transport.

A critical area is the potentially huge increase in demand for space cooling in a globally warming world, especially in India and China. Here future building design will be critical as will the supply of renewable-based electricity through smart grids. These designs will require the skills of a new generation of architects, designers, and business managers with a serious commitment to thermal comfort and the clever use of energy-saving storage and natural cooling systems. All of these transformations will depend on well-thought-through regulation that is properly agreed and enforced. The key is the emergence and retention of an 'aware democracy' with a serious commitment by all urbanites to sustainable urban growth.

Despite a lack of federal support, major cities in the US are taking action. New York City has announced ambitious new fossil fuel caps for thousands of buildings. San Francisco's public transit system will be eliminating fossil fuels by 2045. Atlanta plans to use 100 per cent renewables energy for its functioning by 2035, and Chicago wants to get there even earlier – by 2025.[31] Setting a clear target for delivery of policy is a vital first step. The key is to devise institutions that enforce the necessary transitional pathways.

28   Shell Global, p. 8.
29   100 Resilient Cities.
30   Shell Global, p. 10.
31   Lant.

Redesigning urban transport

In the transport sector, the adoption of more compact urban design, coupled with increased internet use for communication and a massive rise in electric vehicles, walking, and cycling – all connected to smart electric grids fuelled by renewable energy – would cut eight gigatonnes of carbon by 2050, or 40 per cent of current emissions. Much of this is possible in the developed and emerging economy cities, especially if planning and policy focus on restricting cities of around one to five million people to no additional growth. This restriction is particularly important for emerging economies and can best can be achieved by encouraging the more sustainable expansion of attractive smaller cities. For the poorer countries, managing cities in terms of size, density, and energy use is much more problematic, requiring major new levels of investment in urban design, energy supplies, and public and private energy provision.

Two of the most successful examples of innovation in public transportation systems can be found in Curitiba, Brazil, and Bogotá, Colombia. Bogotá's urban transport and cultural overhaul of the early 2000s led to rapid improvements in mobility, decreased air pollution, and increased well-being for its citizens. Bogotá banned the parking of cars on sidewalks, created or renovated 1200 parks, built hundreds of kilometres of bicycle paths and pedestrian streets, and reduced rush-hour traffic by 40 per cent using its 'pico y placa' rush-hour car restrictions.[32] The success of Bogotá's bus rapid transit system, which uses express lanes for buses to move thousands of people each day, was replicated in many other cities, including Mexico City, São Paulo, Hanoi, Seoul, Istanbul, Chicago, Los Angeles, and Beijing. Now, as a result of internal migration due to conflict and, more recently, with migration from Venezuela, Bogotá has begun to grow indiscriminately again, and the mobility and pollution challenges have returned. This situation highlights the importance of aligning urban and national policy frameworks to address the connections between national security and urban development.

In 2001, Paris initiated a major transformation of its transportation system. The first step was to invest in high-quality public transit in the greater Paris area. The next step was to create express lanes for buses and bicycles, reducing the number of lanes for cars and incentivising the use of public transport. Then the city introduced an innovative city bicycle-rental programme with docking stations throughout the city. The popularity of the bike-sharing

32 Peñalosa.

programme has led to its extension into more than 30 of the city's suburbs and inspired hundreds of other cities to adopt similar programmes.[33] Today, there are over 2000 bike-sharing and -rental programmes around the world in operation or under construction.[34]

Among the national leaders in designing bicycle-friendly systems are the Netherlands, where 27 per cent of all trips are by bike, Denmark with 18 per cent, and Germany with 10 per cent.[35] The integration of walkways and bikeways into urban transport systems makes a city more liveable and helps reduce GHG emissions.

The new smart city requires a reduction in the need for movement, an increase in public transport, high financial penalties for the use of fossil fuel-sourced vehicles, and the progressive removal of the diesel engine. There is also much greater use of vehicle sharing and of movement substitution through the use of smart technologies in communication, transport, service provision, and healthcare.

Urban agriculture

Whilst the majority of urban energy use is concentrated in transport and buildings, the industrial and agricultural services that support cities, sometimes beyond their boundaries, are also major energy consumers.

Early cities relied on food from the surrounding countryside, but today cities get their food from distant sources all over the world. The water and oil required to produce and move food also come from faraway places. As people continue to concentrate in urban areas, city managers and other stakeholders are increasingly focusing on ways to address food security challenges. One such way is urban agriculture.

In 2005, the Food and Agriculture Organization of the United Nations (FAO) reported that urban and peri-urban farms (those adjacent to a city) supply food to some 700 million residents.[36] This number has since grown as urbanisation has increased around the world. Today, 800 million people worldwide are involved in urban agriculture.[37] Not only does this practice provide increasing amounts of food, but it has also become an important engine of urban job creation.

---

33 Brown, p. 149.
34 Collinson.
35 Pucher and Buehler, p. 526.
36 Brown, p. 158.
37 FAO.

In Hanoi, 80 per cent of fresh vegetables comes from farms in or adjacent to the city. Fish farmers in Kolkata manage wastewater fishponds that cover nearly 400 hectares and produce 18,000 tonnes of fish per year.[38] Urban Farmers, a Swiss aquaponics enterprise, now operates from the rooftop of De Schilde, a former Philips TV and phone set factory in The Hague. It aims to produce 45 tonnes of vegetables and 19 tonnes of tilapia annually.[39]

Because of its urban-related farming, the Netherlands is now the world's second food exporter by value after the US, though it has only 1/270th of its landmass. The Dutch have designed the country as fragmented cultivated fields, dotted by cities and suburbs. Most of the country's farming is essentially adjacent to cities. In the process, farmers have reduced their dependence on water by up to 90 per cent, virtually eliminated the use of chemical pesticides in greenhouses, and cut the use of antibiotics for poultry and livestock by almost 60 per cent.[40] While the energy use is intensive, it is increasingly being fuelled by renewable means.

Cities are rethinking urban water use

Up to 30 per cent of water used in homes is for flushing – and it takes a lot of energy to deliver the high quantities of drinking-quality water used to flush toilets as well as to operate a sewage treatment facility.[41] An average estimate is one gram of GHG emissions per litre of water supplied. Many cities are beginning to realise that an integrated drinking water system and water-based, waste disposal economy is not a viable option.

The alternative is to separate water-use systems and install the composting toilet. Germany, Sweden, Finland, and other European countries have begun installing composting toilets in cities. Community groups across Chicago, Austin, and Marin County, California, are beginning to lobby their councillors to rethink human manure and encourage excrement collection in one form or another.[42]

Once the toilet is separate from the water-use system in a city, recycling household water becomes a much simpler process. Singapore, which buys water from Malaysia at a high cost, also recycles water very efficiently. Los Angeles and Orange County in California invested in treatment facilities to convert sewage into clean water to replenish the local aquifers.[43]

38 Brown, p. 159.
39 Lovett.
40 Viviano.
41 Brown, p. 156.
42 Barth.
43 Brown, p. 157.

Cities are adapting their infrastructures

Cities act as important nodes within a wider national infrastructure system. Much of the physical infrastructure is fixed and is intended to have very long life spans of hundreds of years. However, the 21st century has seen rapidly shifting flows of capital, people, materials, energy resources, waste, emissions, and culture. The acceleration and intensification of flows has put the fixed nature of physical infrastructure to the test.

City buildings are also now beginning to function as sources of food, drinking water, and energy for the urban spaces they occupy. New 'barn buildings' are popping up in urban environments, providing a source of food and green scenery to local inhabitants. For example, Santalaia, a building in Bogotá, Colombia, is the tallest vertical garden in Latin America, with over 3100 square metres of vegetation. Built in 2015, every year it generates oxygen for more than 3000 people, filters more than 2000 tonnes of gas emissions, captures more than 400 kilograms of dust, and is watered mostly by recycled water. In other words, it serves as the 'lungs' of a mostly cement jungle.[44]

The Hearst Tower, an iconic building in New York, produces all of its own cooling systems from natural resources. It collects rainwater on its roof and transports it to its basement, where over 52,000 litres of water are stored and then used to cool the 46-story building through an evaporation process. Its designer, Vincent Iocovelli, predicts the future of all buildings and even personal housing lies in each building collecting its own water, not only for cooling, draining, and sewage, but also for drinking through filtering systems incorporated as the water descends through the structure.

The majority of materials currently used for the urban built environment – bricks, cement, steel, and asphalt – require a large amount of energy for their production, and, in turn, their production generates large amounts of carbon emissions. However, more than 40 per cent of the materials needed for the projected urbanisation of 2050 still need to be manufactured, providing an enormous opportunity for the replacement of the use of steel and concrete with smarter, sustainable materials.[45] Flexible urban infrastructure built with sustainable and safe materials requires serious policy coordination and sound investments.

Globally, cities are on track to spend upward of US$41 trillion on smart technology – such as the shift to electric vehicles and super grids – within

---

44 Aguilar.
45 Hajer, p. 4.

the next two decades.[46] As automation is on the rise, governments are looking at ways to address the potential job overhaul that it will cause. In Finland, the government is trying out a universal basic minimum income for unemployed citizens. About 70 per cent of people in European countries support such a scheme.[47]

Realising hope through 'smart-with-a-heart', people-centric solutions

In conclusion, the growth of many and more diverse cities seems inevitable and presents an exciting new solution space for addressing climate change. Globally connected cities are also sources of global leadership and incubators of new circular economy solutions to the water-food-energy-security stress nexus. Because cities vary by geography, structure, and culture, no one-size-fits-all solution fits all cases. But among the emerging city-scale solutions, some common interests can be seen:
– City mayors are increasingly powerful actors on the global stage and are standing up when national governments do not.
– Innovative financing is needed that avoids the way private investment often cherry-picks 'winning' cities.
– Urban and national policy frameworks need to be aligned in order to address connected challenges – cities and food, cities and water, and energy security under climate change.
– People-centred governance needs to focus on developing low-carbon, healthy-living environments and circular and locally sourced urban economies, including for migrants and slum dwellers.

Works Cited

100 Resilient Cities. 100 Resilient Cities website. http://www.100resilientcities.org. Accessed 30 Nov. 2017.

Aguilar, Andrea. 'Bogotá tiene el jardín vertical más alto de América Latina'. *Univision*, 23 June 2017. https://www.univision.com/noticias/citylab-arquitectura/bogota-tiene-el-jardin-vertical-mas-alto-de-america-latina. Accessed 2 Oct. 2017.

Appleby, Kyra. 'Cities: Progress and the New Sustainable Economy'. CDP website, 12 Sept. 2017. https://www.cdp.net/en//articles/cities/cities-progress-the-new-sustainable-economy. Accessed 7 Oct. 2017.

46 Radjev.
47 Henley.

Barth, Brian. 'Humanure: The Next Frontier in Composting'. *Modern Farmer*, 7 March 2017. https://modernfarmer.com/2017/03/humanure-next-frontier-composting/. Accessed 2 Oct. 2017.

Brown, Lester. *Plan B 4.0: Mobilizing to Save a Civilization*. New York: W.W. Norton, 2009.

Chinese Ministry of Water Resources. *Country Report of the People's Republic of China*. Marseille: World Water Council, 2003.

Collinson, Patrick. 'On Your Bike: The Best and Worst City Cycle Schemes'. *The Guardian*, 25 Feb. 2017. https://www.theguardian.com/money/2017/feb/25/best-and-worst-city-cycle-schemes-bike-sharing-london. Accessed 2 Oct. 2017.

Creative Science Labs. 'City and County Initiatives'. We Are Still In website. https://www.wearestillin.com/cities-counties/initiatives. Accessed 30 Nov. 2017.

EC. *Global Europe 2050*. Brussels: European Commission, 2012.

Economist Intelligence Unit. 'Empowering Cities: the Real Story of How Businesses and Citizens are Driving Smart Cities'. 2016. http://empoweringcities.eiu.com/wp-content/uploads/sites/26/2016/09/Empowering-Cities.pdf. Accessed 2 Oct. 2017.

FAO. 'Urban Agriculture'. Food and Agriculture Organization of the United Nations. http://www.fao.org/urban-agriculture/en/. Accessed 30 Nov. 2017.

Government Office for Science. *Future of Cities: An Overview of the Evidence*. London: Government of the United Kingdom, 2016.

Hajer, Maarten. 'The Power of Imagination'. Inaugural Lecture on the Occasion of the Acceptance of the Distinguished Professorship in Urban Futures at the Faculty of Geosciences, Utrecht University, 17 March 2017. Personal communication from author.

Henley, Jon. 'Finland Trials Basic Income for Unemployed'. *The Guardian*, 3 Jan. 2017. https://www.theguardian.com/world/2017/jan/03/finland-trials-basic-income-for-unemployed. Accessed 31 October 2017.

Hester, Jessica Leigh, and Martín Echenique. 'Puerto Rico's Grid Needs a Complete Overhaul'. Citylab website, 25 Sept. 2017. https://www.citylab.com/environment/2017/09/hurricane-maria-puerto-ricos-grid-needs-a-complete-overhaul/540969/. Accessed 11 Nov. 2017.

IEA. *World Energy Outlook 2008*. Paris: International Energy Agency, 2008. https://www.iea.org/media/weowebsite/2008-1994/WEO2008.pdf. Accessed 5 June 2018.

JLL and The Business of Cities. 'Benchmarking the Future World of Cities'. Cities Research Center website, 2016. http://www.jll.com/Research/jll-business-of-cities-report-april-2016.pdf. Accessed 21 Dec. 2017.

Kraas F., *et al. Humanity on the Move: Unlocking the Transformative Power of Cities*. Berlin: WBGU – German Advisory Council on Global Change, 2016.

Lant, Karla. 'New Data Shows Progress in the Fight against Climate Change'. *Futurism*, 29 Sept. 2017. https://futurism.com/new-data-shows-progress-in-fight-against-climate-change/. Accessed 11 Nov. 2017.

Light, John. 'The Fires in California, Portugal and Spain Share One Thing in Common'. *UN Dispatch*, 23 Oct. 2017. https://www.undispatch.com/fires-california-portugal-spain-share-one-thing-common/. Accessed 3 Dec. 2017.

Lovett, Gina. 'Is Urban Farming Only for Rich Hipsters?' *The Guardian*, 15 Feb. 2016. https://www.theguardian.com/sustainable-business/2016/feb/15/urban-farming-rich-hipsters-food-affordability-inequality. Accessed 30 October 2017.

McCarthy, Niall. 'The US Cities and States Challenging Trump's Paris Withdrawal'. *Forbes*, 6 June 2017. https://www.forbes.com/sites/niallmccarthy/2017/06/06/the-u-s-cities-and-states-challenging-trumps-paris-withdrawal-infographic/#207bc83e1c0c. Accessed 7 Oct. 2017.

Peñalosa, Enrique. 'Parks for Livable Cities: Lessons from a Radical Mayor'. Keynote address at the Urban Parks Institute's Great Parks/Great Cities Conference, Chicago, 30 July 2001. https://www.pps.org/reference/penalosaspeech2001/. Accessed 8 Oct 2017.

Pucher, John, and Ralph Buehler. 'Making Cycling Irresistible: Lessons from the Netherlands, Denmark, and Germany'. *Transport Reviews* 28.4 (July 2008), pp. 495-528.

Radjev, Naveen. 'Smart Cities Are Great: Human Centric Cities Are (Again) the Future'. *Quartz*, 27 Sept. 2017. https://www.pps.org/reference/penalosaspeech2001/. Accessed 8 Oct. 2017.

Raford, Noah. 'Oxford Future of Cities Scenarios'. Noah Radford (blog), 10 June 2010. http://noahraford.com/?p=558. Accessed 30 Nov. 2017.

Revi, D.S., and D.E. Satterthwaite. 'Urban Areas'. In *Climate Change: Impacts, Adaptation, and Vulnerability. Part A: Global and Sectoral Aspects.* Contribution of Working Group II to the Fifth Assessment Report of the Intergovernmental Panel on Climate Change. Cambridge: Cambridge University Press, 2014, pp. 535-95.

Runyon, Luke. 'Buy and Dry: Farmers Sell Water to Thirsty Cities'. *Earth Eats*, 16 Aug. 2016. https://indianapublicmedia.org/eartheats/water-valuable-crops-farms-compete-thirsty-cities/. Accessed 5 June 2018.

Santiago, Cassandra, and Susan Scutti. 'Week of Wildfires Polluting Air as Much as Year of Cars'. *CNN*, 13 Oct. 2017. https://edition.cnn.com/2017/10/13/health/california-fires-air-pollution-trnd/index.html. Accessed 15 Oct. 2017.

Seto, K.C., and S. Dhakal. 'Human Settlements, Infrastructure and Spatial Planning'. In *Climate Change 2014: Mitigation of Climate Change.* Contribution of Working Group III to the Fifth Assessment Report of the Intergovernmental Panel on Climate Change. Cambridge: University of Cambridge Press, 2014, pp. 923-85.

Shell Global. 'New Lenses on Future Cities'. 2014. https://www.shell.com/energy-and-innovation/the-energy-future/scenarios/new-lenses-on-future-cities.html. Accessed 21 Dec. 2017.

Siddique, Haroon. 'South Asian Floods Kill 1,200 and Shut 1.8 Million Children out of School'. *The Guardian*, 31 Aug. 2017. https://www.theguardian.com/world/2017/

aug/30/mumbai-paralysed-by-floods-as-india-and-region-hit-by-worst-monsoon-rains-in-years. Accessed 20 Sep. 2017.

Thread, Erin A. 'Sea Level Rise: Risk and Resilience in Coastal Cities'. Climate Institute. Oct. 2016. http://climate.org/sea-level-rise-risk-and-resilience-in-coastal-cities/. Accessed 6 Jan. 2018.

UN DESA. *World Urbanization Prospects: The 2014 Revision.* ST/ESA/SER.A/366. UN Department of Economic and Social Affairs, Population Division, 2015. https://esa.un.org/unpd/wup/publications/files/wup2014-report.pdf. Accessed 5 June 2018.

UNEP. *The Emissions Gap Report 2017: A UN Environment Synthesis Report.* UN Environment Programme, 2017. http://www.unep1.org/wordpress/wp-content/uploads/2017/10/Emissions-Gap-Report-2017.pdf. Accessed 9 Jan. 2018.

Viviano, Frank. 'This Tiny Country Feeds the World'. *National Geographic*, Sept. 2017. https://www.nationalgeographic.com/magazine/2017/09/holland-agriculture-sustainable-farming/. Accessed 11 Nov. 2017.

Wile, Rob. 'The Estimated Costs of Hurricanes Irma and Harvey Are Already Higher Than Katrina'. *Money*, 11 Sept. 2017. http://time.com/money/4935684/hurricane-irma-harvey-economic-cost/. Accessed 12 Sep. 2017.

About the Authors

Keith Clarke, CBE, is Chair of Future Cities Catapult and Chair of Forum for the Future.

Viviana M. Jiménez is Senior Consultant and Researcher, UN Environment Programme and the University of Oxford. During the past seventeen years, she has worked with the private sector, academia, governments, and international organisations to further sustainable practices and international conservation efforts.

Tim O'Riordan is Emeritus Professor of Environmental Sciences at the University of East Anglia, a Fellow of the British Academy, and a keen advocate of sustainability science. He has advised business and government on sustainability transitions for over 30 years on three continents.

7 The Future of Global Poverty

Claudia Juech and Chukwudi Onike

Abstract

To achieve the first of the Sustainable Development Goals – to end poverty in all of its forms everywhere by 2030 – will require more than business as usual. Despite uncertain global economic growth we have the financial resources to end extreme poverty. We know more, can predict more, and ultimately can better target the extreme poor. Social entrepreneurship models, machine learning, and robotics are pushing the envelope of what we can do. Using three scenarios, the chapter illustrates what poverty could look like in 2030. Our success will ultimately depend on the levels of global cooperation around conflicts and climate change, economic growth that benefits all segments of society, and the inclusion of minorities and previously excluded groups.

Keywords: extreme poverty, SDGs, poverty scenarios, social exclusion, fragile states, innovative finance, machine learning

From the MDGs to the SDGs: Great progress with greater challenges

The international community reached a major milestone in 2015 in the fight against global poverty. That year marked the end of a fifteen-year movement to achieve the Millennium Development Goals (MDGs) – eight international development goals established by the United Nations – that guided many efforts to alleviate poverty, with a prime objective of cutting in half the proportion of people living in poverty. To many, this effort was seen as the most successful anti-poverty movement in history. Governments, international organisations, and civil society groups all contributed to achieving the target of halving extreme poverty, which was achieved not only in time, but five years ahead of the 2015 deadline. More than a billion people were lifted out of poverty, and the rate of people living under extreme

Wilkinson, Angela, and Betty Sue Flowers (eds.), *Realistic Hope: Facing Global Challenges.* Amsterdam, Amsterdam University Press, 2018.
DOI: 10.5117/9789462987241_CH07

poverty dropped from close to half in 1990 to just 14 per cent in 2015.[1] The success of the MDGs prompted world leaders to launch another set of global goals in 2015 – the Sustainable Development Goals (SDGs) – that build on the momentum of the MDGs but with an even more ambitious goal of eradicating 'poverty in all its forms' by 2030.

Despite progress made, it would be naïve for world leaders to assume that eliminating global poverty entirely can be accomplished by just staying the course. When one considers how the incredible feat of cutting poverty in half was actually achieved, there are very good reasons to be dubious. For one, although globally poverty was halved, in 30 countries – eighteen in Sub-Saharan Africa alone – poverty actually increased.[2] The majority of the population lifted out of poverty came as a result not of widespread global growth, but of economic growth in just a handful of countries, mainly China and India, with macroeconomic conditions that are not necessarily replicable elsewhere. Moreover, the majority of people still living in extreme poverty now live in fragile or conflict states, or in adverse environmental settings, which are typically more challenging for development interventions.

Against this backdrop, it is safe to assume that ending extreme poverty will be even more daunting than cutting it in half – the goal of the past fifteen years. In an era of tepid global growth, with major economies, like that of China, showing signs of contraction, and rising tides of nationalism and populism, which tend to constrain aid funding, it can be hard to envision a future in which poverty becomes a vestige of the past. However, the future of poverty does not need to be grim. Eliminating global poverty is actually achievable, if we seize opportunities for a better future that are masked under challenges of the present.

Who are the global poor?

Since eliminating poverty will require rethinking strategies employed in halving it, it is important to first understand what poverty means, who the poor are, where they are located, and what factors are keeping them in poverty.

Poverty is most commonly understood using a uni-dimensional lens such as income or consumption. The most widely used measure of poverty is the World Bank's global poverty line, which was set in 2008 at $1.25 a day (now $1.90) and is being used to measure progress against the SDGs. This measure characterises the extreme poor, those living in absolute or abject poverty. For

1   UN.
2   Development Initiatives.

example, someone living in rural Ethiopia, deprived of productive means of livelihood, such as having little money or farming land, can be considered extremely poor. However, being poor means much more than having little or no material possessions. It can also be defined by contextual factors that are just as critical to one's well-being and ability to meet basic needs. For example, someone living in New York City, earning US$20,000 a year – less than half of the average New York City household income – can be considered poor. This relative income poverty might not appear as dramatic as living under the global poverty line; but even so, it can have grave implications for the ability to afford adequate housing, food, child care, or healthcare in a neighbourhood where almost everybody else is earning a higher income.

As these examples show, poverty is complex and multidimensional – a state of being that is brought about by many different factors existing at individual and structural levels. Thus, the poor will likely be hit harder by the negative effects of the future trends described in other chapters of this book, such as water scarcity or automation, and will less likely be in a position to benefit from the positive effects of change, such as the envisioned dramatic advances in health.

The characteristics of extreme poverty we highlight are hardly exhaustive. Our goal is by no means to oversimplify the realities of those living in poverty nor to ignore historical factors (e.g., colonialism) that may have contributed to them. Our aim is to call out key contemporary drivers most critical to alleviating global poverty.

What characterises the 'extreme poor'?

Though we know the extreme poor are now located primarily in Sub-Saharan Africa and Southeast Asia, this population is by no means homogenous. However, there are a few characteristics that tend to apply broadly. It is worth noting that it is the confluence of these conditions rather than the presence of any single one that makes extreme poverty so persistent.

First, the extreme poor disproportionately have fewer productive assets (e.g., land or livestock) and financial assets (e.g., access to credit or savings) than the average population. They also tend to have low literacy rates among adults and incomplete primary education, which can prevent upward mobility. Although education requirements for staying out of poverty vary globally, studies show that primary education is a minimum requirement for escaping poverty.[3]

3   Leahardt and Shepherd, p. 6.

Moreover, surveys across the board show that household size is highly correlated with extreme poverty.[4] The extreme poor often have more children, largely due to early marriage. In many developing countries, some families see arranged marriages of their underage daughters as a means to relieve financial stress through marital customs, such as bride prices that involve money or livestock. As a result, girls may be robbed of an education and bear several children, representing an added financial stress to their families, which makes it even harder to escape extreme poverty.

Another important characteristic is that the extreme poor predominantly live in settings that endanger their health. The poor are often relegated to living in hazardous conditions, often without clean water, adequate shelter, or sanitation. As a result, many suffer from or are at high risk of contracting infectious diseases. The health-related expenses and other handicaps (for example, disability or malnutrition) associated with being at that level of poverty can be destabilising to families, plunging them deeper into poverty.

What are the major drivers of extreme poverty?

Looking beyond the broad characteristics that define the extreme poor, at least at the individual level, there are also powerful systemic drivers that make this form of poverty persistent globally. These factors are almost always interrelated and mutually reinforcing, making them especially difficult for world leaders and the development community to contend with. Four fundamental drivers contributing to extreme poverty are: non-inclusive growth, social exclusion, state fragility, and climate change.

Non-inclusive growth

There is a general consensus among experts that economic growth is necessary to bring about reductions in poverty; however, growth alone is hardly sufficient. Studies show that economic growth explains only a quarter of the cross-country variation in poverty reduction.[5] A closer look at countries that have experienced rapid growth in the past decade reveals that growth in itself does not uniformly improve the conditions of the poor. And even when their conditions do improve, progress tends to be much slower for the poor than for the rest of the population. Since 1998, only 0.6 per cent of the benefits of global economic growth have gone to the poorest 20 per cent of

4   *Ibid.*, p. 7.
5   Braun, Hill, and Pandya-Lorch, p. 16.

the world population. In India, for example, though the number of people living in poverty fell at an average 5.7 per cent per year between 2005 and 2012, in eight states, the number of people living in poverty actually rose.[6] This non-inclusive, or unbalanced growth, which leaves out the poorest, is an important driver of poverty because it can effectively mask the subnational inequalities that perpetuate extreme poverty.

Non-inclusive growth occurs when governments fail to invest in sectors, markets, or regions that benefit those living in poverty. For example, it is commonly known that investing in agriculture is closely associated with reducing poverty. The poorest of the poor are predominantly smallholder farmers and are the backbone of agriculture in many low-income countries. In most African countries, agriculture accounts for more than 60 per cent of the labour but only 16 per cent of GDP, demonstrating that these farmers are still struggling with low productivity and could benefit from more targeted investment.[7] Non-farm forms of employment, such as manufacturing or construction, are also important industries that benefit the poor. In the absence of such investments, the livelihoods opportunities that are available to those in poverty end up being mostly informal, poorly paid, and unsafe, without the basic protections of formal employment.[8]

Social exclusion

Social exclusion can be defined as the processes through which groups of people are excluded from full participation in society on the basis of their race, caste, ethnicity, gender, class, or other form of sociocultural identity.[9] Social exclusion is enabled by structures in society that allow for some to progress and others not to. These identity-based inequalities create poverty traps that keep the extreme poor captive in their condition, often for generations. Experts believe that the poorest 5 per cent of the world's population, who failed to benefit from recent declines in global poverty, were most likely from socially marginalised groups.[10] Social exclusion reinforces

6   Development Initiatives.

7   AfDB, OECD, and UNDP.

8   It is worth noting that producing more balanced, pro-poor growth is a challenge. Uneven growth is not always entirely detrimental to the poor if country leaders prioritise redistribution measures. The impact of growth depends on whether countries are ready to confront underlying inequalities that impede the prospects of the poor. It is for this reason that social exclusion is another powerful driver of extreme poverty.

9   Kidd and Hossain.

10   Leahardt and Shepherd.

extreme poverty in two meaningful ways – through exclusion from economic opportunity and exclusion from networks of power and influence.

Social exclusion often leads to exclusion from economic opportunity. Ethnic and minority groups, for example, often face discrimination in labour markets, education, social protection programmes, and other institutions, making them highly vulnerable to shocks that affect their well-being. For example, India experienced a decline of 40 per cent in national poverty rates, but among socially marginalised groups, like the Dalits and Adivasis, poverty declined at a rate at least 5 to 9 per cent less.[11] Moreover, the socially excluded tend to live in remote rural areas and urban slums, intersecting with other disadvantages, such as poor roads, limited access to of public and private services (e.g., health facilities or banks), inadequate communication systems (e.g., internet access), and the absence of proximate employment opportunities.

Social exclusion is also driven by limited access to or involvement in social networks of power and influence. These networks, which include political organisations, civil society and community groups, or even relationships with influential members of society, represent important sources of social capital that are often lacking among the extreme poor. Studies show that when the poor lack access to these types of social capital, they are more likely to lack access to more tangible forms of basic services, such as social protections and resource distribution mechanisms.[12] The absence of these networks often manifests in a lack of political representation or recognition in legislation addressing discrimination (or a lack of access to more tangible forms of basic services, such as social protections enforcement if such legislation exists). Historically, women, people with disabilities, and minorities have been the main victims of this form of exclusion and have found it more challenging to create or gain access to these networks of power, limiting their access to public services or other forms of welfare programmes.[13] This power imbalance is particularly detrimental to the poor because it affects how and whether policies are shaped, how social protection schemes are designed, and how service providers deliver at national and local levels.

State fragility

It is no coincidence that the majority of the extreme poor are now concentrated in fragile or conflict states or countries whose governments are not

11   *Ibid.*
12   Prakash.
13   Braun, Hill, and Pandya-Lorch.

delivering basic public services to the majority of their populations. The inability of public institutions to deliver on their core functions represents a crisis in governance that disproportionately impacts the poor.

Two reinforcing characteristics of state fragility work most powerfully against the poor. The first is a weak rule of law. When state actors are unwilling or unable to ensure that laws are upheld and citizens protected from threats of various kinds, the vulnerabilities of the poor are amplified. In the absence of the rule of law, violent conflict easily escalates, disproportionately affecting the poor and resulting in the loss of life and long-term impacts on livelihoods and well-being. Even when migration is possible, conflict can still exacerbate poverty because the displaced are forced to leave their sources of income, often for overcrowded refugee camps with limited food supply and poor sanitary conditions. For example, since its beginning in 2010, the Syrian conflict has plunged 80 per cent of the population into poverty, reduced life expectancy by 20 years, and led to massive economic losses estimated at over $200 billion.[14]

A second characteristic of state fragility is the existence of weak public institutions, causing failures in the delivery of basic services, such as clean water, sanitation, access to energy, or education – all vital to reducing vulnerabilities faced by the poor. In many developing countries, access to these basic services is not available to the poorest of the poor. This can be as a result of insufficient or misappropriated public funds or inadequate infrastructure and delivery mechanisms. For example, Nigeria, one of the largest economies in Africa, sits on the largest-known natural gas reserves in Africa, but was second only to India in the number of people living without access to electricity in 2013: 82.4 million. Another 117.8 million Nigerians relied on wood and biomass for cooking.[15]

Climate change

Another critical but less obvious driver of extreme poverty is climate change. The resulting climate variability exacerbates the vulnerabilities of the poor, often through natural disasters that threaten life and livelihoods and through adverse impacts on health.

There is broad recognition that the frequency, intensity, and size of natural disasters globally have increased in recent years.[16] The effects of climate

---

14   *The Guardian.*

15   Lavelle.

16   The poor continue to lack the mechanisms to cope with these shocks and stresses, which are only projected to increase in the future. For those living in coastal areas with irreversible damage,

change, such as prolonged drought and floods, make it even harder for the poor to lift themselves out of poverty. In some cases, these effects have even reversed gains previously made. In addition to the immediate effects of natural disasters on the lives of the poor, climate change also threatens food security by reducing access to drinking water and decreasing crop yields. The El Niño-driven drought of 2016, which affected much of Eastern and Southern Africa, caused a national food crisis in Malawi, an impoverished country of eighteen million, where 80 per cent depend on small-scale farming for survival.[17] In response to these adverse conditions, the poor may be forced to sell off the few assets they possess, such as land and farming equipment, which further undermines their ability to sustain themselves over time.

Climate change also disproportionately impacts the health of the poor. Although infectious diseases don't discriminate on the basis of wealth, the poor often do not have health coverage or access to health treatment. The extreme poor also live in adverse ecological conditions, such as near sewage or other forms of pollution, constantly putting their health and well-being at risk. Emerging evidence shows apparent linkages between climatic conditions and the spread of disease. For example, the Planetary Health Alliance – a consortium of universities, NGOs, and other partners, which aims to understand and address the human health implications of accelerating environmental change – has produced research that shows there is a link between deforestation, increasing global temperatures, and the spread of vector-borne diseases like malaria, a leading killer of the poor worldwide.[18]

Seeing poverty through the lens of the future

Applying the drivers of poverty described above to a scenario approach, one could easily paint a dystopian picture of the future of poverty in a low-growth world where we see increasingly severe natural disasters and governments investing less in social protections and pro-poor growth. However, one could also envision a more hopeful future of emerging opportunities amid the challenges ahead, with new forms of development financing, breakthroughs in science for development, data revolution for social impact, and disruptive service delivery models.

---

migration may turn out to be their only solution. It is widely believed that climate-induced migration could be the defining phenomenon of the next 50 years.

17   Rae.

18   Guerra, Snow, and Hay.

New forms of development financing

Development aid has played an important role in reducing poverty. However, funding to least developed countries has been on a downward spiral in recent years. And with global waves of nationalism and populism, that trend is projected to continue, possibly undermining progress on the SDGs, which the UN estimates will cost between $50 and $70 trillion. Fortunately, important shifts in aid flows and new financing mechanisms are emerging that could maximise the utility of current funding and also draw additional funding from unlikely places.

Innovative finance, which represents a diverse set of financial solutions that create opportunities to tap into the more than $200 trillion in private capital invested in global financial markets towards solving social, economic, and environmental challenges, is growing as a powerful force for new funding for development and redefining what development aid means today.[19] These solutions include insurance-linked securities, pay-for-performance schemes, and even new investment models.

One of these instruments is the use of micro-levies, or small taxes on transactions, such as travel, that are relatively painless to consumers and can be repurposed for humanitarian, developmental, and social objectives. For example, in 2015, four African countries decided to create an extractive industries micro-levy covering oil, gold, bauxite, and uranium to help finance the fight against malnutrition in Sub-Saharan Africa. The levy, which could be just a few cents per barrel of oil sold, is the first innovative financing solution created entirely by developing countries. If expanded to eight oil-producing African countries, a ten-cent levy on state-owned companies would generate between $100-200 million per year, and a global oil levy of ten cents would generate at least $1.64 billion a year.[20]

Another promising set of solutions, representing a true break in practice, is unconditional cash transfers. For decades, development aid was distributed in the form of goods (e.g., free rice for the hungry) or services (e.g., providing clean water to rural communities), with mixed results for the long-term prospects of the poor. The assumption behind the practice was probably that the extreme poor could not be trusted to make the right decisions regarding their well-being, or that their current state was largely a reflection of poor decisions they had made. More recently, however, unconditional cash transfers – giving cash to the poor with no strings attached – have

---

19   Rodin and Madsbjerg.
20   *Ibid.*

defied that logic and are showing promise as a viable strategy in the fight against global poverty. Emerging evidence shows that unconditional cash transfers can raise the living standards of the poor as well as increase hours worked and labour productivity. In one case in Uganda, households that received those transfers invested most of the cash in skills and business assets and were more likely to practice a skilled trade, such as carpentry, metalworking, tailoring, or hairstyling. Recipients of the grant overall saw a 49 per cent earning boost in two years and a 41 per cent boost after four.[21] This model bodes especially well for women in developing countries who, studies have shown, reinvest 90 cents for every additional dollar of income they earn in their families' education, health, and nutrition, working to lift not just themselves out of their poverty but their whole families as well.[22]

Breakthroughs in science for development

Just as with development of the yellow fever vaccine, which saved millions of lives from the disease, and the Green Revolution, which saved even more lives from hunger, science has always played an integral role in development. In poverty alleviation, scientific breakthrough has advanced progress in sectors of keen importance to the poor, especially in food, agriculture, and health. And just as science has delivered in past decades, science is still poised to radically change the development practice and the prospects of the poor in the future. With the global population growing and pressures on land and water resources mounting, science looks again like a key tool to address the future's impending problems. The challenge for the future will not only be to produce more food in harsher ecological conditions without further damaging natural ecosystems but also to ensure that the food produced is rich in nutritional value.

Recent breakthroughs in biofortification are showing signs of promise in this arena. Biofortification is a process that improves the nutritional quality of food crops by selective breeding or genetic modification. It is a strategy for combating micronutrient deficiency, a global public health concern of epidemic proportions. Some two billion people around the world, predominantly poor, are deficient in micronutrients (vitamins and minerals) and stand to benefit from this strategy. Recent breakthroughs, like the introduction of scalable vitamin A-enriched sweet potatoes, are poised to potentially reduce malnutrition, especially vitamin A deficiency, which affects children's immune systems and causes blindness. Numerous lives

21   Yglesias.
22   VanderBrug.

have already been positively impacted by these innovations in a number of developing countries, including Ghana, Malawi, and Uganda.

Another breakthrough in food and agriculture is the use of climate-resistant crops, derived from seeds that have been bred to be more tolerant to low water levels and harsh soil conditions. These seeds are designed to use water more efficiently and to mature over shorter periods of time. Major seed giants like DuPont and Syngenta are investing heavily in this space. For example, the Water Efficient Maize for Africa project, a public-private partnership led by the African Agricultural Technology Foundation based in Kenya, with collaborating partners that include the International Maize and Wheat Improvement Centre, Monsanto Company, and five National Agricultural Research Systems for Tanzania, Kenya, Mozambique, Uganda, and the Republic of South Africa, developed a drought-tolerant seed variety that has been used by over 200,000 farmers. Using these hybrids, farmers have been able to harvest significantly more grain under moderate drought conditions as compared to the seeds they had historically planted.[23] These crops have the potential of helping farmers cope with the harsh weather conditions and are already proving to be a viable solution for farmers' livelihoods.

In health, gene-editing tools (like CRISPR) are poised to revolutionise the way the world tackles pandemics. Although the science is still nascent, and the ethics are still being fleshed out, researchers are experimenting with modifying mosquitoes to make them completely resistant to infectious diseases like malaria or Zika. For example, scientists at the University of California, Irvine, have created a malaria-resistant mosquito that does not transmit the disease and also passes on this trait to 99.5 per cent of its offspring. They accomplished this by introducing genes that bind to the malaria parasites, preventing them from recognising their host and moving around in the mosquito's body. As a result, the mosquitoes are unable to transmit the parasites to humans when they do bite.[24] Traditionally, health interventions have focused on treatment and prevention through medication and vaccines, but with such advances in gene editing, in the future, diseases that disproportionately affect the poor may be halted at the source, way before human transmission.

Data revolution for social impact

Until very recently our ability to store and analyse large volumes of data originating from sources as diverse as mobile phones or satellites was limited.

23   Balch.
24   Main.

Today, data analytics and machine learning open up new opportunities for poverty eradication that were formerly not available. Development actors are increasingly becoming armed with better data on what works and what doesn't and with greater insights on how to better target the poor and their interests. Traditional approaches to measuring and targeting poverty rely heavily on census data, which in most low- and middle-income countries are often unavailable or out of date. Studies in Bangladesh,[25] Guatemala,[26] and Senegal[27] have shown the potential of call detail records and geospatial data to provide detailed and reliable estimates of poverty rates in real time and at a far lower cost than traditional surveys – critical in contexts where limited resources both complicate the task of collecting data and accentuate the importance of precisely targeting aid and public spending.

Beyond providing a more current view on the numbers of the poor and where they are located, data analytics and machine learning can also help to make better use of their very limited resources. One of the characteristics of poverty is the lack of access to affordable, high-quality healthcare. Many factors contribute to that lack: a critical one is the dearth of trained health professionals such as doctors and nurses in low-income countries. Large-scale projects implemented in West Africa and India are starting to apply machine learning approaches to support local health workers – alerting them to possible diagnostic mistakes, suggesting treatment options, and providing customized feedback or training options based on individual learning needs.[28]

Another area where data insights can help make better use of constrained resources is in agriculture, which employs many of the poor around the world. A relatively new farming management approach, called precision agriculture, utilizes drones, sensors, and artificial intelligence software to collect data on soil quality, weather, plant growth, and irrigation. The resulting data guide decisions on which crop to plant or when and where to apply fertilizer, allowing farmers to optimize their use of inputs. Although predominantly used by large corporate farms currently, the falling prices for drones and sensors have already spurred the creation of multiple social enterprises that are working on making these techniques available to smallholder farmers.

Through the use of data and fairly rudimentary technology (e.g., SMS-based mobile applications), innovators have also been able to gather and

---

25   Steele *et al.*
26   Hernandez *et al.*
27   Data for Development.
28   IeDA Project.

process disparate forms of data to create digital identities for the extreme poor, under- and un-banked, refugees, and displaced people. These innovations help provide the poor with access to credit and public services and ultimately facilitate broader financial and social inclusion in their locales. A slew of interventions have demonstrated that it is possible to reach the poorest of the poor and at scale. For example, Tala, a data science and mobile technology company, is enabling its users in East Africa and Southeast Asia to download an app that provides them with a new kind of credit score. The app gathers 10,000 data points for each customer, forms a financial identity for them within five seconds, and then uses mobile money or other payment gateways to send capital their way.[29]

Lastly, the use of big data also enables new, often faster and cheaper ways of evaluating the effect of development programmes. For example, AidData's geospatial impact evaluations[30] use long-term data records from satellites in combination with traditional data collections such as surveys to isolate the causal effect of development programmes on outcomes. In a similar example, data from more than 60,000 World Bank infrastucture projects in combination with before and after satellite images made it possible to evaluate the effectiveness of the environmental safeguards implemented by the World Bank.[31] The fact that analysts can implement them retrospectively and remotely makes them particularly useful for studying conflict and fragile state settings, where most of the poorest of the poor are located.

Disruptive service delivery models

In many countries, public services, such as water, sanitation, and health, are not accessible to entire populations due to centralised delivery models, poor infrastructure, and limited resources. In developing countries, this problem is even more acute, especially for the extreme poor living in remote areas or outside of urban centres. The result of these limitations is a form of spatial inequality, where large parts of countries have no access to grid electricity, safe and reliable water, and health services at a proximate distance. Moreover, these spatial inequalities also amount to economic inequalities since the poor, by virtue of their location, are physically excluded from opportunities for upward mobility, such as formal employment or access to

29 Cheney.
30 Custer *et al.*
31 Runfola et al.

financial services. Fortunately, with major advances in technology, recent innovations in distributed and decentralised delivery models are disrupting the way key services are reaching formerly hard-to-reach places at a much cheaper cost than ever before.

Poor infrastructure has always been a challenge in reaching the poorest of the poor in developing countries. Roads and transportation systems often lag in 'last-mile' communities, making it exceptionally difficult for service providers to meet their needs. In many rural communities, the challenges can be life-threatening: for the injured or ill, the nearest hospital could be miles away, women may have to walk miles to reach the nearest source of drinking water, and in some areas, formal waste collection is completely nonexistent. Fortunately, new models of delivery, powered by technology, are leapfrogging traditional transportation infrastructure. One example of these is drone deliveries. In Rwanda, robotics company Zipline is improving medical access by shortening delivery times to rural areas to just fifteen minutes, when they traditionally took hours. The company works with the local health system to deliver blood to patients in need, circumventing dilapidated roads.[32]

Other disruptive delivery models can bring basic services closer to consumers, sometimes at a fraction of the cost and much more sustainably than previous models. For example, advances in energy technology, such as grid-scale battery storage or renewable energy mini-grids, are become viable and relatively affordable alternatives in addressing energy poverty compared to expanding national grids, a highly capital-intensive option. The Rockefeller Foundation has supported this sort of effort through its Smart Power Initiative, which supported over seven energy companies in India to expand electricity service in rural villages across Uttar Pradesh, Bihar, and Jharkhand, India. As of 2016, the initiative has brought power to over 40,000 people, most of whom are poor and from socially excluded groups, by building decentralised clean energy mini-grids in more than a hundred villages. These new mini-grids offer the poor new opportunities for productive living that weren't previously available to them and increase their income prospects in the future. In communities where farming was the only livelihood option, the availability of electricity allows for the new possibilities ranging from garment manufacturing, refrigeration for commercial purposes, and water purification.[33]

32 Walcutt.
33 Khanna.

2030 Scenarios: What poverty could look like

So what does this all mean for the future of poverty, given the major problem drivers and the countervailing forces mentioned above? And what possible scenarios can we expect to see in 2030 vis-à-vis the state of global poverty? Based on our analysis of these trends and forces of change discussed in earlier chapters, we see three possible scenarios for the future of poverty:

1   Resurgence of poverty
One possible, but more dystopian, future is one we call the *resurgence of poverty*. Waves of nationalism and populism lead to retrenchment in foreign aid and protectionist policies. Major setbacks in the fight against global poverty ensue. Already fragile states, like Somalia and Yemen, unravel due to weak governance and lack of economic growth. Global growth stagnates, and income inequality soars to unprecedented levels. A number of conflicts emerge, halting development altogether in many developing countries and rolling back gains in health, education, and livelihoods. Social exclusion increases – with limited resources and ineffective service delivery mechanisms, citizens are pitted against each other to the detriment of the most marginalised in society. New forms of development aid are ineffective due to excessive corruption and misappropriation of funds. A lack of global cooperation by world leaders leads to inaction on climate change, and new scores of poor, due to failing crops, land degradation, and water scarcity, emerge. This scenario may seem like more of a 'doomsday' future but could be a possibility if world leaders forego their commitment to collaboration and the eradication of poverty.

2   Prosperity for 'some'
Another plausible future is one we call the *prosperity for 'some'* scenario, with 'some' representing those in positions of power or with greater access to opportunity. Despite steady global economic growth, it remains non-inclusive because governments fail to address the needs of the socially excluded in a meaningful way. Income inequality sharply increases due to rising wealth of the elites. Much as in previous decades, the result is that in many developing countries, opportunity skips those furthest away from centres of economic power or without enough political representation, such as the rural poor. Though advances in technology increase visibility and access to markets for the extreme poor, a lack of political will, weak ethical frameworks, and an absence of targeted economic and social policies hamper progress on fighting poverty in all its forms. Despite improvements

in governance, public service delivery is likely not to extend beyond cities, where much of the wealth is concentrated. In this scenario, extreme poverty decreases but is not eliminated. The SDGs are not met, and the remaining poor are now further entrenched than before.

3   *Inclusive prosperity*

In this future, extreme poverty in all its forms is eliminated, though some form of income inequality remains. Major improvements in governance across the countries, such as DRC Congo and Haiti, lead to more stable states with a stronger rule of law, where a modicum of security and protection of rights to productive assets (for example, land rights for smallholder farmers) exist. Middle-income countries, like China and India, continue their growth while expanding opportunities within those countries to those initially left behind. Fuelled by the proliferation of new digital and data solutions and innovative delivery models, the formally socially excluded gain greater access to economic opportunity by tapping into digital markets. They also now have access to basic public services, such as clean water, sanitation, health, and energy as well as social protection programmes for those in greatest needed (e.g., the disabled and seniors). Wealth is more evenly distributed globally, and income inequality stagnates and gradually decreases over time. Major breakthroughs in food and agriculture prompts world leaders, both state and non-state actors, to promote more sustainable agricultural practices and climate-adaptation strategies in order to feed the estimated nine billion world population.

Conclusion: What would need to be true for this to happen?

Elements of all of the three scenarios will be present in 2030, but the degree of their presence will depend on our actions until then. We have the financial resources to end extreme poverty. New financing and resource models are emerging that will help close the gap as development aid is declining. We also know more, can predict more, and ultimately can better target the extreme poor and address extreme poverty. Social entrepreneurship models, machine learning, and robotics are pushing the envelope of what we can do. And despite pressures from nationalists and isolationists, world leaders still haven't given up on collaboration. Globally, ramped-up action on climate change and preparation for its impacts are proceeding, driven not only by national governments but also by cities and corporations. Fortunately, these signals bode well for the fight against poverty and are a reminder that an inclusive prosperity future is one we can hope for.

Works Cited

AfDB, OECD, and UNDP. *African Economic Outlook 2017: Entrepreneurship and Industrialisation*. African Development Bank, Organization for Economic Co-operation and Development, and UN Development Program, 2017. https://www.afdb.org/fileadmin/uploads/afdb/Documents/Publications/AEO_2017_Report_Full_English.pdf. Accessed 24 Nov. 2017.

Balch, Oliver. 'Are Drought-Resistant Crops in Africa the Tech Fix They're Cracked Up to Be?' *The Guardian*, 2 Sept. 2016. https://www.theguardian.com/sustainablebusiness/2016/sep/02/drought-resistant-crops-gm-africa-monsanto-syngenta-dupont. Accessed 10 May. 2017.

Braun, Joachim von, Ruth Vargas Hill, and Rajul Pandya-Lorch, eds. *The Poorest and Hungry: Assessments, Analyses, and Actions*. International Food Policy Research Institute, 2009. http://ebrary.ifpri.org/utils/getfile/collection/p15738coll2/id/31334/filename/31335.pdf. Accessed 22 Nov. 2017.

Cheney, Catherine. 'How Alternative Credit Scoring Is Transforming Lending in the Developing World'. Devex, 2016. https://www.devex.com/news/how-alternative-credit-scoring-is-transforming-lending-in-the-developing-world-88487. Accessed 22 Nov. 2017.

Data for Development. 'Orange Data for Development Challenge in Senegal'. Orange, 2015. http://d4d.orange.com/content/download/43330/405662/version/3/file/D4Dchallenge_leaflet_A4_V2Eweblite.pdf. Accessed 6 Jul. 2018.

Development Initiatives. *Investments to End Poverty 2015*. Development Initiatives, 2015. https://www.bond.org.uk/sites/default/files/resource-documents/investments_to_end_poverty_report_2015_0.pdf. Accessed 22 Nov. 2017.

The Guardian. 'Syria's War: 80 Per Cent in Poverty, Life Expectancy Cut by 20 Years, $200bn Lost'. *The Guardian*. 12 March 2015. https://www.theguardian.com/world/2015/mar/12/syrias-war-80-in-poverty-life-expectancy-cut-by-20-years-200bn-lost. Accessed 22 Nov. 2017.

Guerra C.A., R.W. Snow, and S.I. Hay. 'A Global Assessment of Closed Forests, Deforestation and Malaria Risk'. *Annals of Tropical Medicine and Parasitology* 100.3 (2006), pp. 189-204. https://www.ncbi.nlm.nih.gov/pmc/articles/PMC3204444/pdf/ukmss-36379.pdf. Accessed 22 Nov. 2017.

Hernandez, Marco, *et al.* 'Estimating Poverty Using Cell Phone Data: Evidence from Guatemala'. World Bank Policy Research Working Paper No. 7969. 14 Feb. 2017. https://ssrn.com/abstract=2923520. Accessed 9 Jul. 2018.

IeDA Project. 'Improving Primary Health Care through eHealth'. http://ieda-project.org. Accessed 6 Jul. 2018.

Khanna, Deepali. 'How Accelerating Access to Green Energy Is Transforming Lives'.
    The Rockefeller Foundation Blog, 2017. https://www.rockefellerfoundation.org/
    blog/accelerating-access-green-energy-transforming-lives/. Accessed 22 Nov. 2017.

Kidd, Stephen, and Naomi Hossain. *Social Exclusion and Access to Social Protection
    Schemes*. Australian Department of Foreign Affairs and Trade, 2014. http://dfat.
    gov.au/about-us/publications/Documents/social-exclusion-and-access-to-social-
    protection-schemes.pdf. Accessed 22 Nov. 2017.

Lavelle, Marianne. 'Five Surprising Facts about Energy Poverty'. *National Geographic*,
    May 2013. http://news.nationalgeographic.com/news/energy/2013/05/130529-
    surprising-facts-about-energy-poverty/. Accessed 22 Nov. 2017.

Leahardt, Amanda, and Andrew Shepherd. 'What Has Happened to the Poorest 50
    Per Cent?' University of Manchester Brooks World Poverty Institute, Working
    Paper 184, 2013. http://hummedia.manchester.ac.uk/institutes/gdi/publications/
    workingpapers/bwpi/bwpi-wp-18413.pdf. Accessed 22 Nov. 2017.

Main, Douglas. 'Researchers Genetically Modify Mosquitoes to be Malaria-
    Resistant'. *Newsweek*, 28 Nov. 2015. http://www.newsweek.com/2015/12/11/
    researchers-genetically-modify-mosquitoes-be-malaria-resistant-398998.html.
    Accessed 22 Nov. 2017.

Prakash, Sanjeev. 'Social Capital and the Rural Poor: What Can Civil Actors and
    Policies Do?' *Social Capital and Poverty Reduction*. UNESCO, 2002. http://unesdoc.
    unesco.org/images/0013/001325/132556e.pdf. Accessed 22 Nov. 2017.

Rae, Kenny. 'Widespread Drought Threatens Farmers in Malawi'. Oxfam, 2016.
    https://www.oxfamamerica.org/explore/stories/widespread-drought-threatens-
    farmers-in-malawi/. Accessed 22 Nov. 2017.

Rodin, Judith, and Saadia Madsbjerg. 'Closing the Funding Gap: Development
    in the 21st Century Is about Financing, Not Giving'. *Foreign Affairs: Special
    Issue on Innovative Finance*, Council on Foreign Affairs, 2017. https://www.
    foreignaffairs.com/sites/default/files/rockefellerinnovativefinancespecialissue.
    pdf.pdf. Accessed 22 Nov. 2017.

Runfola, Daniel, *et al.* 'A Top-Down Approach to Estimating Spatially Heterogeneous
    Impacts of Development Aid on Vegetative Carbon Sequestration'. *Sustainability*.
    9. 409. 9 Mar. 2017. http://www.mdpi.com/2071-1050/9/3/409. Accessed 9 Jul. 2018.

Steele, Jessica, *et al.* 'Mapping Poverty Using Mobile Phone and Satellite Data'.
    The Journal of the Royal Society Interface. 3 Jan. 2017. https://doi.org/10.6084/
    m9.figshare.c.3662800.v1. Accessed 6 Jul. 2018.

UN. *The Millennium Development Goals Report: 2015*. United Nations, 2015. http://
    www.un.org/millenniumgoals/2015_MDG_Report/pdf/MDG%202015%20
    rev%20(July%201).pdf. Accessed 22 Nov. 2017.

VanderBrug, Jackie. 'The Global Rise of Female Entrepreneurs'. *Harvard Business Review*, 4 Sept. 2013. https://hbr.org/2013/09/global-rise-of-female-entrepreneurs. Accessed 22 Nov. 2017.

Walcutt, Leif. 'Future of Healthcare Takes to the Skies'. *Forbes*, 24 May 2017. https://www.forbes.com/sites/leifwalcutt/2017/05/24/future-of-healthcare-takes-to-the-skies/#9a2bff82e2d1. Accessed 22 Nov. 2017.

Yglesias, Matthew. 'The Best and Simplest Way to Fight Global Poverty'. *Slate*, 29 May 2013. http://www.slate.com/articles/business/moneybox/2013/05/unconditional_cash_transfers_giving_money_to_the_poor_may_be_the_best_tool.html. Accessed 22 Nov. 2017.

About the Authors

Claudia Juech is CEO of the Cloudera Foundation and former Associate Vice President for Strategic Insights, The Rockefeller Foundation. She pioneered the use of foresight methods to identify global impact opportunities for the philanthropic sector and established the Searchlight network, the first-of-its-kind horizon scanning and trend monitoring effort in the social sector.

Chukwudi Onike is Program Associate, The Rockefeller Foundation, where he manages early stage explorations into potential opportunities for impact. He was previously a Research Consultant for the Public Sector and Governance Practice at the World Bank.

8 Transcending Boundaries: The Realistic Hope for Water

Alejandro Litovsky

Abstract

The impacts of water scarcity are increasing the likelihood of resource conflicts. However, emerging institutional processes and business models show that a sustainable water future is possible. These models assume well-functioning, transboundary hydrological systems as the basis for human innovation. The Blue Peace model brings together the governments of riparian states to see shared water resources as a source of trans-boundary cooperation rather than conflict. Second, new water investment funds create economic incentives among upstream and downstream users of water to ensure water quality and availability. Third, proven technological solutions, such as hydroponic agriculture, are mainstreamed across sectorial divides in regions that face acute water shortages in the next two decades.

Keywords: water scarcity, business risk, investors and water funds, water governance, trans-boundary cooperation, Blue Peace approach, hydroponic agriculture

A silent emergency

A 'silent emergency' is taking place as many countries around the world deplete or heavily pollute their water resources. The World Bank recently reported that emerging, populous countries, such as Nigeria and Indonesia, must invest close to US$150 billion a year to deliver safe and clean water to their populations, or risk an economic crisis due to the costs and impacts of their people drinking filthy water.[1]

---

1   World Bank Group, p. 52.

Wilkinson, Angela, and Betty Sue Flowers (eds.), *Realistic Hope: Facing Global Challenges.*
Amsterdam, Amsterdam University Press, 2018.
DOI: 10.5117/9789462987241_CH08

In the next twelve years, humanity's demand for fresh water is expected to exceed supplies by over 40 per cent.[2] Water is at the centre of climate change impacts, as weather extremes amplify droughts and floods. Despite the unpredictability, a near-certain water crisis is looming as the functioning of the economy is misaligned with the functioning of the Earth's water systems. This will require the development of political, enterprise, and investment models that align economic growth with the stability of hydrological cycles.

Today over 1.7 billion people are living in river basins where water use is exceeding the natural recharge rates.[3] Four billion people face severe water scarcity at least a month every year.[4] In California, droughts and retreating groundwater tables have accentuated the trade-offs between agriculture and household water use. Water scarcity cost the agriculture sector an estimated US$1.5 billion in 2014, including lost revenues and additional operational costs.[5]

In India, the World Bank estimates that parts of the country will have exhausted their available water supplies by 2050.[6] Conflicts over water are multiplying. Most industry sectors in India are exposed to water shortages, from power generation to materials. Companies in these sectors are under significant political pressure to reduce their water use, but the underlying problem will be resolved only by also addressing agricultural water use. In India, agriculture consumes nearly 80 per cent of the country's available water, largely from groundwater sources.

According to the United Nations, 70 per cent of industrial waste in developing countries is being discharged untreated into rivers and lakes.[7] But water pollution occurs in advanced economies as well.[8] For example, in the US, electric power plants are major sources of heavy metal pollution in waterways and account for 94 per cent of all water releases of arsenic.[9]

Glaciers, which hold up to 80 per cent of our drinking water reserves, are already receding due to climate change. In Central Asia, where water conflicts are a driver of geopolitical risks, 50 per cent of glaciers could disappear by as soon as 2035, and glaciers could disappear entirely in parts

2   WSG, 'Charting Our Water Future', p. 5.
3   UN.
4   Mekonnen and Hoekstra, p. 1.
5   Welsh.
6   World Bank, p. xi.
7   Pacific Institute, p. 2.
8   Earth Security Group, 'The Earth Security Report 2017', p. 6.
9   Barton, p. 55.

of Pakistan.[10] The rest of our global freshwater reserves are largely stored underground, in aquifers that straddle country borders. Of the world's largest 37 trans-boundary aquifers, 21 are already being heavily depleted and polluted due to the absence of any oversight.[11] At this point, one has to acknowledge the view of global security analysts, who see water shortages as one of the leading threats of future global security.[12]

Opening up the future

The future for water feels bleak and doomed. The *Financial Times* reports that multinational companies are moving to invest billions of dollars in projects to secure their water supplies, demonstrating the scale of companies' concerns over global warming and ensuing droughts that could hurt their operations.[13] In many contexts where water is becoming a scarce resource, the security of supply of one will happen at the expense of others and hence exacerbate conflict. In 2015, the UN World Water Assessment Programme concluded that business-as-usual scenarios for water, even with optimistic assumptions on economic growth and adoption of water technologies, end in the best of cases in a situation with regional water crises and, in the worst case, in a global crisis.[14]

In 2017, a scenario planning exercise for the future of water in South Africa, developed jointly by WWF South Africa and the Boston Consulting Group, was launched to feed into the debates of the National Water Week. The initiative illustrates how scenarios can help decision-makers to immerse themselves in new frames of systems thinking. The process defined four alternative scenarios. And while the outcome focuses on practical proposals, one wonders if the definition of these scenarios suggests an underlying absence of hope in the potential to realise a sustainable water future for the country[15]:

—   In the first scenario, *Down the Drain*, South Africa has ample water availability nationwide, but an excessive amount of water is wasted due to poorly maintained water infrastructure.

10   Dawn.
11   Earth Security Group, 'CEO Briefing: Global Depletion of Aquifers', p. 4.
12   Goldenberg.
13   Mooney.
14   Alcamo and Gallopín, p.3.
15   WWF-SA, p.11.

- In the second, *Big Fish, Growing Pond*, South Africa has adequate clean water, and the economy is thriving, but economic growth is driving water demand to outpace supply.
- In the third, *Illiquid Assets*, South Africa experiences strong economic growth, but clean water is increasingly scarce and costly due to recurring drought and high levels of pollution.
- Finally, in the fourth, *Cry Me a River*, a devastating drought strikes South Africa, the economy is weak, and the country is ill-equipped to survive a destructive water crisis.

The complexity of water trends is perhaps inevitably leading water scenarios to paint a picture of ensuing disasters. Water conflicts are compounded by climate change, food shortages, and mass migration. The alternative, plausible scenarios can be used to inform and navigate the pathways towards a *desired* sustainable and inclusive water future, as defined by aspirations of the UN Sustainable Development Goals.

The World Business Council for Sustainable Development (WBCSD) scenarios, *Business in the World of Water*, describe three plausible alternative water futures that are relevant to many different types of industry and businesses.[16] The three scenarios are not designed as either business-as-usual projections or 'heaven vs. hell' visions. Instead they enable a new sense of plausibility by using future perspectives to develop deeper, shared understanding of the current situation. Using scenarios to support a whole systems appreciation, in turn, enables new intervention points to be discovered and opens up discussions about existing solutions to the consideration of new and more options. In the WBCSD initiative, new solutions were identified in relation to the challenges of water efficiency, water security, and water access – for example, unlocking legacy systems and new approaches to water governance and accountability tools. The WBCSD scenarios recognise that one does not have to be in the water business to have a water crisis. In reality, all businesses are in the water business, often in ways they take for granted.

By looking beyond visions of heaven vs hell, and working with pragmatic and plausible alternative futures, which make assumptions about the wider situation and underlying system model explicit, testable, and contestable, we can enhance our understanding of the present situation and promote better and collaborative action.

---

16   WBCSD.

Managing interconnected systems

On the face of it, water disputes are a zero-sum game. However, water originates, flows, and cycles through natural systems: glaciers, rivers, aquifers,
clouds, soil. These interconnected processes involving water, with humans
using it in various ways along the way, mean that managing water really
ought to be about managing interconnected systems.

Take the example of groundwater aquifers. They cross the political
boundaries of nations, complicating the role of governments in ensuring a
rational use of water, especially when their administrations are organised in
siloed ministries and agencies. The borders of modern countries have been
redrawn over the past 500 years using either straight lines or geographic
dividers such as rivers, but not taking into account the boundaries needed
for a proper functioning of those ecosystems.

This misalignment of human governance and ecological systems is
nowhere more apparent than in the challenge of governing transboundary
aquifers, which hold the majority of fresh water that is not stored in glaciers.
Of the 37 largest transboundary aquifers on Earth, 21 are already being
depleted and polluted. This is due to two fundamental governance failures:
the lack of governance systems to manage transboundary jurisdictions; and
the absence or weakness of existing transboundary institutions.

1   *The lack of governance systems to manage transboundary*
         jurisdictions
There are over 500 transboundary aquifers, but only five of these are covered
by formalised trans-boundary agreements or institutional arrangements.
These include the treaties on the Geneva Aquifer between Switzerland and
France, the Guarani Aquifer Agreement in South America, and the Al Sag/Al
Disi Aquifer agreement between Jordan and Saudi Arabia. Non-treaty-based
cooperation frameworks include the Strategic Action Programme for the
Nubian Sandstone Aquifer in North Africa and the consultation mechanism
for the North-Western Sahara Aquifer System. Within countries, agencies
face the difficulty of managing trade-offs among multiple industries and
populations using land and water. The ability to manage this complexity
of issues and levels usually exceeds the capacity of individual agencies.

2   *The absence or weakness of existing transboundary institutions*
Groundwater abstraction has happened at a much faster speed than the
creation of regimes and agreements to manage it, leaving groundwater
systems under-regulated, undervalued, and poorly understood. Ownership

rights have historically been linked to land rights. Where permit-based rights to groundwater have come into effect, ensuring adequate law enforcement and defining the proper baseline to allocate such permits remain a challenge. Only a few countries have set up dedicated groundwater agencies for monitoring and permitting, such as India's Central Groundwater Board and Authority. However, even in these cases, given the complexity of these systems, implementation capacity is usually insufficient.[17]

Water flows in a circular way; our economic and industrial systems do not. Even proponents of 'circular economy' systems, which focus on the reuse of resources and materials, tend to think about closed-loop use of materials rather than the broader synchronisation of industrial processes and ecological systems. Today we understand better than we did 500 years ago that river basins and aquifers, whose ecological integrity is needed to sustain the water cycle, require redefinition of how to connect political and ecological boundaries so as to ensure a sustainable development.

The water nexus

Water is not a stand-alone resource. It is a crucial input to many global industries, and requires a coordinated approach to managing trade-offs, risks, and opportunities. For example, the energy system is acutely dependent on water. But lower reservoir levels in hydropower dams in countries like Colombia and Brazil are already leading to electricity shortages. And coal-fired power generation in countries like China, South Africa, and India competes with agriculture for water use, leading to water shortages and the need to rethink allocation.[18]

The agriculture sector uses up to 70 per cent of water globally. Companies in the food and agriculture industry are the most impacted by water issues. Rising operational costs, production losses due to drought, and, in some cases, challenges to the social license to operate are increasingly common for business. In the case of mining, the six largest global mining companies have 70 per cent of their combined operations in countries that already face water scarcity risk. In 2014 alone, mining companies globally spent more than US$12 billion on water infrastructure in water-stressed regions, a 253 per cent increase from 2009.[19] Social opposition to mining projects has

---

17   See Earth Security Group, 'CEO Briefing: Global Depletion of Aquifers', for a discussion of these two governance failures.

18   Schneider.

19   Park *et al.*, p. 9.

increased exponentially in recent years, driven mainly by competition for water with local populations.[20] Of the water-related risks identified as critical to their business by over 600 corporate respondents to the Carbon Disclosure Project (CDP) survey, respondents expect half of them to materialise within the next six years.[21] Global investors are following these signals. In 2013 and 2014 Norges, the manager of Norway's US$900 billion sovereign wealth fund, divested from 35 companies over water risks.[22]

Water scarcity is having serious effects on the viability prospects of some megacities. Out of the world's 100 largest cities, 30 are reported to be experiencing some level of water stress.[23] Growing cities are hotspots for water challenges. The World Bank estimates that water availability could be reduced by as much as two-thirds in cities by 2050 compared with 2015 levels.[24]

The technology sector also faces key water challenges. In Asia-Pacific, where eleven of the world's fourteen largest semiconductor factories operate, requiring vast amounts of ultra clean water for manufacturing, 80 per cent of wastewater being discharged in water bodies gets little or no primary treatment.[25] Nearly 70 per cent of companies in the materials sector are identifying higher operating costs from exposure to water risk, according to the CDP.[26] Wastewater is the largest untapped waste category in the circular economy.[27]

In sum, we know that the effective allocation of water has to balance competing demands from different users and different industries, such as agriculture and energy, and growing populations in cities, while managing the trade-offs. Managing this complexity vastly exceeds the capacity of the systems that are in place today.

A possible paradigm shift

While there is urgent cause for concern, a number of emerging models are demonstrating that such a paradigm shift is possible. With the impacts of scarcer resources already being felt in large cities and populous states around

20   *The Economist.*
21   CDP, p. 4.
22   Chaudhary.
23   McDonald and Shemie, p. 6.
24   Clark.
25   ADB, p. 7.
26   CDP, p. 46.
27   Stuchtey, 'Four Ways Water Can Join the Circular Economy Revolution'.

the world, these models provide political and economic benefits that are needed in order to build a sustainable long-term future. Considering the water cycle as an integral part of a circular economy is driving the creation of new technological solutions to improve water management, and these solutions are already being integrated into the redesign of business models.[28]

Models of realistic hope

Radical innovation is possible. Many of the technologies available today, such as water desalination, will evolve rapidly when coupled with other technologies such as renewable energy. Water reuse and recycling is becoming more common and opening up new possibilities for industrial innovation. But even those individual firms adopting disruptive innovations for water are facing political challenges to their license to operate in water-stressed regions. In other words, finding solutions at a system level is critical to the success on this agenda. Three models discussed here offer a glimpse into how such reorganisation of interests might look.

1   Rethinking political boundaries: The Blue Peace
The Blue Peace approach calls for engagement of high-level political leaders to promote water cooperation and requires the establishment of sustained mechanisms for regional cooperation, including agreements on trade-offs, the development of joint investment programmes, and the dissemination of modern technologies for renewing water resources.[29]

Joint investment programmes are emerging as a good way to approach shared infrastructure projects because they offer a practical way to overcome financing constraints and create incentives for cooperation. They allow governments to pool their capacity to underwrite risk and create attractive propositions for multilateral financial institutions and banks.

In West Africa, joint investment plans have been developed for the Senegal and Gambia River basins. The Islamic Development Bank has financed transboundary projects with the Senegal River Basin Development Authority. This success model is a beacon of hope for the rest of the developing world. Of the 80 trans-boundary water basins in Africa, fewer than 10 per cent have any kind of inter-country mechanism or agreement for the coordination of integrated development efforts.[30]

28 Stuchtey, 'Rethinking the Water Cycle'.
29 Waslekar.
30 INBO, p. 1.

The Blue Peace model is now operational in several regions, encouraging a shared political vision for water management that supports the necessary technical cooperation.[31] For instance, in Central Asia, the Blue Peace Initiative facilitated by the Swiss government has pioneered a political dialogue among the five Central Asian countries on the challenges and potential solutions to managing transboundary water resources. This process is beginning to cross-connect the insights and opportunities across river basins of the world, effectively turning the Blue Peace into a global movement.[32]

2   *Creating new investment models: Water funds*
A water fund is essentially a trust fund that water users pay into, which in turn pays for conservation and agriculture investments in the upper watershed in order to secure water quality and, in some cases, water quantity improvements. River basins span large areas of territory and encompass a multitude of water users. Water funds that cross-connect upstream and downstream actors with a common focus on conservation have successfully shown a way to organise interests and invest to protect and preserve water sources.

Payments into water funds are made by companies in different industries and involve partnerships with water utilities and other stakeholders. The funds create incentives for upstream actors to avoid land degradation and pollution and therefore improve the quality of water flowing downstream. These funds are also demonstrating that investing in sustainable land and agriculture practices upstream is cheaper and more effective for down-stream companies than investing to treat polluted water arriving at their manufacturing facilities.

In Colombia, the beer company Bavaria found that rising water pollution levels affected one of its breweries and increased the costs of water treatment. Miles upstream, unsustainable land and farming practices were key contributors to this pollution.

Most of Bogotá's water originates high above the city in Chingaza National Park. Forest clearing for cattle ranching and farming occurs in and around the park, and that has taken its toll on water quality. Plant roots act as natural sieves that retain and release water. With them gone, erosion and mudslides have harmed water quality and wildlife. Bavaria partnered with The Nature Conservancy, providing seed funding of US$150,000 to set up the Bogotá Water Fund in cooperation with the local water utility. The fund

31   Cuppari, p. 3.
32   FDFA.

pays farmers to use their land more sustainably.[33] Once the pilot moved to the 60,000 hectares of the water catchment area, the improvement in water quality saved the company three times the money that would have been needed for treating the water.[34]

3   *Mainstreaming new technologies: Hydroponic agriculture*
Jordan was already depleting its scarce water resources before the Syrian conflict broke out. Now, the influx of refugees has additionally triggered 20-40 per cent increases in water demand in different regions.[35] Most of Jordan's water comes from underground aquifers. The vast majority is used for agriculture. Water is being withdrawn twice as fast as it can replenish, wasted through inefficient agricultural techniques. At the current rate, Jordan's supply of fresh water will be completely depleted by 2060.[36] With less water available for irrigation, food security and jobs in agriculture are at risk. This is a sector that employs many migrant workers. Water scarcity will trigger a series of associated social conflicts that quickly escalate.

USAID's Hydroponic Green Farming Initiative in Jordan has demonstrated the economics and viability of new farming models such as hydroponic agriculture, together with local farming entrepreneurs. With savings in water use ranging between 50 per cent and 80 per cent, hydroponic farming uses mineral nutrient solutions instead of growing in the soil. In Zarqa, for example, a 300-square-metre greenhouse can produce 29,000 heads of lettuce (six harvest cycles) using only 216 cubic metres of water per year through hydroponics, which would require 1160 cubic metres of water using conventional irrigation in the soil.[37]

In the United Arab Emirates, the Khalifa Fund for Enterprise Development funded 130 farms using hydroponic technology as part of an initiative to reduce water consumption and enhance food security. The fund also works on creating a national standard for hydroponic farming to guarantee that the quality of the products is aligned with international standards.[38]

The value chain associated with efficient irrigation, from suppliers to farms, means that this nascent sector can offer job opportunities in a wide range of skill levels, with a positive impact on refugees, women, and youth.

33 Pearce.
34 Earth Security Group, 'CEO Briefing: Food and Agriculture', p. 9.
35 *Jordan Times*.
36 MercyCorps, p. 12.
37 USAID.
38 AMEinfo.

Innovation in agriculture has the potential to create up to 15,000 new jobs in Jordan.[39]

However, to help consolidate Jordan's nascent hydroponic industry, an enterprise development programme is needed that tackles the barriers to scale. On one hand, greater awareness of farmers of the economic benefits is needed to scale the demand. On the other, the availability of financing for SME suppliers and customers is needed to enable service providers to support growth along the hydroponics value chain – from farmers to the suppliers of greenhouses and nutrients to packing houses and cold storage facilities. Proposals have been made for the Jordanian Loan Guarantee Corporation, which offers SME guarantees, to focus on hydroponics and for the Jordan Enterprise Development Corporation (JEDCO) and the Agricultural Credit Corporation to address gaps in access to finance in the governorates where the business environment is particularly difficult.[40]

Looking ahead: Aligning the economics with the politics

Conflicts over water resources no longer belong to a fictional dystopian future. The global water crisis is playing out, and its contours and consequences are all too clear. The clock is ticking. As with other related systemic transformations, the next few decades will tell if the models described here can be mainstreamed at the speed that is required before water runs out.

In the face of increasing water scarcity, the growing demand from civil society for water to become a fundamental human right makes much sense. This creates the political imperative for no person to have to go without access to fresh water. At the same time, the business and investment community calls for clearer water pricing, to send the right signals and incentivise more rational water consumption.

Fears that water pricing could lead to excluding poorer populations from accessing water are understandable. However, the way forward requires a blend of political and economic incentives. Better water pricing is needed to reflect water scarcity. This is a necessary economic organising principle. At the same time, enshrining an inalienable right to access to fresh water provides a political organising principle to ensure that, whatever the solution taken, principles of fairness and inclusiveness in the access to water will remain a top priority for decision-makers. Reconciling economic and political incentives is a vital compass for the turbulent decades to come.

39   WSG, 'The Water Resources Group', p. 32.
40   Earth Security Group, 'Forced Displacement and Development', p. 11.

Water intersects critically with other challenges, such as climate change, food security, energy, and security. These new models of coordination are operationalising the idea of systemic thinking across political, investment, and technological boundaries. They are the only realistic hope we have to create lasting solutions to the impending global water crisis.

Works Cited

ADB. 'Asian Water Development Outlook 2016: Strengthening Water Security in Asia and the Pacific'. Mandaluyong City, Philippines: Asian Development Bank, 2016. https://www.adb.org/sites/default/files/publication/189411/awdo-2016.pdf. Accessed 7 Nov. 2017.

Alcamo, Joseph, and Gilberto Gallopín. 'Building a 2nd Generation of World Water Scenarios'. UN World Water Assessment Programme (WWAP), 2015.

AMEinfo. 'Khalifa Fund Approves Funding for 130 Farms Using Hydroponics System'. *AMEinfo*, 19 Jan. 2015. http://ameinfo.com/money/economy/khalifa-fund-approves-funding-130-farms-using-hydroponics-system/. Accessed 7 Nov. 2017.

Barton, B. 'Murky Waters? Corporate Reporting on Water Risk'. Ceres, UBS and Bloomberg, February 2010. http://waterfootprint.org/media/downloads/Barton_2010.pdf. Accessed 7 Nov. 2017.

CDP. *Thirsty Business: Why Water is Vital to Climate Action: 2016 Annual Report of Corporate Water Disclosure*. London: Corporate Water Disclosure, 2016. https://b8f65cb373b1b7b15feb-c70d8ead6ced550b4d987d7c03fcdd1d.ssl.cf3.rackcdn.com/cms/reports/documents/000/001/306/original/CDP-Global-Water-Report-2016.pdf?1484156313. Accessed 7 Nov. 2017.

Chaudhary, A. 'A 23 Billion Stock Drop Shows India's Rising Water Risks'. Bloomberg, 17 June 2015. https://www.bloomberg.com/news/articles/2015-06-17/a-23-billion-stock-drop-shows-rising-india-water-risks. Accessed 7 Nov. 2017.

Clark, P. 'Water Scarcity Threatens Growth and Stability, Study Warns'. *Financial Times*, 3 May 2016.

Cuppari, R. 'Water Diplomacy: International Centre for Water Resources and Global Change'. International Centre for Water Resources and Global Change and UNESCO, Policy Brief Number 1, June 2017. http://www.waterandchange.org/wp-content/uploads/2017/06/PB_WaterDiplomacy_lowres.pdf. Accessed 7 Nov. 2017.

Dawn. 'Pakistan's Glaciers Will Melt by 2035'. *Dawn*, 6 Nov. 2013.

Earth Security Group. 'CEO Briefing: Food and Agriculture'. London: Earth Security Group, 2016. https://earthsecuritygroup.com/strategy-briefs/ceo-briefing-food-agriculture. Accessed 7 Nov. 2017.

Earth Security Group. 'CEO Briefing: Global Depletion of Aquifers'. London: Earth Security Group, 2016. https://earthsecuritygroup.com/strategy-briefs/ceo-brief-global-depletion-aquifers. Accessed 7 Nov. 2017.

Earth Security Group. 'The Earth Security Report 2017: Sustainable Development Goals for Business Diplomacy and Growth'. London: Earth Security Group, 2017. https://earthsecuritygroup.com/strategy-briefs/earth-security-report-2017. Accessed 7 Nov. 2017.

Earth Security Group. 'Forced Displacement and Development: Public-Private Partnerships for Sustainable Solutions'. London: Earth Security Group, 2016. https://earthsecuritygroup.com/strategy-briefs/forced-displacement-development. Accessed 7 Nov. 2017.

The Economist. 'From Conflict to Co-operation'. *The Economist*, 6 February 2016. https://www.economist.com/news/americas/21690100-big-miners-have-better-record-their-critics-claim-it-up-governments-balance. Accessed 7 Nov. 2017.

FDFA. 'Federal Councilor Didier Burkhalter Launches "Blue Peace" Initiative for Transboundary Water Management in Central Asia'. Swiss Development Cooperation, Federal Department of Foreign Affairs, 19 June 2017. https://www.admin.ch/gov/en/start/documentation/media-releases.msg-id-67098.html. Accessed 7 Nov. 2017.

Goldenberg, S. 'Why Global Water Shortages Pose Threat of Terror and War'. *The Guardian*, 9 Feb. 2014.

INBO. 'Transboundary Water Management and Regional Integration in Africa'. 4th World Water Forum, International Network of Basin Organisations, Session FT218 Report. http://www.riob.org/IMG/pdf/FT2-18_Session_repor__final.pdf. Accessed 7 Nov. 2017.

Jordan Times. 'Refugee Crisis Pushes Water Demand Up by 21 Per Cent'. *Jordan Times*, 21 March 2015.

McDonald. R.I., and Daniel Shemie. 'Urban Water Blueprint: Mapping Conservation Solutions to the Global Water Challenge'. Washington, DC: The Nature Conservancy, 2014.

Mekonnen, M., and A.Y. Hoekstra. 'Four Billion People Facing Severe Water Scarcity'. *Science Advances* 2.2, 12 Feb. 2016.

MercyCorps. 'Tapped Out: Water Scarcity and Refugee Pressures in Jordan'. Portland: MercyCorps, March 2014. https://www.mercycorps.org/sites/default/files/MercyCorps_TappedOut_JordanWaterReport_March204.pdf. Accessed 7 Nov. 2017.

Mooney, Attracta. 'Big Companies Invest Billions to Secure Water Supplies'. *Financial Times*, 6 Nov. 2017.

Pacific Institute. 'World Water Quality Facts and Statistics'. Pacific Institute, 22 March 2010. http://pacinst.org/wp-content/uploads/2013/02/water_quality_facts_and_stats3.pdf. Accessed 7 Nov. 2017.

Park, A., *et al.* 'Water Risk Valuation Tool: Integrating Natural Capital Limits into Financial Analysis of Mining Stocks'. Bloomberg and Natural Capital Declaration, Sept. 2015. https://www.bbhub.io/sustainability/sites/6/2015/09/Bloomberg_WRVT_09162015_WEB.pdf. Accessed 7 Nov. 2017.

Pearce, F. 'How Beer Money Can Help Save a Nation's Water Supply'. *Conservation Magazine*, 11 Dec. 2013.

Schneider, K. 'As Drought Grips South Africa, a Conflict over Water and Coal'. *Yale Environment* 360, 16 May 2016.

Stuchtey, M. 'Four Ways Water Can Join the Circular Economy Revolution'. *Guardian Sustainable Business*, 5 March 2015.

Stuchtey, M. 'Rethinking the Water Cycle'. McKinsey & Co., May 2015. https://www.mckinsey.com/business-functions/sustainability-and-resource-productivity/our-insights/rethinking-the-water-cycle. Accessed 7 Nov. 2017.

UN. 'Goal 6: Ensure Access to Water and Sanitation for All'. UN Sustainable Development Goals. http://www.un.org/sustainabledevelopment/water-and-sanitation. Accessed 18 April 2017.

USAID. 'USAID Hydroponic Green Farming Initiative (HGFI)', US Agency for International Development, 24 May 2017. https://www.usaid.gov/jordan/fact-sheets/usaid-hydroponic-green-farming-initiative-hgfi. Accessed 14 Mar. 2018.

Waslekar, S. 'Blue Peace Approach Is the Way to Go'. *Gulf News*, 21 March 2013.

WBCSD. *Business in the World of Water: WBCSD Water Scenarios to 2025.* World Business Council for Sustainable Development, 2006.

Welsh, J. 'California's Drought Is the Greatest Water Loss Ever Seen, and the Effects Will Be Severe'. *Business Insider*, 15 July 2014.

World Bank. 'India's Water Economy: Bracing for a Turbulent Future'. World Bank, 22 Dec. 2005. http://documents.worldbank.org/curated/en/731801468033688876/pdf/34750.pdf. Accessed 7 Nov. 2017.

World Bank and PIK. 'Turn Down the Heat: Confronting the New Climate Normal: The Climate Challenge for Central Asia'. World Bank and Potsdam Institute for Climate Impact Research, 2014. http://documents.worldbank.org/curated/en/294131467991967756/The-climate-challenge-for-Central-Asia. Accessed 7 Nov. 2017.

World Bank Group. *Reducing Inequalities in Water Supply, Sanitation, and Hygiene in the Era of the Sustainable Development Goals: Synthesis Report of the Water Supply, Sanitation, and Hygiene (WASH) Poverty Diagnostic Initiative.* Washington, DC: World Bank Group, 2017.

WSG. 'Charting Our Water Future: Economic Frameworks to Inform Decision-Making'. Washington, DC: 2030 Water Resources Group, 2009. https://www.2030wrg.org/portfolio-item/charting-our-water-future/. Accessed 7 Nov. 2017.

WSG. 'The Water Resources Group: Background, Impact and Way Forward'. 2030
    Water Resources Group, 26 Jan. 2012. http://www3.weforum.org/docs/WEF/
    WRG_Background_Impact_and_Way_Forward.pdf. Accessed 7 Nov. 2017.
WWF-SA. *Scenarios for the Future of Water in South Africa*. South Africa: World
    Wildlife Fund South Africa and Boston Consulting Group, 2017.

About the Author

Alejandro Litovsky is the Founder and Chief Executive of Earth Security
Group, a strategic advisory firm innovating on business intelligence for
sustainable development impact. He previously held senior positions at
London-based sustainability consultancies AccountAbility and Volans
Ventures, advancing the strategic collaboration of business, governments,
and civil society in emerging markets. He holds an MSc in political sociology
from the London School of Economics and Political Science, which awarded
him the Hobhouse Memorial Prize in 2004.

9 Health Systems: Doomed to Fail or About to Be Saved by a Copernican Shift?

Kristel Van der Elst and Rudi Pauwels

Abstract

Advances in health and healthcare have added about 35 years of life expectancy worldwide over the last century alone. This success has come with a rising cost that is quickly becoming unsustainable. Efficiency gains in our current system, while absolutely necessary, are in themselves insufficient. Our future healthcare system needs to be an actual '*health*' system rather than a 'disease care' system – and it needs to be financially sustainable. Such a transformation requires new ideas, structures, mindsets, and actions. Across the world we see increased investments in prevention, growing innovation and entrepreneurship in public and private sectors in health tech, health data, and health culture, and shifts towards value-based and outcome-based health systems.

Keywords: health system, prevention, disease care, value-based healthcare, patient-focused care, healthcare innovation, future of health

The evolution of the healthcare system

Advances in health and healthcare have been significant during the last two centuries. Over the last 100 years we have gained worldwide about 35 years of life expectancy as a result of increases in sanitation, decreases in poverty, the lowering of child mortality, and evolutions in medicine and healthcare systems.

These successes have not come without cost. For example, in 2016, OECD countries spent an average of 9 per cent of our gross domestic product (GDP) on health, with wide variations from country to country.[1] The US,

---

1   OECD, 'OECD Health Statistics 2017'.

Wilkinson, Angela, and Betty Sue Flowers (eds.), *Realistic Hope: Facing Global Challenges*. Amsterdam, Amsterdam University Press, 2018.
DOI: 10.5117/9789462987241_CH09

for example, spent 2.5 times the OECD average. Over the past decades total healthcare expenditure in OECD countries has climbed faster than GDP. Projections for the coming 20 years suggest that the cost of healthcare will rise by another 50 to 100 per cent.[2] Outside the OECD costs are also expected to rise. Some forecasts suggest that the BRICS countries will more than double their healthcare costs over the next 40 years.[3] This increasing cost is driven by both demand and supply factors.

An ageing population

By 2030, people aged over 60 are expected to account for one in six globally, which is a 56 per cent increase from 2015 – 1.4 billion people. In Europe and North America people over 60 will comprise more than one in four of the total population. The global population of people over 80 years is rising even faster and is expected to increase by 61 per cent between 2015 and 2030 to nearly 202 million people.[4] A fundamental question is whether these additional years of life expectancy will be lived in good or ill health.

An increase in chronic diseases and multi-morbidity

The increase in chronic diseases is partly linked to the ageing population but also finds its origin in other causes, such as unhealthy lifestyles and air and chemical pollution. At present in Europe chronic diseases account for 80 per cent of the EU health budget. In the US, more than half of the population has at least one chronic disease while one in four Americans has multiple chronic diseases, rising to three in four among people aged 65 and over. In most of the OECD countries, over 50 per cent of the burden of disease comes from people with multiple chronic diseases. Low- and middle-income countries are also significantly affected. An estimated 80 per cent of 'premature' deaths attributed to chronic diseases occurring between the ages of 30 and 96 years take place in those countries.

A rise in public expectations for healthcare

In many societies health is seen as a right that should be provided equitably and independent of cost. With the introduction of new, advanced technologies,

2   World Economic Forum.
3   De la Maisonneuve and Martins.
4   UN DESA.

diagnostics, and treatments, the consumption of health-related products and services increases. With increased health literacy the public also makes more demands on health professionals, taking a more proactive role in their desired treatment.[5] Consumers often do not have strong price signals and incentives to make cost or value-based decisions. Advances in what is possible in curing disease also increase our desire to try all possibilities, at any cost.

Increasing prices for healthcare products and services

Medical prices have risen yearly. How this will play out in the future will be a balance between factors such as general inflation, the evolution in proportionality of costs born by the different stakeholders, the level and nature of innovation, the number of drugs coming off patent, and scrutiny on prices by the payers.

Inefficient resource allocation and incentive systems

The health sector has a reputation for being very adverse to change because of strong vested interests, practitioners' habits, and so on. Optimising health value and relating outcomes to inputs and costs are further complicated because of the lack of transparency across the value chain.

Rising anti-microbial resistance (AMR)

Drug-resistant infections are on the rise and said to claim possibly ten million lives annually by 2050. Every year up to 50,000 people in Europe and the US and 7,000,000 globally die from infections that have become resistant to antibiotics.[6] In addition to claiming many lives, AMR can have a damaging impact on the health system as hospital stays will be needed for illnesses that now are handled without hospitalisation, and will become longer. There will also be a significant impact on countries' economies as people will take longer to recover from even simple infections.

Our unsustainable healthcare system

In light of increasing overall budgetary pressures on public funds, the healthcare system as it currently stands is unsustainable and in need of

5   King's Fund.
6   Review on Antimicrobial Resistance.

deep transformation, including significant innovations. The health systems of emerging and developing countries cannot afford to follow the model of the developed countries. Realistic alternatives to the traditional healthcare system must be explored to ensure that progress in healthcare transformations is made across the world in an equitable way.

Visions of a sustainable health system

Hope for the better starts with the fact that the future bankruptcy of our current healthcare systems is now a commonly accepted truth. If the current healthcare system is unsustainable, we have to rethink it. What would be a better system? And what pathways and actions could lead to it?

The World Economic Forum's Sustainable Health Systems project noted four key elements of a vision for sustainable national health systems across stakeholders and nations:

1   Individual empowerment and responsibility, with patients having greater control over treatment and management of conditions and taking greater responsibility over life choices to reduce the burden on the health system;
2   Greater accountability of governments and healthcare providers to deliver effective, sustainable health services;
3   Data-driven/evidence-based value and outcomes;
4   Multi-stakeholder responsibility.[7]

Underlying all of these is a shift in mind-set about what a 'healthcare' system is. Our current model of a 'healthcare' system is more a 'disease care' system – a system of institutions, facilities, and actors that delivers products and services for health problems. Our future healthcare system must be rather a *'health'* system that includes the preservation of health and addresses aspects of society that directly or indirectly affect our health (e.g., food and beverage companies, wellness providers, prevention providers).

Another piece of a new transformative health-system vision is described in Goal 3 of the UN Sustainable Development Goals: 'Ensure healthy lives and promote well-being for all at all ages'.[8] This vision sets out a number of specific targets to achieve globally by 2030 in order to eradicate diseases and address a set of health issues, and includes advances in mortality rates, prevention and treatment of chronic diseases, access to healthcare services, universal health coverage, healthcare capacity, and the development of

7   World Economic Forum.
8   UN, 'Goal 3'.

vaccines and medicines. This goal is part of the 17 Sustainable Development Goals and 169 related targets agreed on in 2015 and to be achieved by 2030. These goals are designed to provide direction for individual and collective action across governments, the private sector, civil society, and individuals to end poverty, protect the planet, and ensure prosperity for all.[9]

Exogenous factors offering realistic hope

Three factors largely outside the control of the health system will influence its nature and shape: health tech, health data, and health culture.

1   Health tech: The convergence of health and technology
Advances in technologies such as artificial intelligence, big data, sensors, nanotechnology, synthetic biology, genomic sequencing, additive manufacturing, blockchain, and a host of other technology-related developments are beginning to have a big impact on health systems. In addition, technology firms such as Amazon, Google, Apple, and Qualcomm are beginning to act in the health system. For example, Alphabet – Google's parent company – is devoting research teams and resources to work on initiatives such as contact lenses, the measurement of blood sugar, anti-ageing, bioelectronics, symptom searches, health-tracking watches, and much more. Former Google employees are also highly represented in health-related start-ups in Silicon Valley. Collaborations between the traditional players and the technology industry multiply while commercially driven health systems have been setting up their own venture capital arms to discover solutions to their problems, becoming, in effect, incubators and accelerators.

The new insights into the molecular causes and mechanisms of disease and disease progression together with increased adoption of existing technological innovations and the emergence of new ones open the door for innovations in which, how, where, and when health services are provided. These insights and innovations also allow for more prevention and timely disease interception, faster, better, and more personalised treatments, better utilisation rates of caregivers and healthcare infrastructures, more patient participation, and so forth. They might even allow for the substitution of medicine by non-medicine options in certain cases.

How fast technological innovation will penetrate the health system and industries will converge depends in part on regulation and the willingness for stakeholders to adopt or adapt to those innovations. For example, the

---

9   UN, 'Sustainable Development Goals'.

newer, more targeted pharmaceutical drugs that have entered the market in recent years and the many more to be launched in the coming decade require, from a clinical and regulatory standpoint, a much more detailed, high-quality, and timely diagnostic assessment of the disease of each individual patient. This requires a more convergent R&D, regulatory, and marketing approach by the pharmaceutical, biotech, and diagnostic players who have traditionally operated separately. Moreover, this convergence requires greater alignment at the reimbursement level. The jury is still out on whether these innovations will decrease or increase cost over the long term. Cost savings will be possible only if they are not offset by increased demand. And treatments that help people live longer can push up the overall healthcare cost, depending on the future need for health services.[10]

How this new ecosystem will play out might be uncertain, but, as the saying goes, we tend to overestimate the effect of a technology in the short run and underestimate it in the long run.

2   *Health data collection, access, and usability*
Increasingly, a wide set of players from both public and private organisations is collecting and sharing data across the health system. Health data collection offers opportunities for generating increased efficiency and better outcomes.

Health data is only one of the types of data in the explosion of data, estimated by some to have quadrupled globally in just a span of five years. Whether this data will continue to be collected easily, who will own it, who can harvest it and under which circumstances, and whether its use will create real disruptive change in the health system will be conditioned, in part, by regulation, standards, and consumer stances. The health data context will also be influenced by a more general appreciation of data collection, ownership, access, and usability, as well as of cybersecurity.

3   *Health culture: Solidarity, inclusiveness, and other social values*
How the health system will play out in the future also depends on the evolution of societal values. For example, staying healthy to reduce the burden on the health system is an important step. Health education, policies, urban design, and general attitudes towards valuing being healthy can significantly affect the transformation of the health system.

Attitudes towards solidarity and inclusiveness are shifting. Whether societies and communities will see health as a universal right or an individual

10   Rauch.

responsibility – and more generally the strength of the social cohesion within societies – will influence who has access to what health services and at what cost. Where universal healthcare is still a prominent aspiration, it is often cited as unaffordable, resulting in a push towards a commodified and privatised healthcare system. Although increased stratification of societies might well favour less inclusive systems, several studies show that it is in the interest of wealthier populations to support the less wealthy.

Endogenous change

Because the health system is made up of many diverse subsystems, no magic pill or panacea can transform it overnight so that it can achieve desired outcomes for all in a financially sustainable way. The health system transformation will require new ideas, changes in power, incentive structures, mind-sets, and actions, and the influence of visionaries, entrepreneurs in public and private sectors, public-private collaborations, and societies at large.

Pessimistic stakeholders argue that vested interests, the complexity of the system, the rigidity of actors in the system, the reluctance to take political and commercial risks, and the relative lack of evidence for the success of new ideas all make such a transformation unlikely. Taking a more optimistic perspective, we can suppose people are naturally problem solvers, well intentioned to avoid pain and failure, and striving to grow and strive for progress. Additionally, as noted by Peter Diamandis, 'The world's biggest problems represent the world's biggest opportunities'.[11] Whether change, disruption, and innovation will bring about the best and most sustainable health system for all will need to be seen, but what is certain is that change is happening.

Transformational spaces offering realistic hope

1   *From volume to outcomes and value*
The traditional healthcare systems give incentives to health providers to maximise the number of 'interventions', with revenues based on volume. This system has created significant waste. For example, sources estimate that about one-fifth to one-third of health expenditures do not result in improved health. A major transformation occurring now is a shift away from these fee-for-service or volume-based health systems and towards value-based and outcome-based health systems.

11   Diamandis and Kurzweil.

This trend arises from the interaction of a number of factors: governments aiming to decrease their health expenditures, commercial payers (such as corporate payers and private insurers) adopting reimbursement schemes to decrease cost and improve service offerings, the consumerisation of healthcare, and the growing demand by both individuals and communities for patient empowerment.

Although many definitions exist, in essence, *value-based healthcare* is the optimisation of health outcomes in relation to the cost. Across health system stakeholders the meaning given to 'outcomes' and 'values' varies. For example, while some refer to 'outcomes' as clinically meaningful medical results, others talk about patient-experience satisfaction and cost, while others include concepts such as the experienced healthcare and treatment options being congruent with one's personal daily life and life objectives.

Moving towards value-based healthcare raises a number of challenges: for example, defining and measuring outcomes, measuring cost, linking cost with outcomes, implied investments in IT and data infrastructure, the development of standards, data protection and privacy rules, intellectual property protection, and human capacity building. Challenges also arise from those who fear that shifting to a value-based revenue model means cutting into short-term profits. Another challenge is rooted in mental models: some stakeholders see increasing positive outcomes and decreasing costs as mutually exclusive, while others see this opposition as a false dichotomy – improving outcomes and decreasing costs can be achieved together.

In spite of these challenges, there are signs of realistic hope that we might be moving towards a world where health systems manage to lower the cost of the burden of disease, produce better, evidence-based health outcomes, and improve the experience of both patient and caregiver. In response to the challenge of defining and measuring outcomes, for example, the International Consortium for Health Outcomes Measurement (ICHOM) is working to create global standards, defining health outcomes as 'the results people care about most when seeking treatment, including functional improvement and the ability to live normal, productive lives'. In relation to each specific disease, ICHOM is creating a standard set of outcomes through consultations with both physicians and patients. Measuring outcomes through these standard sets would allow health providers to compare results and learn from each other, improve their performance, and provide a means to demonstrate superior outcomes as a competitive advantage in the market place – and thus to facilitate value-based payment.[12]

12   ICHOM.

A 2016 study done by The Economist Intelligence Unit (EIU) shows that at varying speeds across the world, governments are implementing value-based approaches.[13] EIU measures alignment with value-based approaches through four criteria:

1   The enabling of context, policy, and institutions for value in healthcare;
2   The level of measurement of outcomes and costs;
3   The level of integrated and patient-focused care;
4   The focus on outcome-based payment approaches.

Experimentation is more diverse in private health systems, where moving from siloed, single-provider-based care to co-ordinated, team-based care is seen as a business opportunity in a dysfunctional market. These experiments are spearheaded by large integrated health provider groups, such as Kaiser Permanente, as well as by entrepreneurial providers backed by venture capital.

This shift is driving innovation in healthcare delivery models, which can be seen not only in developed markets but also in emerging and developing countries less restrained by existing legacy structures and where out-of-pocket health expenditure is more prevalent.

Given the trend of payers to move into value-based reimbursement, it is a strategically smart, forward-looking action for providers to reflect on how to adapt as soon as possible. Providers who have started moving in this direction note that it makes them more competitive and financially sustainable in the long term as they attract consumers with lower prices for higher-quality services. As they make this shift, they gain expertise in managing service delivery under cost restrictions and get a head start on the long process of building new relations with all required stakeholders.[14]

2   *From disease care systems to health systems*
A second significant transformation underway in the health system is the increased focus on preserving health and increasing well-being rather than merely treating illness. This shift emerges from the realisation that focusing on efficiency gains and cost containment measures alone will not achieve long-term sustainability of health systems – it is essential to ease the demand for care.

---

13   In the majority of countries, the enabling components for this new approach to healthcare still need to be assembled. In the assessed panel, Sweden made it to the category of 'very high' alignment with value-based approaches while the UK qualified in the 'high' category.
14   Kaiser and Lee.

Such a realisation requires a significant mental shift within the health system, changing its purpose as well as how it operates. The new paradigm addresses unhealthy lifestyles – changing what we consume, how we think, how we live – and it requires a broader set of actors to be involved and collaborate, including policymakers, health system leaders, industry, the civil society, and individuals. With this shift in focus from illness treatment to well-being, many more domains of society must be involved – education, urban planning, the food and beverage industry, transportation, leisure, technology, and many more.

In developed nations, chronic, or non-communicable diseases (NCDs) are the main cause of death, disability, and health expenditure. Beyond the realm of health expenditures, the prevalence of chronic diseases also has secondary impacts. For example, in the EU, non-communicable diseases account annually for a loss of about 3.4 million potential productive life years and €115 billion (0.8 per cent of EU GDP). The burden on social benefit expenditure is 1.7 per cent of GDP spent on disability and sick leave annually in the EU – more than what is spent on unemployment.[15]

Major risk factors associated with those diseases – such as tobacco smoking, alcohol use, physical inactivity, unhealthy diets, environmental factors, and social and emotional skills – are considered largely preventable.[16] Out of the total burden of disease 45.2 per cent is accountable to risk factors linked to attitudes and behaviours, while 32.7 per cent of disease can be linked to purely behavioural risk factors, excluding environmental and occupational and metabolic risks.[17]

Despite all these facts, prevention is still a health area that lacks investment. For example, in OECD countries in 2015, health expenditure on preventive care via government and compulsory schemes represented between 0 and 0.4 per cent of GDP, compared to between about three and 9.5 per cent of GPD for all health expenditure.[18]

For such a transformation, government intervention is important. Factors hindering political advancements in this area are the lack of evidence about what interventions work and which do not, and the entrenched interests of those who profit from the current system.

15   OECD and EU.
16   WHO and OECD.
17   GBD 2016 Risk Factors Collaborators. Note on cited percentages: they represent the population-attributable fraction for DALYs in 2016 for all ages and both sexes combined: 45.2 per cent (95 per cent UI 43.2-47.3 per cent); 32.7 per cent (30.7-34.8 per cent).
18   OECD, 'OECD Health Expenditure Indicators'.

One of the countries that has made prevention a clear priority is Singapore. Singapore has a long tradition of promoting a healthy lifestyle in its population, beginning in 1992 when the Ministry of Health launched the National Healthy Lifestyle Programme focusing on physical, social, and mental well-being. At the 20-year celebration of this launch, the ministry started a number of new initiatives that included the nationwide roll-out of the Healthy Living Index (a questionnaire on ten health domains participants can fill in to obtain advice on appropriate health improvement actions), healthyMEtv (a digital TV health and wellness channel to increase health literacy), and the Healthy Shopper Programme (guiding grocery shoppers to make healthier choices).

The Healthy Living Master Plan was developed in response to 'Our Singapore Conversation' – a national-level public engagement process initiated by the prime minister of Singapore in 2012. This plan, which envisions Singapore in 2030, is a multi-stakeholder initiative across government agencies, the private sector, and communities. It aims to provide healthy living for all Singaporeans at the 'doorstep' – accessible, affordable, and participative at work, in the community, and in schools. It builds on the country's experience that disease-specific strategies were insufficient, and a systemic approach was needed. Healthy choices need to become easy choices. Recognising that health consciousness and challenges start at an early age, the government has initiated NurtureSG in a collaboration between the Ministry of Health and the Ministry of Education. It aims to address Singapore's second biggest cause of ill-health and death – mental health concerns among the young, like cyberbullying and suicide, and sleep health. Deaths from these causes were estimated to be 440,000 in 2014 and projected to grow to 1 million by 2050.

In addition to the public sector, the private sector is also beginning to focus on health prevention, in part motivated by the billion-dollar growth opportunities forecast for the preventive healthcare technologies and services market. In the 'healthy diet' solution space, for example, companies such as Coca-Cola and Pepsi have started cutting sugar from their sodas, and companies such as Mars and General Mills have pledged to reduce salt in their products. Preventive services and programmes – such as health coaches and early diagnostics – are also becoming more commonplace as part of providers' and payers' offerings, while some variation of workplace wellness programmes are in place in many companies that provide health benefits.

Although deep understanding of what incentive systems work on individuals to adapt their behaviours and make better health life choices is still nascent, over time and with experimentation we can see how solutions and best practices will emerge.

Works Cited

De la Maisonneuve, C., and J.O. Martins. 'Public Spending on Health and Long-Term Care: A New Set of Projections'. OECD Economic Policy Paper No. 6, June 2013. https://www.oecd.org/eco/growth/Health%20FINAL.pdf. Accessed 30 Oct. 2017.

Diamandis, Peter, and Ray Kurzweil. 'Singularity University: Founder's Video'. https://player.vimeo.com/video/187563875. Accessed 7 July 2018.

GBD 2016 Risk Factors Collaborators. 'Global, Regional, and National Comparative Risk Assessment of 84 Behavioural, Environmental and Occupational, and Metabolic Risks or Clusters of Risks, 1990-2016: A Systematic Analysis for the Global Burden of Disease Study 2016'. *The Lancet* 390, 16 Sept. 2017, pp. 1084-1150. http://www.thelancet.com/pdfs/journals/lancet/PIIS0140-6736(17)32366-8.pdf. Accessed 30 Oct. 2017.

ICHOM. 'Why Measure Outcomes'. International Consortium for Health Outcomes Measurement, n.d. http://www.ichom.org/why-measure-outcomes/. Accessed 30 Oct. 2017.

Kaiser, L.S., and T.H. Lee. 'Turning Value-Based Health Care into a Real Business Model'. *Harvard Business Review*, 8 Oct. 2015. https://hbr.org/2015/10/turning-value-based-health-care-into-a-real-business-model. Accessed 30 Nov. 2017.

King's Fund. 'Public Attitudes and Expectations: Future Trends'. In 'Time to Think Differently', The King's Fund, 2012/2013. https://www.kingsfund.org.uk/time-to-think-differently/trends/public-attitudes-and-expectations. Accessed 30 Oct. 2017.

OECD. 'OECD Health Expenditure Indicators'. Organisation for Economic Co-operation and Development, 2017. http://www.oecd-ilibrary.org/social-issues-migration-health/data/oecd-health-statistics/system-of-health-accounts-health-expenditure-by-function_data-00349-en. Accessed 30 Oct. 2017.

OECD. 'OECD Health Statistics 2017'. Organisation for Economic Co-operation and Development, 2017. http://www.oecd.org/els/health-systems/health-data.htm. Accessed 30 Oct. 2017.

OECD and EU. *Health at a Glance: Europe 2016: State of Health in the EU Cycle*. Paris: Organisation for Economic Co-operation and Development and European Union, 2016.

Rauch, J. 'Disruptive Entrepreneurship in Transforming US Health Care'. Brookings Institution, Center for Effective Public Management, 2005. https://www.brookings.edu/research/disruptive-entrepreneurship-is-transforming-u-s-health-care/. Accessed 30 Oct. 2017.

Review on Antimicrobial Resistance. 'Tackling Drug-Resistant Infections Globally: Final Report and Recommendations', May 2016. https://amr-review.org/sites/default/files/160518_Final%20paper_with%20cover.pdf. Accessed 30 Oct. 2017.

UN. 'Goal 3: Ensure Healthy Lives and Promote Well-being for All at All Ages'. UN Sustainable Development Goals. https://www.un.org/sustainabledevelopment/health/. Accessed 30 Oct. 2017.

UN. 'Sustainable Development Goals'. UN Sustainable Development Goals, 25 Sept. 2015. http://www.un.org/sustainabledevelopment/sustainable-development-goals/. Accessed 30 Oct. 2017.

UN DESA. 'World Population Ageing, 2015'. UN Department of Economic and Social Affairs, Population Division (ST/ESA/SER.A/390), 2015. http://www.un.org/en/development/desa/population/publications/pdf/ageing/WPA2015_Report.pdf. Accessed 30 Oct. 2017.

World Economic Forum. 'Sustainable Health Systems – Visions, Strategies, Critical Uncertainties and Scenarios'. World Economic Forum, 2013. http://www3.weforum.org/docs/WEF_SustainableHealthSystems_Report_2013.pdf. Accessed 30 Oct. 2017.

WHO and OECD. 'Promoting Health, Preventing Disease. The Economic Case'. World Health Organization and Organisation for Economic Co-operation and Development, 2015. http://www.euro.who.int/__data/assets/pdf_file/0006/283695/Promoting-Health-Preventing-Disease-Economic-Case.pdf?ua=1. Accessed 30 Oct. 2017.

About the Authors

Kristel Van der Elst is CEO of The Global Foresight Group, Visiting Professor at the College of Europe and the London School of Hygiene and Tropical Medicine, member of the Independent Advisory Committee for the Global Burden of Disease, and former Head of Strategic Foresight of the World Economic Forum.

Rudi Pauwels is Founder and President of the Praesens Foundation, co-founder of biotech companies Biocartis, Tibotec, Virco, and Galapagos Genomics, and a member of Boards such as A*STAR and Imec.

10 Seeding the Future: Challenges to Global Food Systems

Ariella Helfgott and Joost Vervoort

Abstract

Food poses a massive challenge globally. Many people are either food insecure or suffering from nutritional problems, including overconsumption. At the same time, the fulfilling of growing food demand has enormous environmental impacts. In this chapter, we urge individuals and organisations around the world to start looking at everything to do with food as interconnected, taking a 'food systems' perspective to start solving the deeper problems. Using hopeful and powerful examples, we show how looking at food systems can help transform food economics, politics, technologies, habits, and cultures.

Keywords: food systems, diet change, food waste, cities and food, food politics, education, gender gaps

Something's rotten

Food security underpins the stability and prosperity of entire societies. The aphorism 'Every society is only three missed meals away from revolution'[1] is evidenced by the unrest surrounding food price spikes around the world.[2] Food is central to every aspect of human life.

Today's food systems face unprecedented and ever-increasing pressure from population growth, climate change, and environmental degradation more broadly. The world's population is projected to grow to almost ten billion by 2050, and demand for food will increase accordingly.[3] According

---

1   Burgess, p. 333.
2   McKie and Stewart.
3   Godfray *et al.*

Wilkinson, Angela, and Betty Sue Flowers (eds.), *Realistic Hope: Facing Global Challenges.* Amsterdam, Amsterdam University Press, 2018.
DOI: 10.5117/9789462987241_CH10

to one of the UK's chief scientists, by 2030 the world will need to *produce* 50 per cent more food and energy together with 30 per cent more fresh water, whilst mitigating and adapting to climate change.[4]

Poignantly, many of the advances in food systems productivity and efficiency have contributed to the environmental challenges and population growth that now threaten them.[5] Food production is the primary driver of biodiversity loss, responsible for at least 60 per cent of global terrestrial biodiversity loss and full or over-exploitation of around 90 per cent of commercial fish stocks.[6] Marine ecosystems are quite literally dying due to the combined effects of overfishing, ocean acidification, and pollution.[7]

The agriculture sector worldwide directly contributes around 30 per cent of global greenhouse gas emissions when fuel use, fertiliser production, and land-use changes are included.[8] Crop-livestock production systems are the largest driver of changes to global nitrogen and phosphorus cycles,[9] which are already well outside of the safe operating space for the planet.[10]

Food processing uses large amounts of energy and water – for example, accounting for 10 per cent of industrial use of the public water supply and around 10 per cent of the industrial waste stream in the UK.[11] The waste from food processing also contains large amounts of organic material and high levels of suspended oil or grease, which contribute to phenomena like the enormous 'fatbergs' under London and other cities and other significant environmental impacts.[12]

The packaging of food is responsible for marine pollution, including the world's growing ocean garbage patches. The majority of seafood consumed today contains plastic.[13] Food packaging also uses large amounts of raw materials and alone is responsible for 7 per cent of greenhouse gas (GHG) emissions from the UK food system.[14]

Food distribution and retail also have significant impacts. One-quarter of all the lorries on the road in the UK are involved in food transport, and refrigerant leakage contributes nearly one-third of the direct GHG emissions

4   Beddington.
5   Matthew *et al*; see Millennium Ecosystem Assessment.
6   Westhoek *et al.*; EEA.
7   Nellemann *et al.*, *In Dead Water.*
8   Bellarby *et al.*
9   Bouwman *et al.*
10   Rockström *et al.*
11   DEFRA.
12   Edmond; DEFRA.
13   Van Cauwenberghe *et al*; Swerdloff.
14   Garnett.

of all UK supermarkets.[15] All together, food-related activities contribute 40 per cent of all GHG emissions in the EU – 25 to 31 per cent from the food system and an extra 9 per cent arising from the food service sector.[16]

In developing countries post-farm-gate GHG emissions are significantly less, although there is a trade-off here with food spoilage. In India an estimated 35 to 40 per cent of fresh produce is lost because neither wholesale nor retail outlets have cold storage.[17] Even with grains that can be stored more readily, as much as one-third can be lost after harvest in Southeast Asia due to pests and spoilage.[18]

Inequalities in the food system are not limited to developed-versus-developing country comparisons. Many developed countries suffer from quite extreme dietary inequality. The term 'food desert' was coined to describe an urban area, especially one with low-income residents, that has little to no access to affordable, nutritious food.[19] In fact, the advances in food-system profitability over the past decades have so far involved increases in inequality in both power and distribution of food from local to global scales, which create enormous concerns about food-system performance and associated threats of social unrest, even in the absence of all of the other issues.[20]

Around one billion people across the world have insufficient calories and suffer from micronutrient deficiencies, affecting their growth and development. On the other hand, almost two billion people are overweight with excess calories. The impacts on the health of modern diets that are rich in fats, sugar, salt, and meats are striking. Obesity is the number one killer of people today. Some parts of the world waste and over-consume while others starve. Despite the fact that more than enough food is currently produced per capita to adequately feed the global population, about 925 million people were food insecure in 2010.[21]

Opening the can

The challenges raised by our food systems can seem almost overwhelming. Can we feed the growing world population sustainably, equitably,

---

15   Wood.

16   Tukker *et al.*

17   Nellemann *et al.*, *The Environmental Food Crisis.*

18   FAO, *The State of Food and Agriculture 2009.*

19   Butler; Stuart.

20   McMichael.

21   Ingram, 'A Food Systems Approach'.

and nutritiously? How can we transform the increasingly unsustainable, inequitable, and unhealthy trends that currently exist?

Food systems involve more than production. They include processing, packaging, retail, distribution, consumption, and waste – all of which are shaped by culture, environment, policies, laws, and many other factors.[22] But that also means that it is possible to identify leverage and to develop new and better solutions at many different points in food systems.

Advanced industrial economies tend to focus on supply side concerns and productivity boosts that increase the production of calories through the commercialisation and intensification of farming. This narrow focus itself has either created or worsened many of the problems we are facing today. Other points of focus include isolated parts and specific actors in the system – for example, critics blame farmers or supermarkets or consumers. The need to engage with the many-to-many interactions that contribute to connected challenges can be overwhelming and confounding, because as individuals we feel relatively powerless even though we all share responsibility for the way things are. But by shifting to thinking about more than one different food system future, we can avoid narrow, quick fix solutions that exacerbate disconnects, inequalities, inefficiencies, and conflicts and discover new and integrated solutions.[23]

Of course, adopting a food-systems futures approach does not mean that everyone across the entire system has be involved in doing all the thinking. But if people with specialised expertise and more localised and/ or hands-on positions work together to exchange top-down and bottom-up perspectives, a new shared understanding of the whole food system can provide the foundation for discovering new pathways to more sustainable, inclusive, and secure food futures.

During the last decade, the new food-systems foresight approach has become more common in the work of many different national governments, international organisations, and public-private partnerships. Using new opportunities for global community networks and multi-stakeholder platform-based approaches, these groups have discovered promising integrated solutions. For example, in 2011, the UK Government Office for Science completed a comprehensive foresight study and scenario-based exploration to 2050 of the future of food and farming.[24] The study engaged the perspectives of 400 leading experts and stakeholders from about 35 low-,

---

22   Ingram, 'Sustainable Food Systems for a Healthy World'.
23   Ingram, 'A Food Systems Approach'.
24   Government Office for Science.

middle-, and high-income countries across the world. The report identifies key strategic choices relating to the global sustainability of food systems and identifies actions to address the connected challenges – ending hunger, introducing better nutrition and improving diets, tackling climate change by reducing GHG emissions, securing rural livelihoods, and improving environmental sustainability. The conclusions emphasise the need to raise the profile of food systems security and sustainability on political agendas and to develop more inclusive and effective approaches to global food systems governance.

Other examples of new approaches include the work of the FAO's Global Panel on Food Systems and Nutrition,[25] large collaborative trans-disciplinary programmes such as TRANSMANGO, SUSFANS, and FOODSECURE,[26] and the recent formation of the International Panel of Experts on Sustainable Food Systems (IPES-Food).[27]

Planting hope

With a more inclusive approach to food systems foresight a number of systemic challenge-and-opportunity spaces become clear. Lifecycle assessments of individual food products reveal that meat and dairy products have *by far* the highest GHG emissions burden. Currently, per capita consumption of animal products is exceedingly high in developed countries and on the increase in developing countries. The conversion efficiency of plant into animal matter is about 10 per cent – thus, *prima facie*, more people could be supported from the same amount of land if they were vegetarians or at least ate less meat.[28]

There are far fewer people in the developed than in the developing world, and the population growth rates are also different, such that even though developed per capita intakes are very high, the effects of cutting consumption here are minimal in the face of the large absolute projected increase in developing world consumption.[29] The environmental consequences of this are dire. Therefore, not only do we face the challenge of cutting meat and dairy consumption dramatically in the developed world, but there is also the challenge of moderating increases in the developing world.

25 Global Panel on Agriculture and Food Systems for Nutrition.
26 Zurek *et al.*
27 IPES-Food.
28 FAO, *World Agriculture Towards 2030/2050.*
29 Garnett.

Diet change towards more plant-based diets is certainly underway in developed countries, and though the change is still primarily within niche communities, it is spreading to the mainstream. The number of vegans in the UK increased by 350 per cent in the last decade.[30] The total number is still only half a million out of roughly 66 million people. Similarly, veganism has grown by 500 per cent in the US. The total number is still only 6 per cent, but that is a dramatic increase from 1 per cent in 2014.

In the past decade, the number of restaurants catering to vegans and vegetarians (exclusively or not) has grown significantly in the majority of cities in the developed world.[31] Animal-free versions of almost anything can be found in businesses in Europe's major cities.[32] The UK's number one food retailer, Tesco, has highlighted the greater environmental impact of meat on its consumer-facing website, indicating that in the UK, at least, the discussion is becoming more mainstream.[33] Other indications are increasing as well:

– The global meat-alternative market will reach $5.2 billion by 2020.
– The plant-milk sector is poised to reach $11 billion by 2019.
– Vegan products grew by 92 per cent in Australia last year.
– UK plant-based foods sales grew 1500 per cent in the last year.[34]

Governments across the developed world are considering policy interventions from food-system education and awareness-raising programmes to cooking-skill development programmes to meat taxes. The major international institutions, including the United Nations Environment Programme and the World Bank, have highlighted the environmental impacts of high levels of meat consumption.[35] There has been substantial talk about 'meat taxes' in Scandinavian countries, but no specific policies have been implemented yet. New Zealand's proposed tax on GHG emissions from livestock, mockingly called a 'fart tax', was proposed but blocked in 2003.[36] To date, no specific policies have been implemented on the consumption side in high-income countries, but at least they are being discussed.

30 Marsh *et al.*
31 Campbell.
32 O'Malley.
33 Garnett.
34 Plant Based News.
35 Nellemann *et al.*, *The Environmental Food Crisis*; Hertwich *et al.*; Bierbaum *et al.*; Secretariat of the Convention on Biological Diversity.
36 Fickling.

In developed countries, where a large variety of foods are accessible, little or no consumption of animal products can result in increased health if well managed,[37] whereas in low-income countries, where seasonal and chronic malnutrition exist, and where people don't have access to such a variety of foods, animal products often make a critical difference to the nutritional adequacy of diets.[38] According to the Food and Agricultural Organization of the United Nations (FAO), roughly 987 million people, or about 70 per cent of the world's 1.4 billion 'extreme poor', depend on livestock for their livelihoods.[39]

So the answer is not as simple as everyone, everywhere suddenly stopping eating meat. While the need to significantly reduce (in the developed world) and moderate (in the developing world) is clear, the question of eating animal products depends very much on who, where, and in what kind of agro-ecological system. In certain contexts, careful inclusion of animals within integrated permaculture-type food production systems can actually support an increase in biodiversity, but this is far from the industrial approach to livestock in the developed world. For those of us living in the developed world, the general imperative to reduce consumption of animal products is a no-brainer.

Sugar, loneliness, and overconsumption

Across the developed world there have been initiatives to raise awareness about the health impacts of high-sugar foods, their propensity to drive ever higher levels of consumption, and the high levels of sugar in processed foods, even so-called 'healthy' foods.

There is a social tendency to blame people who are overweight and to assume they are either lazy or greedy. In fact, the high fructose content of processed foods thwarts human biochemical signalling mechanisms that control energy balance, causing us to eat more while simultaneously causing serious deleterious health effects, including increased lethargy, mood swings, reduced concentration, visceral fat, reduced liver function, type 2 diabetes, and heart disease – even with the same overall amount of exercise and calories as a healthy person. Without a doubt there is an

37 Friel *et al.*
38 Neumann *et al.*
39 FAO, *The State of Food and Agriculture 2009.*

individual responsibility to maintain a healthy diet and exercise daily. However, there is much more to this issue.[40]

To address the obesity epidemic many governments have implemented or are considering implementing a sugar tax. The World Health Organization (WHO) publicly urged all countries to tax sugary drinks to curb growing obesity rates, particularly in children. The WHO claims a tax of 20 per cent or more will result in reduced consumption of sugary drinks.[41] In 2013, Mexico introduced a tax of one Mexican peso per litre of sugary drink, leading to a 5.5 per cent drop in purchases in the first year and a 9.7 per cent drop in the second. Mexican advocates of the tax argue that it is still too low to have a significant impact and that only the poorest households are affected. France implemented a sugary drinks tax in 2012 and in 2017 banned all public eateries from selling unlimited sugary drinks at a fixed price or free. Brunei introduced a tax for drinks with more than 6g of sugar per 100ml in 2017.

In 2016 the UK announced the introduction of a sugar tax (the Soft Drinks Industry Levy) and put it into effect on 6 April 2018. Hungary's public health product tax, introduced in 2011, not only covers sugary drinks but also energy drinks, alcoholic beverages, salted snacks, fruit preserves, and pre-packaged sweetened products.[42]

The sugar tax is an excellent idea with demonstrated impacts. However, it still places the blame and the cost on the consumer, and gives no responsibility for metabolic disruption and addiction creation to the food companies that aggressively advertise and supply these products in the majority of public spaces, often to the exclusion of healthier options. In some places, at least, conversations are shifting to regulating the amount of sucrose and fructose included in processed foods. In Singapore soft drink manufacturers have agreed to cut down the sugar content of their drinks.[43] There are also policies to limit access to fast and sugary foods in the vicinity of schools and other places children and adolescents are cared for in the US, UK, and Europe.[44]

There are significant emotional drivers of overconsumption operating at a societal level. Levels of loneliness, feelings of isolation, and disconnection are higher than ever in modern developed societies, much higher than in

---

40   Mini Medical School for the Public.
41   Boseley.
42   *The Economist.*
43   Kok.
44   Glickman *et al.*

developing countries. Dubbed 'the loneliness epidemic', loneliness has been identified as one of the main problems facing developed societies today[45] with terrible impacts on health and well-being.[46] Emotional pain and loneliness drive overconsumption of food.[47] Food is one of the ways people create and express feelings of love, well-being, and belonging.[48] All of the environmental policies that tell people to stop consuming can't possibly work if the reason why people are consuming is to cope with the pain of being alive.[49] Studies investigating loneliness, social integration, and consumption of sugary beverages demonstrate that perceived loneliness is associated with elevated intake of all sugary beverages, while relationship satisfaction is negatively associated with all sugary beverages. Being married or cohabitating, having supportive friends, and having a sense of togetherness at work are also associated with lower intake of sugary beverages. These associations were significant, even after controlling for factors such as body mass index, weight-related self-image, depression, physical activity, educational level, age, and income.[50]

Sugar taxes by themselves can't address the underlying drivers of overconsumption of sugary products. However, programmes aimed at addressing loneliness, reinvigorating community, and developing social networks that involve face-to-face contact have been shown to have positive impacts. There is a real opportunity for change in an aspect of food systems that has, so far, been ignored in many policies and strategies – the 'food environment' or 'foodscape', which is the world of food that we interact with as consumers on a daily basis. This foodscape could be shaped to steer consumers towards food choices that are healthier and more sustainable.

Cutting waste

As already discussed, almost half of the food in both developed and developing countries is lost to waste – but the causes are very different.[51] In the developing world losses occur on the farm and in getting the food to market. In India an estimated 35-40 per cent of fresh produce is lost because neither wholesale nor retail outlets have cold storage – an interesting trade-off when

45   Harris; De Jong-Gierveld.
46   Gil; Knapton.
47   Monbiot.
48   Troisi and Gabriel.
49   Confino.
50   Henriksen *et al.*
51   Nellemann *et al.*, *The Environmental Food Crisis.*

you consider the percentage of GHG emissions that come from refrigeration in developed countries.[52] Even with grains, which can be stored more readily, as much as a third can be lost after harvest in Southeast Asia due to pests and spoilage.[53] In contrast, in the developed world, pre-retail losses are low, but those arising in the retail food service, and home stages of the food system are quite dramatic. Consumers have become accustomed to the highest cosmetic standards, meaning that products that are only slightly blemished are discarded. The food service industry frequently uses large or even 'supersized' portions as a selling point, and 'Buy one, get one free' offers have the same function for retailers. Litigation and lack of education on food safety have led to reliance on 'use by' dates whose safety margins mean that food that is fit for consumption is often thrown away. In most developed countries limiting legislation means that unwanted food goes to landfill instead of being used for animal feed or compost. In the US more than 60 per cent of food waste occurs after food has been purchased.

The number of innovative actions underway to reduce food waste, from households through municipal, national, regional, and global scales and across all sectors, is manifold. Starting from the household level, research has shown that allowing the time to plan meals before shopping and education about 'use by' and 'best before' dates makes quite some difference to household food waste. Programmes that provide education and development of cooking skills can help people know how to recombine leftover ingredients into delicious meals. Other skills such as pickling, fermenting, and composting also help to reduce household food waste. Pickles and ferments also improve digestive health, which helps us to absorb more nutrients from the foods we do eat.

The European Commission is considering a number of options to simplify date-marking on food stuffs while maintaining food safety standards. In Europe, regional and national laws are also being reviewed to examine where other food safety regulations actually contribute to food waste. For example, allowing edible food waste to be fed to livestock could significantly reduce waste.

Food service providers are reducing portion size to deal with both overconsumption and waste.[54] Numerous food service providers have sustainability strategies that include the goal of zero waste for food, water, energy, and packaging. Some are using creative ways to reduce waste, such as novel reuse – for example, using steamed milk from coffee machines to

52 *Ibid.*
53 FAO, 'Estimated Post-Harvest Losses of Rice in Southeast Asia'.
54 Young and Nestle; Juul.

make ricotta, or using coffee grounds to grow mushrooms, and so forth. Some feed non-edible food waste to mechanical biodigesters to produce energy. This approach can also be used to convert domestic waste to energy and in some places is being used to provide cheap (or even free) heating to buildings.[55] Household-level waste separation is crucial for municipal composting or waste-to-energy programmes. Unfortunately, there are still far too many people across the developed world who do not separate their trash to any degree.

More importantly than all of this is a culture of appreciation for food. When people have a culture of appreciation for food, they are far more likely to pay attention to food purchasing, preparation, and eating – all of which are crucial to reducing waste. Currently, there are even niche movements advocating mindful eating from an environmental perspective. Though that may sound New Agey, it's actually profoundly sensible because at the household level in the developed world, food waste is a consequence of mindlessness with respect to food. Reducing developed country waste is closely linked to individual behaviour and attitudes towards food.

In the developing world the issue of food waste is being addressed, though arguably not equally, by public investment in transport infrastructure, better access to markets, and the possible introduction of cold storage (though this has implications for GHG emissions). There is a large gap in extension services in many parts of the developing world, however, even though the spread of existing knowledge, technology, and best practice through education and extension services is a crucial way to improve both productivity and post-harvest management. Market and finance mechanisms to protect farmers from having to sell at peak supply, leading to gluts and wastage, are also helpful, and many trials exist. Post-harvest storage technologies and improved technology for small-scale storage in poorer contexts have the potential to greatly reduce waste. State incentives for private innovation on all of these fronts, with the involvement of small-scale traders, millers, and producers, also have promise. Conducting value-adding activities locally makes a huge difference. To illustrate the point – Ghana and Nigeria both are large tomato producers, whose tomatoes are shipped to Italy to be processed into tomato paste, which is then shipped back to Ghana and Nigeria for sale. Ghana and Nigeria are also two of the top tomato paste importers in the world – so it would make sense to have tomato-paste manufacturing facilities in Ghana and Nigeria.[56] The CGIAR Research Program on Climate Change,

55 Hardcastle; STREFOWA.
56 Gro Intelligence.

Agriculture and Food Security (CCAFS) is an example of an international programme working to support such value-adding actions.

Organically reorganising

Food and nutritional insecurity exist in places where there is an abundance of food. Food and nutritional security are not issues that relate just to food; they also relate to income security and education about healthy food. If stable and supportive incomes are made possible through economic policies, food and nutritional security will increase in a way that is more sustainable than supporting only short-term solutions, like food banks for the poor.[57]

Currently, the global food economy is highly centralised, with only a relatively small number of global businesses making up the key players that link food producers and consumers. Reorganising food economies means reorganising the ways economies are governed in a broader sense: supporting small and medium enterprises, for example, or offering spaces for niche food initiatives to flourish.

Food system policies and strategies, from local to international levels, are extremely important for providing the confidence among policymakers, voters, businesses, and others that food systems can be transformed through strategic collaboration.

At the city level throughout the world, urban agriculture programmes are being used to help educate people about food and to build a culture of appreciation for food while simultaneously building community and social cohesion. In these ways food waste is reduced, and healthy and sustainable consumption patterns are promoted. Urban agriculture has other benefits in that it offers poorer people a means of diversifying their diets and decreasing nutritional insecurity; it adds to urban ecosystems; it plays a role in climate adaptation to heat waves by 'greening' cityscapes; and it provides an opportunity for local composting.[58]

Food policy councils represent a concrete example of city-level food system governance. Brighton, Toronto, New York, and a number of other cities across the world have established 'food policy councils' and 'urban food strategies' in which local governments, companies, entrepreneurs, community organisations, consumers and researchers work together.[59]

57   De Schutter.
58   Ackerman *et al.*
59   Sonnino.

Networks of such food policy councils and urban food strategy initiatives have been created, linking cities all around the world and creating massive opportunities for learning between urban centres. One prominent example is the Milan Urban Food Policy Pact that involves 159 cities globally in efforts to create more sustainable, nutritionally secure, social cities.[60]

National and regional governments have direct influence over the public procurement of food for government-supported institutions, such as schools, hospitals, prisons, and aid provided for food-insecure groups. Many places around the world, from Sweden to Colombia, have been introducing public food procurement policies that integrate nutrition with sustainability and often go further by integrating the education of school children with food procurement and taking the support of local livelihoods into account.[61] The combination of public procurement and education – eating and learning about healthy and sustainable food – is especially powerful.[62]

Large food industry platforms for collaboration on sustainability and food security, such as the FReSH project organised by the World Business Council for Sustainable Development (WBCSD), are publically recognising the need for transformative change in the current global food system to make it significantly more sustainable, fair, and health-oriented.[63] It is up to leaders in such companies, but also up to governments and private individuals as consumers and as politically engaged citizens, to press hard for real and rapid change without using the way global markets are currently organised as an excuse.

Minding the gender gap

In the developed world, studies show that while there are 'changes in the activities and representation of women and men in society', gender stereotypes are as strong today as they were 30 years ago, and people are even more likely now to believe that men avoid 'traditional' female roles.[64] This stereotyping includes gender-based resistance to sustainable and healthy diet change. Even in the developed world women still do the bulk of food-related and domestic chores, and are more likely than men to be food insecure as they are more likely to have a disproportionate share of care-giving roles and receive lower wages.

60 Milan Urban Food Policy Pact.
61 Ashe and Sonnino; Smith *et al.*
62 TRANSMANGO Research Program.
63 WBCSD.
64 Haines *et al.*

In the developing world context, the Millennium Development Goals Gender Chart 2015 indicates that while progress has been made in basic education, where the gender gap in youth literacy has narrowed substantially, and in maternal mortality, which has declined by nearly 44 per cent since 1990, little progress has been made in other dimensions, and more needs to be done. Women and girls need to be at the centre of any development imperative.

Every single food system activity – from access to education and farm inputs, to what is produced, how it is produced, who takes what to the market, who receives what benefits for labour, all the way through to who eats what – is gendered. Women do most of the work involved in sowing, weeding, fertilising, and harvesting staple crops such as rice, wheat, and maize, but are not responsible for the sale of these crops. Women are almost exclusively in charge of the household garden, growing legumes and vegetables. Most of the produce from household gardens goes to feeding the household and is critically important to nutritional security. In rural areas women produce most of the food consumed locally. These gardens are surprisingly productive, and sometimes women are able to sell excess in the market. Research shows that where women are selling agricultural products in the market place, almost all of that money is channelled into the well-being of the household, which is not the case with male income.

In many societies, tradition and in some cases law bars women from owning land. In South and Southeast Asia more than two-thirds of the female labour force is engaged in agricultural production, but in India, Nepal, and Thailand, for example, fewer than 10 per cent of women farmers own land. Without land to serve as collateral, women are cut off from access to credit. Even in cases where women do own land, they are frequently barred from access to credit. Without credit, they often cannot buy essential inputs such as seeds, tools, and fertiliser, or invest in irrigation and land improvements. Because their role in food production is seldom recognised, women rarely benefit from extension and training services that would teach them about new crop varieties and technologies. A recent FAO survey found that female farmers receive only 5 per cent of all agricultural extension services worldwide.

Globally, women's empowerment is considered a 'prerequisite' for achieving food security.[65] Removing the obstacles faced by women improves all parts of the food system, from farm yields to nutritional outcomes.[66] In both

---

65 Akter *et al.*
66 FAO, 'Women, Agriculture and Food Security'.

developed and developing world contexts, targeted education of both men and women about the destructive and limiting nature of gender norms for both sexes could make an enormous difference.

Furthermore, global population models have found that population growth is now above all else underpinned by the education level of women.[67] In countries where women are educated, population has already plateaued or declined, whereas population growth is concentrated in areas where education levels of women are low – the so-called 'education effect'. According to the International Institute for Applied Systems Analysis (IIASA), by the end of the century the global population could plateau as high as 9.84 billion or as low as 8.87, which will have major implications on our capacity to feed the global population sustainably and equitably – yet another reason why educating women everywhere is essential.[68]

Food action

It is certainly possible to imagine a world where we can achieve food and nutritional security for a potential population of ten billion sustainably, equitably, and ethically.

In this new vision, food systems will play a role in social inclusion. Food system policies will exist and be integrated with education, health, and environmental policies. Significant economic and associated dietary inequality will no longer exist. Informed men and women will value their health, their community, and their environment. Communities will build food cultures rather than filling loneliness with calories. There will be diversity of agro-ecological systems in urban, peri-urban, and rural landscapes. All people will have the basic food system education and cooking skills they need to prepare nutritious, seasonal, predominantly plant-based meals. In this new vision, there is a positive role for the private sector: biodegradable food packaging, tracking to ensure fairness of global food system actors, space for innovation, and opportunities for small-to-medium enterprises to flourish alongside larger organisations.

There is hope for the future of food – but whether or not we act has everything to do with whether that hope will be realised.

67 Templeton.
68 *Ibid.*

Works Cited

Ackerman, K., *et al.* 'Sustainable Food Systems for Future Cities: The Potential of Urban Agriculture'. *Economic and Social Review* 45 (2014), pp. 189-206.

Akter, Sonia, *et al.* 'Women's Empowerment and Gender Equity in Agriculture: A Different Perspective from Southeast Asia'. *Food Policy* 69 (May 2017), pp. 270-79. http://www.sciencedirect.com/science/article/pii/S0306919217303688. Accessed 29 Jan. 2018.

Ashe, L.M., and R. Sonnino. 'At the Crossroads: New Paradigms of Food Security, Public Health Nutrition and School Food'. *Public Health Nutrition* 16 (2013), pp. 1020-27.

Beddington, John. 'Food, Energy, Water and the Climate: A Perfect Storm of Global Events?' London: Government Office for Science, Kingsgate House, 2009.

Bellarby, J., B. Foereid, A. Hastings, and P. Smith. *Cool Farming: Climate Impacts of Agriculture and Mitigation Potential.* Amsterdam: Greenpeace, 2008.

Bierbaum, Rosina M., Marianne Fay, and Bruce Ross-Larson, eds. *World Development Report 2010: Development and Climate Change.* World Bank, 2009.

Bosely, Sarah. 'World Health Organisation Urges All Countries to Tax Sugary Drinks'. *The Guardian*, 11 Oct. 2016. https://www.theguardian.com/society/2016/oct/11/world-health-organisation-who-countries-tax-sugary-drinks. Accessed 29 Jan. 2018.

Bouwman, Lex, *et al.* 'Exploring Global Changes in Nitrogen and Phosphorus Cycles in Agriculture Induced by Livestock Production over the 1900-2050 Period'. *Proceedings of the National Academy of Sciences* 110.52 (2013), pp. 20,882-87.

Burgess, Mark. *Analytical Network and System Administration: Managing Human-Computer Systems.* Chichester: Wiley, 2004.

Butler, Peter. 'Britain in Nutrition Recession as Food Prices Rise and Incomes Shrink'. *The Guardian*, 18 Nov. 2012. https://www.theguardian.com/society/2012/nov/18/breadline-britain-nutritional-recession-austerity. Accessed 28 Jan. 2018.

Campbell, Denis. 'Vegetarians Gain More Options for Fine Dining with 50 Per Cent Rise in Foodie Eateries'. *The Guardian*, 30 Apr. 2010. https://www.theguardian.com/lifeandstyle/2010/apr/30/vegetarian-restaurants-uk-boom. Accessed 29 Jan. 2018.

Confino, Jo. 'Zen and the Art of Protecting the Planet'. *The Guardian.* 26 Aug. 2010. https://www.theguardian.com/sustainability/environment-zen-buddhism-sustainability. Accessed 29 Jan. 2018.

DEFRA. 'Food Industry Sustainability Strategy 2006'. UK Department for Environment, Food and Rural Affairs. https://www.gov.uk/government/publications/food-industry-sustainability-strategy-fiss. Accessed 29 Jan. 2018.

De Jong-Gierveld J., T.G. Van Tilburg, and P.A. Dykstra. 'New Ways of Theorizing and Conducting Research in the Field of Loneliness and Social Isolation'. In *Cambridge Handbook of Personal Relationships*, ed. A.L. Vangelisti and D. Perlman, 2nd rev. ed., Cambridge: Cambridge University Press, 2018.

De Schutter, Olivier. 'Food Banks Can Only Plug the Holes in Social Safety Nets'. *The Guardian*, 27 Feb 2013. https://www.theguardian.com/commentisfree/2013/feb/27/food-banks-social-safety-nets. Accessed 29 Jan. 2018.

The Economist. 'Taxes to Trim Waistlines are Spreading throughout Europe'. *The Economist*, 10 June 2017. https://www.economist.com/news/europe/21723119-hungary-fattest-eu-member-leading-charge-taxes-trim-waistlines-are-spreading. Accessed 29 Jan. 2018.

Edmond, Charlotte. 'The Nausea-Inducing Energy Source That Lurks Beneath Our Feet'. World Economic Forum, 2017.https://www.weforum.org/agenda/2017/08/from-fatberg-to-fuel-the-nausea-inducing-energy-source-that-lurks-beneath-our-feet/. Accessed 29 Jan. 2018.

EEA. 'Seafood in Europe: A Food System Approach for Sustainability'. EEA Report no. 25, European Environment Agency, 2016. http://agricultura.gencat.cat/web/.content/de_departament/de02_estadistiques_observatoris/27_butlletins/02_butlletins_nd/documents_nd/fitxers_estatics_nd/2016/0184_2016_Pesca_Recursos-marins-sistemes-alimentaris-UE-2016.pdf. Accessed 29 Jan. 2018.

FAO. 'Estimated Post-Harvest Losses of Rice in Southeast Asia' [image]. Food and Agricultural Organization of the United Nations, 1997. www.fao.org/english/newsroom/factfile/IMG/FF9712- e.pdf. Accessed 29 Jan. 2018.

FAO. *The State of Food and Agriculture 2009: Livestock in the Balance.* Rome: Food and Agriculture Organization of the United Nations, 2009.

FAO. 'Women, Agriculture and Food Security'. Food and Agricultural Organization of the United Nations, 2001. http://www.fao.org/worldfoodsummit/english/fsheets/women.pdf. Accessed 29 Jan. 2018.

FAO. *World Agriculture towards 2030/2050*. Rome: Food and Agricultural Organization of the United Nations, 2006.

Fickling, David. 'Farmers Raise Stink over New Zealand "Fart Tax"'. *The Guardian*, 5 Sept. 2000. https://www.theguardian.com/world/2003/sep/05/australia.davidfickling. Accessed 29 Jan. 2018.

Friel, S., *et al.* 'Public Health Benefits of Strategies to Reduce Greenhouse-Gas Emissions: Food and Agriculture'. *The Lancet* 374 (2009), pp. 2016-25.

Garnett, Tara. 'Where Are the Best Opportunities for Reducing Greenhouse Gas Emissions in the Food System (Including the Food Chain)?' *Food Policy* 36, Supplement 1 (2011), pp. S23-32.

Gil, Natalie. 'Loneliness: A Silent Plague That Is Hurting Young People Most'. *The Guardian*, 20 July 2014. https://www.theguardian.com/lifeandstyle/2014/jul/20/loneliness-britains-silent-plague-hurts-young-people-most. Accessed 29 Jan. 2018.

Glickman, D., *et al.*, eds. *Accelerating Progress in Obesity Prevention: Solving the Weight of the Nation.* Committee on Accelerating Progress in Obesity Prevention,

Food and Nutrition Board, and Institute of Medicine, Washington, DC: National Academies Press, 2012. https://www.ncbi.nlm.nih.gov/books/NBK201134/. Accessed 29 Jan. 2018.

Global Panel on Agriculture and Food Systems for Nutrition. 'Food Systems and Diets: Facing the Challenges of the 21st Century'. 2016. http://glopan.org/news/foresight-report-food-systems-and-diets. Accessed 29 Jan. 2018.

Godfray, H., *et al.* 'Food Security: The Challenge of Feeding 9 Billion People'. *Science* 327 (12 Feb. 2010), pp. 812-18. http://science.sciencemag.org/content/sci/327/5967/812.full.pdf. Accessed 28 Jan. 2018.

Government Office for Science. 'Foresight: The Future of Food and Farming: Final Project Report'. London: UK Government Office for Science, 2011. https://assets.publishing.service.gov.uk/government/uploads/system/uploads/attachment_data/file/288329/11-546-future-of-food-and-farming-report.pdf. Accessed 29 Jan. 2018.

Gro Intelligence. 'You Say Tomato, I Say Tomato Paste'. *Gro Intelligence,* 5 Nov. 2014. https://gro-intelligence.com/insights/nigeria-tomato-consumption. Accessed 29 Jan. 2018.

Haines, Elizabeth L., Kay Deaux, and Nicole Lofaro. 'The Times They Are a-Changing … Or Are They Not? A Comparison of Gender Stereotypes, 1983 to 2014'. *Psychology of Women Quarterly* 40.3 (2016), pp. 253-63.

Hardcastle, Jessica Lyons. 'NY Food-Waste-to-Energy Pilot Expands'. *Environmental Leader,* 15 Aug. 2014. http://www.environmentalleader.com/2014/08/ny-food-waste-to-energy-pilot-expands/. Accessed 29 Jan. 2018.

Harris, Rebecca. 'The Loneliness Epidemic – We're More Connected than Ever but Are We Feeling More Alone'. *The Independent,* 30 Mar. 2015. http://www.independent.co.uk/life-style/health-and-families/features/the-loneliness-epidemic-more-connected-than-ever-but-feeling-more-alone-10143206.html. Accessed 29 Jan. 2018.

Henriksen, R.E., T. Torsheim, and F. Thuen. 'Loneliness, Social Integration and Consumption of Sugar-Containing Beverages: Testing the Social Baseline Theory'. *PLoS ONE* 9.8 (2014). https://doi.org/10.1371/journal.pone.0104421. Accessed 29 Jan. 2018.

Hertwich, E., *et al.* 'Assessing the Environmental Impacts of Consumption and Production: Priority Products and Materials: A Report of the Working Group on the Environmental Impacts of Products and Materials to the International Panel for Sustainable Resource Management'. UN Environment Programme, 2010. http://www.unep.fr/shared/publications/pdf/dtix1262xpa-priorityproductsandmaterials_report.pdf. Accessed 24 June 2018.

Ingram, J.S.I. 'A Food Systems Approach to Researching Food Security and Its Interactions with Global Environmental Change'. *Food Security* 3.4 (2011), pp. 417-31. https://doi.org/10.1007/s12571-011-0149-9. Accessed 29 Jan. 2018.

Ingram, J.S.I. 'Sustainable Food Systems for a Healthy World'. *Sight and Life* 30.1 (2016), pp. 28-33.

IPES-Food. 'International Panel of Experts on Sustainable Food Systems (IPES-Food)'. N.d. http://www.ipes-food.org. Accessed 29 Jan. 2018.

Juul, Selina. 'How to Control Portions and Reduce Food Waste'. *Huffington Post*, 20 Jan. 2016. https://www.huffingtonpost.com/selina-juul/portion-control-reduse-food-waste_b_9022674.html. Accessed 29 Jan. 2018.

Knapton, Sarah. 'Loneliness Is Deadlier Than Obesity, Study Suggests'. *The Telegraph*, 6 Aug. 2017. http://www.telegraph.co.uk/science/2017/08/06/loneliness-deadlier-obesity-study-suggests/. Accessed 29 Jan. 2018.

Kok, Lee Min. 'Sugar Tax to Curb Soft Drink Consumption? Here's How It Works in Some Countries'. *Straits Times*, 21 Aug. 2017. http://www.straitstimes.com/world/sugar-tax-to-curb-soft-drink-consumption-heres-how-it-works-in-some-countries. Accessed 29 Jan. 2018.

Marsh, Sarah, and Guardian readers. 'The Rise of Vegan Teenagers: "More People Are into It Because of Instagram"'. *The Guardian,* 27 May 2016. https://www.theguardian.com/lifeandstyle/2016/may/27/the-rise-of-vegan-teenagers-more-people-are-into-it-because-of-instagram. Accessed 29 Jan. 2018.

Matthew, Richard A., Jon Barnett, Bryan McDonald, and Karen L. O'Brien, eds. *Global Environmental Change and Human Security.* Cambridge, MA: MIT Press, 2010.

McKie, Robin, and Heather Stewart. 'Hunger, Strikes, Riots: The Food Crisis Bites'. *The Guardian*, 13 April 2008. https://www.theguardian.com/environment/2008/apr/13/food.climatechange. Accessed 28 Jan. 2018.

McMichael, P. 'The Power of Food'. *Agriculture and Human Values* 17.1 (2000), pp. 21-33.

Milan Urban Food Policy Pact. http://www.milanurbanfoodpolicypact.org/. Accessed 29 Jan. 2018.

Millennium Development Goals Gender Chart 2015. http://mdgs.un.org/unsd/mdg/Resources/Static/Products/Progress2015/Gender_Chart_Web.pdf. Accessed 7 July 2018.

Millennium Ecosystem Assessment. *Ecosystems and Human Well-being: Synthesis.* Washington, DC: Island Press, 2005. http://www.millenniumassessment.org/documents/document.356.aspx.pdf. Accessed 29 Jan. 2018.

Mini Medical School for the Public. 'Sugar, the Bitter Truth'. UCSF Center for Integrative Medicine, 27 July 2009. Video. https://www.uctv.tv/shows/Sugar-The-Bitter-Truth-16717. Accessed 29 Jan. 2018.

Monbiot, George. 'The Age of Loneliness Is Killing Us'. *The Guardian*, 14 Oct. 2014. https://www.theguardian.com/commentisfree/2014/oct/14/age-of-loneliness-killing-us. Accessed 29 Jan. 2018.

Nellemann, C., *et al.*, eds. *The Environmental Food Crisis: The Environment's Role in Averting Future Food Crises.* Nairobi: UN Environment Programme (UNEP), 2009. https://www.researchgate.net/publication/304215848. Accessed 29 Jan. 2018.

Nellemann, C., S. Hain, and J. Alder, eds. *In Dead Water: Merging of Climate Change with Pollution, Over-Harvest, and Infestations in the World's Fishing Grounds*. Grid-Arendal, Norway: UN Environment Programme (UNEP), 2008.

Neumann, C., D.M. Harris, and L.M. Rogers. 'Contribution of Animal Source Foods in Improving Diet Quality and Function in Children in the Developing World'. *Nutrition Research* 22.1-2 (2002), pp. 193-220.

O'Malley, Elizabeth. 'Europe Is Seeing a Growing Interest in Veganism, and Berlin Is at the Centre of It'. *The Journal*, 21 Aug. 2016. http://www.thejournal.ie/flexitarians-vegan-berlin-2931005-Aug2016/. Accessed 29 Jan. 2018.

Plant Based News. 'Five Surprising Statistics that Prove that Veganism Is Growing Around the World'. *Plant Based News*, 7 June 2017. https://www.plantbasednews.org/post/5-surprising-studies-that-prove-veganism-is-growing-around-the-world. Accessed 29 Jan. 2018.

Rockström, Johan, *et al*. 'A Safe Operating Space for Humanity'. *Nature* 461, 24 Sept. 2009, pp. 472-75.

Secretariat of the Convention on Biological Diversity. *Global Biodiversity Outlook 3*. Montreal, 2010. https://www.cbd.int/doc/publications/gbo/gbo3-final-en.pdf. Accessed 29 Jan. 2018.

Smith, J., *et al*. 'Balancing Competing Policy Demands: The Case of Sustainable Public Sector Food Procurement'. *Journal of Cleaner Production* 112 (2016), pp. 249-56.

Sonnino, R. 'The New Geography of Food Security: Exploring the Potential of Urban Food Strategies'. *Geographical Journal* 182 (2016), pp. 190-200.

STREFOWA. 'Pilot Actions to Optimize Separate Collection or Special Treatment of Food Waste'. Interreg Central Europe, European Commission, STREFOWA. http://www.reducefoodwaste.eu/pilot-actions-food-waste-separate-collection.html. Accessed 29 Jan. 2018.

Stuart, Hunter. 'The Percentage of Americans Who Can't Afford Food Hasn't Budged since the Recession Peaked'. *Huffington Post*, 18 Aug. 2014. https://www.huffingtonpost.com/2014/08/18/american-recession-food-insecurity_n_5681559.html. Accessed 29 Jan. 2018.

Swerdloff, Alex. 'This Study Says Almost All the Seafood We Eat Contains Tiny Pieces of Plastic'. *Munchies*, 25 Jan. 2017. https://munchies.vice.com/en_us/article/ypegyx/this-study-says-almost-all-the-seafood-we-eat-contains-tiny-pieces-of-plastic. Accessed 20 Jan. 2018.

Templeton, Graham. 'The Education Effect: Global Population to Plateau by 2070'. *Geek.com*, 25 Oct. 2014. https://www.geek.com/news/the-education-effect-global-population-to-plateau-by-2070-1607645/. Accessed 29 Jan. 2018.

TRANSMANGO Research Program. http://www.jamtoday.eu/. Accessed 29 Jan. 2018.

Troisi, Jordan D., and Shira Gabriel. 'Chicken Soup Really Is Good for the Soul: "Comfort Food" Fulfills the Need to Belong'. *Psychological Science* 22.6, 2 May 2011, pp. 747-53. http://journals.sagepub.com/doi/abs/10.1177/0956797611407931. Accessed 29 Jan. 2018.

Tukker, A., *et al.* 'Analysis of the Life Cycle Environmental Impacts Related to the Total Final Consumption of the EU25'. Environmental Impact of Products (EIPRO), European Commission Technical Report (EUR 22284 EN), May 2006. http://ec.europa.eu/environment/ipp/pdf/eipro_report.pdf. Accessed 29 Jan. 2018.

Van Cauwenberghe, Lisbeth, and Colin R. Janssen. 'Microplastics in Bivalves Cultured for Human Consumption'. *Environmental Pollution* 193 (Oct. 2014), pp. 65-70.

WBCSD. FReSH Program. World Business Council for Sustainable Development. http://www.wbcsd.org/Projects/FReSH. Accessed 29 Jan. 2018.

Westhoek, H., J. Ingram, S. Van Berkum, L. Özay, and M. Hajer. *Food Systems and Natural Resources: A Report of the Working Group on Food Systems of the International Resource Panel.* UN Environment Programme (UNEP), 2016.

Wood, Zoe. 'Supermarket Fridges as Polluting as Their Plastic Bags, Study Claims'. *The Guardian*, 1 Feb. 2010. https://www.theguardian.com/business/2010/feb/01/supermarket-fridges-pollution. Accessed 29 Jan. 2018.

Young, L.R., and M. Nestle. 'The Contribution of Expanding Portion Sizes to the US Obesity Epidemic'. *American Journal of Public Health* 92.2 (2002), pp. 246-49. https://www.ncbi.nlm.nih.gov/pmc/articles/PMC1447051/. Accessed 29 Jan. 2018.

Zurek, M., J. Vervoort, and A. Hebinck. 'A Systematic Review of Existing EU-Wide Scenarios Related to the EU Sustainable Food and Nutrition Security, Identification of Most Salient Features, and Resulting Synthesis Scenarios for Exploring Sustainable Diets'. Deliverable No. 6.2. SUSFANS, 2017. http://susfans.eu/portfolio/deliverable-62-systematic-review-existing-eu-wide-scenarios-related-eu-sustainable-food. Accessed 29 Jan. 2018.

About the Authors

Ariella Helfgott is a Senior Researcher in the University of Oxford's Food Systems Research Group. Her work spans conceptual and mathematical modeling of food systems and participatory multi-stakeholder approaches for the creation of sustainable and equitable food futures. She specialises in bringing together stakeholders across sectors and scales and engaging them in systemic processes designed to develop strategic capacity. She has extensive experience in East and West Africa, South and Southeast Asia, Latin America, Europe, and Australia from individual, through community to national and international scales.

Joost Vervoort is Assistant Professor at the Copernicus Institute, Utrecht University, and Honorary Research Associate, Environmental Change Institute, University of Oxford. He has led research programmes that use future scenarios to guide policy and planning with national governments in more than 30 countries in efforts to ensure food and nutrition security in the face of global environmental and economic change.

11   The Great Livestock Trade-off: Food Production, Poverty Alleviation, and Climate Change

Luke York and Claire Heffernan

Abstract

The chapter explores the future of the global livestock sector and the trade-offs policymakers, particularly those in developing economies, will need to consider to meet the unprecedented global demand for animal protein against a backdrop of climate change, animal welfare, and broader environmental concerns. Approaches to climate change adaptation and mitigation are discussed along with key uncertainties around synthetic and insect protein sources. The chapter concludes that the drivers impacting livestock development in the industrial vs developing economies vary widely. However, there is realistic hope that the global livestock sector and related management practices will transform to meet the climate change agenda, provided domestic trade-offs are acknowledged alongside global stewardship.

Keywords: livestock scenarios, climate warming, synthetic protein, insect protein, adaptation, mitigation, animal welfare

Livestock and livelihoods

Feeding the world's projected population of nine billion people in 2050 is not optional – but *how* to feed this population remains a question. And when the challenge of sustainability is added to this necessity, the predicted outcome is even less clear.

Historically, the global livestock sector has been an important driver of both economic growth and food security. Scientific advances since the 1960s have led to a quadrupling of global livestock production. Commercial

Wilkinson, Angela, and Betty Sue Flowers (eds.), *Realistic Hope: Facing Global Challenges.* Amsterdam, Amsterdam University Press, 2018.
DOI: 10.5117/9789462987241_CH11

production aside, livestock for two-thirds of the 2.1 billion households living on less than $2 dollars a day is critical to livelihoods. Livestock ownership offers households a source of animal protein, improved purchasing power (from sales of milk, meat, eggs, and manure), and a mobile, inflation-resistant store of wealth, draft power, fertiliser, and fuel (from the burning of manure). Because of its many benefits to livelihoods, livestock as a key 'pathway out of poverty' has underpinned development praxis since the 1980s. Most national development plans across Africa include the livestock sector as a crucial means of economic growth.

The role livestock play in safeguarding food and livelihood security is particularly important to policymakers in the developing economies. Livestock-keeping creates a more robust livelihood strategy by diversifying income and acting as a source of financial capital that decreases vulnerability to shocks from ill health, crop failures, and other risks. Simply put, livestock-keeping can help households escape poverty and prevent declines into poverty.

Livestock and climate change

Yet the public discourse from the industrially developed economies is clear: livestock in an era of climate change are unsustainable. Commercial livestock production, in particular, has large animal welfare and resource implications. There is also increasing concern that as the human population increases, the competition for land will intensify. Indeed, land use for biofuel production is already an issue as is the need to protect remnant biodiversity.

Such public pressure has had an impact on the funding of livestock development projects in the developing economies. Over the past fifteen years, the number and size of livestock projects and programmes have decreased. Despite the desire of many developing- economy governments to increase national livestock production as a contributor to livelihoods and food security, concerns from the industrially developed economies regarding sustainability have had a substantial impact on livestock as a tool for poverty alleviation.

This is not to say that environmental and resource concerns are invalid. Commercial livestock production globally is a large user of agricultural land and water resources and has a role in both water and soil pollution. Yet while the poor have been impacted by the public discourse, the commercial sector continues to grow. For the past 50 years, almost the same fifteen countries (industrially developed and emerging economies) have accounted for 70 per cent of total global production.[1] As the global population grows, and demand for milk and meat increases, the response has been more intensive livestock production by the same national industries, not less.

At the same time, in many geographic areas, especially Africa, the efficiency of production has declined dramatically despite smallholder producers attempting to replicate commercial production practices. For example, in Nigeria, while the number of cattle has followed overall human population increases, the quantity of beef produced has remained static since the 1960s.[2] Within such a context of lowering productivity, food gaps are rapidly increasing. In 1984, Sub-Saharan Africa had an estimated food gap in dairy products of over ten million metric tons.[3] This figure is now the food gap for dairy in West Africa alone.

Climate change is another polarising issue. Ruminants excrete a range of greenhouse gases (GHGs), which contribute to climate warming. Increased livestock production also leads to land-use change, which then drives increased GHG emissions. While emission measurement is contentious due to recognised data gaps, the science appears, at least ostensibly, to justify commercial production because dairy scientists have spent decades improving the feed efficiency (and, by proxy, lowering GHG emissions) of the Holstein Friesian.[4] The role of small-scale livestock production on the environment is much less clear – low-yielding animals owned by developing economy farmers are often assumed to be the biggest polluters.

While the evidence base on the global level for both aspects of GHG emissions could be strengthened, on an individual animal level, the evidence is much clearer. Climate warming has a range of negative impacts on livestock production: animals under heat stress are less productive and are more susceptible to disease, an outcome that is broadly similar for milk, beef, pig, and poultry production systems. Hence, the varied livelihood benefits that the poor, especially, derive from livestock ownership are in the front line of climate change impacts.

Is the future of livestock, no livestock?

The role of livestock has come under increasing scrutiny as consumers are cautioned to consider the real 'cost' of production by weighing dietary,

1   FAO, *FAOSTAT Emissions Database*.
2   *Ibid.*
3   Von Massow.
4   Capper *et al.*; Herrero *et al.*; O'Brien *et al.*

animal welfare, and environmental concerns. The extent such concerns drive consumption patterns differs markedly among countries and households. Within the industrially developed economies, trends of vegetarianism, veganism, and the mainstreaming of issues in 'expose-style' documentaries, such as *Cowspiracy: The Sustainability Secret* (2014), would suggest a growing impetus for a future without livestock.[5] In developing and emerging economies, increased production and, therefore, the consumption of livestock products is viewed as critical to meeting present and future food security. As noted above, animal-source protein is a critical constituent of diets, and removing or limiting this source of protein is likely to increase levels of malnutrition and stunting among vulnerable populations.

Yet what are the options for a livestock-less future? The replacement of livestock products with synthetic milk or meat or other protein substitutes, which is often proffered as a 'solution', raises a variety of unknowns.

Key uncertainties

1   Synthetic protein

It is almost certain that a portion of the market currently occupied by traditional meat and milk products will be replaced by the synthetic version – provided these products can be grown with high levels of food safety, limited environmental impact, and at low cost.

However, consumer acceptance for synthetic animal proteins is largely unknown, even though it will ultimately determine the viability of these products. Lessons from the debate around the role of genetically modified organisms (GMOs) within agriculture may prove useful. With over 30 years of research into GMOs indicating no negative impacts on human health from their consumption, many nations continue to maintain bans on the use of GMOs in agriculture.[6] In this context, it seems unrealistic to assume that laboratory-grown animal products will entirely side-step this debate. If consumers struggle to accept consuming an organism that has had DNA modifications, how will products grown entirely in a laboratory be viewed?

Yet even if only a portion of the population that currently consumes animal products switches to the (hopefully) more 'sustainable' synthetic version, this switch could lessen the pressure on the livestock sector to keep pace with demand. Thus, synthetic animal products may not compete with traditional ones but rather serve to complement them. For example, the demand for meat

5   Ruby *et al*. Also see Raphaely and Marinova.
6   National Academies of Sciences, Engineering, and Medicine.

met by synthetic products may remove the need for industrialised ruminant production.[7] The lower demand may result in pasture-based systems being sufficient to meet demand, with improved sustainability outcomes as ruminants in these systems perform important nutrient-cycling functions.

If the livestock sector were freed from the focus on productivity improvements to meet demand, environmental and animal welfare implications would likely be more easily met. For example, in Australia the move towards cage-free egg systems was blamed for egg shortages in southern states when the onset of winter significantly reduced production levels.[8] Caged systems, with their controlled climate and lighting, largely protect production levels from the effects of seasonality. Synthetic eggs could potentially fill the gap between supply and demand. However, it's unclear whether there is sufficient incentive for livestock producers to shift their focus away from increased outputs as a means of increasing income levels. In this circumstance, there may be a role for government to further regulate or incentivise animal welfare and environmental standards to ensure conformity.

2   *Insect protein*

The use of insects as a protein source is also viewed as a potential protein option for nutritionally threatened populations. This is unsurprising because insects have formed part of the diet of many societies for centuries.[9] However, it is the potential for insects to act as a protein source within livestock feed which may hold the most promise. Early indications suggest that insects could be produced at a large scale at relatively low cost with the use of waste from industrial processing.[10] Like synthetic meats, the generation of a dietary protein source that does not rely on cropping could mitigate perceptions of competition between livestock and humans for land.

However, the great limitation for both synthetic meats and insects is the likelihood that the manufacturing processes will be controlled by large companies and protected by patents, leading to greater levels of livestock-system industrialisation. Although monogastric systems, the primary users of these products, are largely already industrialised, neither option leaves much opportunity for smallholder producers to participate. It seems highly unlikely that the rural poor of the developing economies will become synthetic protein or insect farmers.

7   Alexander *et al.*
8   Ly.
9   Raubenheimer *et al.*
10   Gahukar.

Even if synthetic proteins or insect feeds complement livestock production, the impact on the livestock sector's contribution to climate change
may be minimal. Indeed, for the monogastric species, a significant proportion of emissions are associated with feed production.[11] However, the use
of synthetic or insect protein as a dietary component for ruminants does
not address enteric or manure emissions. The environmental impact of
livestock will likely still need to be addressed.

Lowering environmental impacts

Clearly technological solutions to deal with GHG emissions without the
need to radically redesign livestock systems are appealing for policymakers.
Early examples that may hold promise include the use of animal genetic
resources to breed appropriate animal types (particularly dairy cattle) and
the use of technologies such as methane capture. Emission trading schemes
are also an option.

1   Animal genetic resources

Breeding has long been used to improve genetic merit and increase milk
yield. Theoretically, this reduces the number of animals needed to produce a
specified quantity of milk. Fewer animals mean fewer emissions. However,
if the improved productivity is not accompanied by a decline in population
size, total dairy sector emissions will increase.

The breeding of cows with high genetic merit is appealing as farmers
are likely to already be undertaking genetic improvement programmes.
But achieving increased milk production is more complex than simply
improving genetic merit because a number of interlocking variables (mild
temperatures, high-quality feeds, veterinary services) are required to ensure
that high levels of genetic merit can be translated into high milk yields.[12]
Within large sections of the developing economies, such inputs are not
available, particularly for the rural poor. Additionally, as previously noted,
to achieve an overall reduction in emissions via improved genetic merit, the
increased levels of milk production must be accompanied by a reduction
in total herd size. Questions remain as to whether a reduced population
size would ever be socially or politically acceptable to rural households and
governments within the developing economies.

11   Zervas and Tsiplakou.
12   Hristov *et al.*

Given the absence of supportive inputs within the developing economies, breeding animals for improved feed efficiency (that is, a low-emission animal) rather than improved genetic merit (or yield) could be pursued to reduce methane yield.[13] Early indications suggest low GHG emission is partly heritable.[14] Because this field of study is relatively new, the potential magnitude with which reductions can be achieved is largely unknown[15] – but preliminary studies suggest that potential emissions reduction could be in the range of 40-45 per cent.[16]

Realising any significant level of emission reduction from the breeding of a low-emission cow is unlikely to be a realistic option in the short-term because significant methodological limitations need to be overcome: for example, techniques to accurately measure methane emissions from the animal, the requirement for sufficient measurement over time to rank sires in terms of methane emission level, and the practical difficulties of measuring emissions on-farm.[17]

Furthermore, without financial incentives, farmers are unlikely to switch to low-emission cows. Even with the financial incentive of improved yields, it has taken over 30 years to increase India's crossbred dairy cow population to 28.4 per cent of the total dairy cow population.[18]

2   *Technological fixes for emission reduction*

A range of technologies could be used to reduce emissions because they offer the opportunity to reduce emissions without changing long-held production paradigms, such as a focus on milk yield as a measure of success. Technological fixes, such as installing anaerobic digesters, are already favoured by international policymakers.[19] However, the applicability of such a technology to some production systems, particularly pasture-based systems, is questionable. Additionally, manure methane emissions account for only a small proportion of total methane emissions. Therefore, it is necessary for policymakers to target those sites of greatest emission for greatest reduction impact.

It is unclear whether the ambition of existing technological fixes can be translated to realised emission reduction. For example, vaccination against

13   Vellinga *et al.*; Pickering *et al.*; Webb *et al.*
14   Lassen and Løvendahl.
15   Hristov *et al.*
16   Pickering *et al.*
17   *Ibid.*
18   Ministry of Agriculture.
19   York *et al.*, 'A Systematic Review'.

methanogens is the most developed rumen modification technique available, but recent investigations have yielded mixed results.[20] In addition, the impact of such a technology is likely limited at a global scale. Therefore, a one-size-fits-all approach to technological solutions is unlikely to yield the results needed to ensure a low-emission livestock production system in the longer term. However, if livestock systems converge into a 'gold standard' single industrialised model, as the industrial chicken meat industry has, several key technologies could be widely dispersed. The impact of such convergence on rural livelihoods, particularly in the developing economies, would be profound.

3   *Emission trading schemes*

The participation of the livestock sector within Emission Trading Schemes (ETSs) is another area of uncertainty. There is a clear aversion to the inclusion of livestock production within ETSs. This may be due to the limited strategies available to reduce emissions from the sector[21] or alternatively, the significant political will required to implement a tax on the livestock sector that may be passed onto consumers via food price.

The 'carbon farming initiative' implemented by the Australian government may avoid such difficulties.[22] Financial incentives (via carbon credits) are offered to livestock producers who undertake emission-reduction strategies. This approach offers an alternative to direct taxation. However, such an initiative is likely to be expensive for governments to implement at a large scale.

Nonetheless, the unintended (or perhaps intended) consequence of including livestock production in ETSs will be an increase in the price of animal products. The increased price may reduce demand, particularly for ruminant products. Although this may be insignificant for consumers in the industrially developed economies, those in the developing economies are highly sensitive to changes in price. Great care would be required to ensure that the benefits from the consumption of animal products are not pushed beyond the means of the poor.

---

20   Vaccination attempts to stimulate an immune response in the animal to produce antibodies against methanogens (Wright *et al.*) The antibodies enter the digestive system (via saliva) to inhibit the activity of methanogens and/or reduce the methanogen population size (Williams *et al.*). Early evidence for the vaccination against methanogens appeared particularly promising (Wright *et al.*). However, more recent investigations were unable to elicit a reduction in methane production, which increased by 18 per cent in vaccinated animals (Williams *et al.*). Williams *et al.* concluded that for methane reductions to be achieved via vaccination, 'certain undefined conditions' will need to be met and that vaccination type may need to differ based on the diet of the animal (p. 1864).

21   Gerber *et al.*, *Tackling Climate Change through Livestock*, and Hristov *et al.*

22   Department of Environment and Energy.

A change in consumer demand (due to increased price) may also instigate a change in high-emission production systems, namely specialised beef production units. Within industrially developed economies, beef has a particularly high-emission intensity due to the length of production. Beef producers may commence milk production to ensure emissions can be allocated between meat and milk products. Although this will not reduce total emissions, it will ensure that beef has a lower-emission intensity (and is less negatively affected by an ETS). In the developing economies, there is generally no segregation between beef and dairy production. However, emission allocation methods that effectively consider the diverse livelihood benefits derived from livestock ownership may be an effective way of avoiding product price rises instigated by ETSs.

At the forefront of change: A case study from India

The Indian dairy sector offers a useful example of how sustainability issues are playing out at both a household and sectoral level as a consequence of climate change. The Indian dairy sector is the largest in the world (approximately 44.5 million milking cows[23]) and represents 16.7 per cent of the world's dairy cattle population.[24] The Indian 'white revolution' began in the 1970s with the implementation of Operation Flood, a government anti-poverty programme to increase the food and livelihood security of smallholder farmers.[25] A key feature of that programme was the introduction of exotic germ plasm for crossbreeding with indigenous *Bos indicus* breeds. As a result of the programme, the crossbred population increased from 4.6 per cent to 16.6 per cent of the total cattle population over a 25-year period (1982-2007).[26] Current estimates indicate that the crossbred population is 28.4 per cent of the dairy cow population and supplies 54.2 per cent of India's cow milk (59.81 million tonnes).[27]

In the 20 years following Operation Flood, the Indian dairy sector sustained annual growth rates of 5.6 per cent, ensuring that the dairy sector made a significant contribution to India's food security.[28] Unsurprisingly, the increase in milk production resulting from Operation Flood increased milk availability and household income from the sale of milk. However, it

23   Ministry of Agriculture.
24   FAO, *FAOSTAT Emissions Database*.
25   Gautam *et al.*
26   Working Group on Animal Husbandry and Dairying.
27   Ministry of Agriculture.
28   Ali.

is the impacts on nutrition, school attendance (particularly among girls), employment, and female empowerment that demonstrate the importance of Operation Flood as a driver of transformation.[29] For example, the World Bank estimates that Operation Flood resulted in between 350,000 and 1.1 million additional children attending school.[30]

Nonetheless, the growth rate is now slowing in all aspects of the production system, including feeding, breeding, health, and management due to the impact of climate change. Indeed, by 2020, climate change is expected to reduce India's milk production by 1.6 million tonnes.[31] Even with adaptation, milk yields at a household level are expected to be irrevocably reduced.[32] But within this context of climate change, Operation Flood's focus on productivity gains via improved 'exotic' animal genetics has reduced the resilience of dairying-based livelihoods and constrained the efficacy with which the poor can access and implement adaptation options.

Changing the system requires a variety of considerations. Dairying and dairy products are a feature of the Indian cultural identity and essential for food security. Despite urbanisation trends and an increasingly affluent middle class, the multifunctional role dairying plays within India is unlikely to change in the near future. The centrality of cattle within the national psyche is particularly well illustrated by the recent ban on the slaughter of cows and buffalo (including exports).[33]

In addition to supporting livelihoods and food security through income generation, draft power, and soil nutrient cycling, and increasing the availability of high-quality animal proteins, the over-grazing of livestock also plays a role in land-use change. Few studies however, have explored the benefits of livestock in the recycling of industrial processing by-products and crop residues, which are important sources of feed for Indian cattle.

Given these roles, it is unlikely that a future without dairy cattle will ever be achievable or desirable. The increasing threat of climate change will force Indian policymakers to implement strategies to safeguard food security by addressing the diverse range of challenges presented (including heat stress, reduced feed availability and quality, changed disease and pest prevalence, and distribution) while also reducing contributions of the sector to GHG emissions.

---

29 Candler and Kumar.
30 *Ibid.*
31 Upadhyay *et al.*, p. 26.
32 York *et al.*, 'A Deterministic Evaluation'.
33 Biswas.

Yet climate-change action within the livestock sector of India (and the developing economies more generally) is further complicated by gaps in knowledge. Estimates of impact and emissions are absent or demonstrate methodological shortcomings. As a result, adapting livestock production systems to deal with climate change impact and/or emission mitigation cannot be undertaken with any level of certainty.

Trade-offs for the future

It is indisputable that crossbreeding India's indigenous breeds with high-yielding exotic breeds has successfully increased milk yields. Although there remains disagreement as to the comparative importance of productivity (level of milk production) and genetics (physiological characteristics of *Bos taurus* breeds compared with *Bos indicus* breeds) in determining tolerance to heat stress, it can be assumed that those breed types that are more sensitive to heat stress are ill-equipped to deal with increased temperature. The overall usefulness of crossbreeding in a context of climate change is limited if increased milk yields cannot be maintained when cows are challenged by increasing temperatures. Thus, the traditional single-trait policy focus on milk yield as a measure of success limits the ability of the sector both in India and globally to respond to this challenge.

However, if the Indian dairy sector continues to be characterised by a large number of lower-yielding cows, it will have a high-emission intensity when compared with a sector composed of fewer, higher-yielding cows.[34] The direct impact of climate change (increased risk of heat stress) suggests the need to consider more heat-tolerant, lower-yielding breeds. However, to do so will increase the emission intensity of the milk production. Thus, trade-offs exist between the need to manage the effects of heat stress and the creation of a low-emission dairy sector. Great care will be required as attempts to deal with the effects of climate change may inadvertently increase climate change itself.

Are adaptation and mitigation mutually exclusive? The advocacy (and implementation) of adaptation strategies without considering mitigation (or vice versa) is likely to be highly unsustainable. Thus, a balance must be sought to ensure that adaptation and mitigation can be achieved simultaneously.

Herein lies the difficulty for all stakeholders into the future. Important questions need to be addressed about what role livestock, specifically dairy

34   Capper *et al.*; Gerber *et al.*; 'Productivity Gains'; and Kiefer *et al.*

production, will play in safeguarding food security, and what constitutes 'sustainable intensification' within the context of climate change.[35] The traditional livestock development paradigm has advocated improved animal genetics (often derived from 'exotic' breeds) as an integral feature of sustainable intensification. Clearly this needs to be revisited on a global scale.

Realistic hope

The challenges faced by the livestock sector have created a 'perfect storm' of trade-offs as the global community will be forced to weigh the demand for animal protein against both climate change and wider environmental concerns. As with most large challenges, no single, simple solution will ensure that the demand for animal products can be met under the guise of 'sustainable intensification'.

The opportunity offered by synthetic and insect proteins to complement rather than compete with the livestock sector may be an attractive option. For policymakers in the industrially developed economies, the integration of synthetic and insect proteins into livestock and food systems could avoid the expenditure of valuable political capital to restructure livestock systems to address issues associated with livestock production. Focusing on livestock consumption rather than human consumption could also help policymakers avoid debates such as those surrounding GM food products. However, for policymakers in the developing economies, the move to synthetic and insect proteins is complicated by the resilience function fulfilled by livestock within the livelihoods of the poor. Thus, the future is highly nuanced in the developing economies because a move away from livestock production to address contributions to climate change and other environmental concerns may risk the diverse livelihoods benefits derived from livestock keeping.

Although the livestock sector may continue to contribute to climate change in the near future, there is realistic hope – and even a kind of inevitability – that livestock management practices will be modified to adapt to the effects of climate change. Yet a scarcity of social and financial resources means that such modifications will be particularly difficult for livestock producers in developing economies. Therefore, it may be necessary for the global community not only to consider domestic trade-offs but also to acknowledge the importance of global stewardship.

---

35 'Sustainable intensification' is defined as 'producing more from the same area of land while reducing negative environmental impacts and increasing contributions to natural capital and the flow of environmental services' (FAO, 'Save and Grow', p. 9).

Works Cited

Alexander, P., *et al.* 'Could Consumption of Insects, Cultured Meat or Imitation Meat Reduce Global Agricultural Land Use?' *Global Food Security* 15 (2017), pp. 22-23.

Ali, J. 'Livestock Sector Development and Implications for Rural Poverty Alleviation in India'. *Livestock Research for Rural Development* 19.2 (2007), pp. 1-14.

Biswas, S. 'Is India's Ban on Cattle Slaughter "Food Fascism"'? *BBC News*, 2 June 2017. http://www.bbc.com/news/world-asia-india-40116811. Accessed 21 Nov. 2017.

Candler, W., and N. Kumar. *India: The Dairy Revolution*. Washington, DC: The World Bank, 1998.

Capper, J.L., R.A. Cady, and D.E. Bauman. 'The Environmental Impact of Dairy Production: 1944 Compared with 2007'. *Journal of Animal Science* 87 (2009), pp. 2160-67.

Department of Environment and Energy. *About the Carbon Farming Initiative.* Australian Government, Department of Environment and Energy, 2014. http://www.environment.gov.au/climate-change/government/emissions-reduction-fund/cfi/about. Accessed 24 June 2018.

FAO. *FAOSTAT Emissions Database*. Rome: Food and Agricultural Organization of the United Nations (FAO), 2013.

FAO. 'Save and Grow: A Policymaker's Guide to the Sustainable Intensification of Smallholder Crop Production'. Rome: Food and Agricultural Organization of the United Nations, 2011.

Gahukar, R.T. 'Edible Insects Farming: Efficiency and Impact on Family Livelihood, Food Security, and Environment Compared with Livestock and Crops'. In *Insects as Sustainable Food Ingredients*, ed. A.T. Dossey, J.A. Morales-Ramos and M.G. Rojas. San Diego: Academic Press, 2016, pp. 85-111.

Gautam, R.S. Dalal, and V. Pathak. 'Indian Dairy Sector: Time to Revisit Operation Flood'. *Livestock Science* 127.2-3, 2010, pp. 164-75.

Gerber, P., *et al.*, eds. *Tackling Climate Change through Livestock: Global Assessment of Emissions and Mitigation Opportunities*. Rome: UN Food and Agricultural Organization (FAO), 2013.

Gerber, P., T. Vellinga, C. Opio, and H. Steinfeld. 'Productivity Gains and Greenhouse Gas Emissions Intensity in Dairy Systems'. *Livestock Science* 139 (2011), pp. 100-108.

Herrero, M., *et al.* 'Biomass Use, Production, Feed Efficiencies, and Greenhouse Gas Emissions from Global Livestock Systems'. *Proceedings of the National Academy of Sciences* 110 (2013), p. 20,888-93.

Hristov, A.N., *et al.*, eds. *Mitigation of Greenhouse Gas Emissions in Livestock Production: A Review of Technical Options for Non-CO_2 Emissions*. Rome: UN Food and Agricultural Organization (FAO), 2013.

Kiefer, L., F. Menzel, and E. Bahrs. 'The Effect of Feed Demand on Greenhouse Gas Emissions and Farm Profitability for Organic and Conventional Dairy Farms'. *Journal of Dairy Science* 97 (2014), pp. 7564-74.

Lassen, J., and P. Løvendahl. 'Heritability Estimates for Enteric Methane Emissions from Holstein Cattle Measured Using Noninvasive Methods'. *Journal of Dairy Science* 99 (2016), pp. 1959-67.

Ly, P. 'New Free Range Rules "Lead to Egg Shortage"'. *SBS News*, 9 June 2016. http://www.sbs.com.au/news/article/2016/06/09/new-free-range-rules-lead-egg-shortage. Accessed 12 Nov. 2017.

Ministry of Agriculture. *Basic Animal Husbandry & Fisheries Statistics*. New Delhi: Government of India, 2013.

National Academies of Sciences, Engineering, and Medicine. *Genetically Engineered Crops: Experiences and Prospects*. Washington, DC: The National Academies Press, 2016.

O'Brien, D., J.L. Capper, P.C. Garnsworthy, C. Grainger, and L. Shalloo. 'A Case Study of the Carbon Footprint of Milk from High-Performing Confinement and Grass-Based Dairy Farms'. *Journal of Dairy Science* 97 (2014), pp. 1835-51.

Pickering, N.K., *et al.* 'Animal Board Invited Review: Genetic Possibilities to Reduce Enteric Methane Emissions from Ruminants'. *Animal* 9 (2015), pp. 1431-40.

Raphaely, T., and D. Marinova. 'Flexitarianism: Decarbonising through Flexible Vegetarianism'. *Renewable Energy* 67 (2014), pp. 90-96.

Raubenheimer, D., J.M. Rothman, H. Pontzer, and S.J. Simpson. 'Macronutrient Contributions of Insects to the Diets of Hunter-Gatherers: A Geometric Analysis'. *Journal of Human Evolution* 71 (2014), 70-76.

Ruby, M.B., S.J. Heine, S. Kamble, T.K. Cheng, and M. Waddar. 'Compassion and Contamination: Cultural Differences in Vegetarianism'. *Appetite* 71 (2013), 340-48.

Upadhyay, R.C., *et al. Final Report of the Network Project on Climate Change*. Karnal: National Dairy Research Institute, 2007.

Vellinga, T.V., *et al.* 'Implementation of GHG Mitigation on Intensive Dairy Farms: Farmers' Preferences and Variation in Cost Effectiveness'. *Livestock Science* 137 (2011), pp. 185-95.

Von Massow, V. 'Dairy Imports into Sub-Saharan Africa and Their Policy Implications'. *ILCA Bulletin* 21 (1985).

Webb, J., E. Audsley, A. Williams, K. Pearn, and J. Chatterton. 'Can UK Livestock Production Be Configured to Maintain Production While Meeting Targets to Reduce Emissions of Greenhouse Gases and Ammonia?' *Journal of Cleaner Production* 83 (2014), pp. 204-11.

Williams, Y.J., *et al.* 'A Vaccine against Rumen Methanogens Can Alter the Composition of Archaeal Populations'. *Applied and Environmental Microbiology* 75 (2009), pp. 1860-66.

Working Group on Animal Husbandry and Dairying. 'Report of the Working Group on Animal Husbandry and Dairying, 12th Five Year Plan (2012-17)'. Submitted to Planning Commission, Government of India, New Delhi, 2012. http://planning-commission.gov.in/aboutus/committee/wrkgrp12/agri/AHD_REPORT_Final_rev.pdf. Accessed 24 June 2018.

Wright, A.D., *et al.* 'Reducing Methane Emissions in Sheep by Immunization against Rumen Methanogens'. *Vaccine* 22 (2004), pp. 3,976-85.

York, L., C. Heffernan, and C. Rymer. 'A Systematic Review of Policy Approaches to Dairy Sector Greenhouse Gas (GHG) Emission Reduction'. *Journal of Cleaner Production* 172 (2018), pp. 2,216-24.

York, L., C. Heffernan, C. Rymer, and N. Panda. 'A Deterministic Evaluation of Heat Stress Mitigation and Feed Cost under Climate Change within the Smallholder Dairy Sector'. *Animal* 11 (2017), pp. 900-09.

Zervas, G., and E. Tsiplakou. 'An Assessment of GHG Emissions from Small Ruminants in Comparison with GHG Emissions from Large Ruminants and Monogastric Livestock'. *Atmospheric Environment* 49 (2012), pp. 13-23.

About the Authors

Luke York holds a PhD from the Livestock Development Group, School of Agriculture, Policy and Development, University of Reading and has conducted research for a range of international organizations from the Australian Centre for International Agricultural Research (ACIAR) to the International Livestock Research Institute (ILRI). He is currently advising a national government on sustainable livestock development.

Claire Heffernan holds a Personal Chair in International Development and is Director of London's International Development Centre, a consortium of seven University of London institutions.

12 Rethinking Economics for Global Challenges

Christian Kastrop

Abstract

This chapter tries to check the wisdom of 'standard' economics against global megatrends, such as globalisation, digitalisation, and other future technologies, as well as ecological challenges. The result is rather negative. For many aspects of these new developments, standard economics isn't able to give the necessary description of the upcoming 'new world'. Given this diagnosis, the policy recipes derived from standard economics for expected economic and societal problems will not fly. The chapter discusses the need for a paradigm change in economics and for more interdisciplinary work, and explores possible avenues of progress.

Keywords: failure of standard economics, holistic versus restricted approaches, paradigm change, crises of capitalism

The challenges to the practice of economics in the new global economy

The global economy is experiencing rapid worldwide upheaval. The radical changes taking place are also leading to greater insecurity and inequality, while populism and nationalism are on the rise. Advanced OECD economies, especially those that have no raw materials, must examine whether their economic model is sustainable in the long term. Both emerging countries and developing countries need to develop quickly, raising living standards and well-being while encouraging inclusiveness and open societies.

This upheaval has to be seen in conjunction with emerging megatrends, including those that lie outside economics, such as continuing digitalisation and the challenge of climate change. These megatrends can create great opportunities for countries – but at the same time, the associated risks and difficulties must be taken seriously.

Wilkinson, Angela, and Betty Sue Flowers (eds.), *Realistic Hope: Facing Global Challenges*. Amsterdam, Amsterdam University Press, 2018.
DOI: 10.5117/9789462987241_CH12

In the last two centuries, starting with Adam Smith and David Ricardo, economic policy and piecemeal economic 'engineering', backed up by economic theory within the typical rationalistic and instrumentalist methodological approaches, have been very influential in shaping these processes. There is no standstill in the development of theories and of better and more sophisticated analytical tools to conduct empirical research and create evidence-based policy advice. But there is an important question: is this piecemeal engineering approach sufficient and the only thing we can do or realistically hope for? Or do we need a fundamental rethinking of economics in a more holistic and less imperialistic mode so that it can be much more helpful in shaping the future, with better policies for better lives?

The starting position for answering this question is clear: no, current standard economics is not yet able to do the job required by the new global economy – so yes, we do need a paradigm shift in economics. Economics and economists must undergo a fundamental paradigm shift, not only leaving the neo-liberal paradigm but also accepting a completely new and much more modest – although still important – role as an integral part of solving future problems.

The underlying problem

Economics was developed in the 18th century as an offspring of philosophy. As a 'social science', it was embedded in a strong normative background, as developed in Adam Smith's other major book besides *The Wealth of Nations – The Theory of Moral Sentiments*.

Beginning with David Ricardo from 1799 onwards, and developed by other classical and neoclassical economists, the economic mainstream moved away from its original philosophical and social science foundations and began developing a rationalist methodological approach based on rather artificial and narrow assumptions of people's economic behaviour. The originally much broader methodological concept of economics was narrowed, focusing more and more on logical relations and empiricist analyses with mathematical terms and equations, and with the logical or statistical results then being used for forward-looking policy advice.

The main feature of this classical and neoclassical mainstream economic paradigm is a focus on the individual. Solipsistic individuals exhibit a very simple rational behaviour – they always maximise their individual utility with private and public goods and services via individual decision-making. These 'rational agents' also have rather stable preferences about the utility of these different goods and stable expectations about the future.

With this mix of inductive empirical design and deduction of the fundamental human economic behaviour from very few eternal principles, nearly everything in economics could be put into an equation, and models of economic behaviour could be developed, including models for market equilibrium, supply and demand curves, how the price mechanism balances supply with demand and clear markets, or how a monopoly works, and why it's bad.

Later, in the 20th century, less weight was put on these theoretical approaches, which used deductive logic. Economics shifted to a more 'scientific' inductive approach using data-based econometric research and modelling using micro/macro panel data within fundamental economic relations. Economists built a hypothesis, put the hypothesis into the form of an equation, and then tested it using advanced applied statistical methods. If a regression showed significance, the 'experiment' had produced a correlation, or, even better, a causality and a piece of truth, building on and enhancing further an economic theory of economic reality. This methodology is still used today, although with better data and ever more sophisticated methods of econometrics.

The mathematicisation of economics resulted in a nice halo effect, leading to the belief among politicians, in civil society, and, not least, among economists themselves that economics comes much closer to being a natural science than other social sciences. Economists tend to think very highly of their numeric results and the derived policy conclusions.

Of course, evidence-based economics is welcome against just guessing and speculating, and economic modelling and empirical research is a very useful exercise as a heuristic structural concept. It may be sophisticated and intellectually thrilling on the frontier – but in a sense it will always deliver what you put in or leave out. And what you put in needs to be correct and stable in an increasingly dynamic world. This is the famous Lucas critique: at the very moment of a change in economic policies, the expectations of the people will change, and the policy reaction will not be the same as before; so the policy-change goal may not be achieved because it is based on the old reaction assumption.[1] In other words, the relation between a policy and expected outcome might not be stable in the future. Economic behaviour is endogenous not exogenous, as standard theory presumes. And this means: economics isn't like engineering or physics.

Again, the need for stable numbers in an unstable world doesn't mean that the effort is useless – on the contrary, these models can show fundamental

---

1   Lucas, p. 263.

structural relations of how the economy might work under restricted and ideal assumptions. But they are by no means sufficient for explaining the reality or for policy advice at any given point in time – and even less so for predicting the future.

The challenge of data

There are also problems with the available data. In contrast to empirical research in the natural sciences, data in the social sciences depend not so much on controlled experiments as on the quality of the assembled macro- or micro-data. And, in addition to other quality criteria, any given database depends on the institutional quality of the data-delivering stations on all levels.

Another challenge is that for a lot of issues we do not have the exact data we need, so we build bridges from other related data. We 'clean' or 'smooth' data if they look odd and make them match our econometric needs. And when we use questionnaires for data creation, we rely on the right understanding of a question and the reader's honesty in giving a real answer rather than a strategic or 'fake' one.

We can also use different types of statistical methods to create significant results – which means having a certain maximum level of error probability. Of course, we choose the method that will give us the results we expect. We can also change the set of cases in a panel or change the timeline we are looking at. Results and their significance may look rather different in different set-ups, and there is no empirical basis for what to use – just judgement or forced judgement, if a specific result is expected up front. In academia these choices must be made transparent and are reviewed by the academic community. But will these specialists, who are also divided in their sympathy for certain methodological approaches, always be open and fully transparent in their final judgement about a method chosen when underpinning political advice?

The challenge of the assumption of rational behaviour

And then there's the fundamental assumption of rational behaviour. Do people really prefer more rather than less, or cheap rather than expensive for the same quality? They know a market price of a 'product' in manufacturing or services or digital – but has this price factored in, for instance, a monopolistic supply, the use of your personal data, the use of our natural environment, or child labour? Do consumers even know what is 'more' or 'less', now and in the future? How do they perceive, expect, or judge the behaviour of others in reaction to their own behaviour? Even if there is a typical – and tested – behavioural pattern, is it stable? Under what conditions will it remain stable or become unstable?

There are even more fundamental problems when we look into the future. Can any backwards-looking empirical result tell us something about the future? How much is individual behaviour shaped by the surroundings, the group the individual likes or belongs to, and the reality the individual inhabits, especially as it is constructed by social media in a new digital environment? When individual behaviour is unstable, why not manipulate it? Manipulating for good may be fine and helpful (i.e., 'nudging'[2]), behavioural economics tells us, but then what about the 'dark side' – manipulating with fake news and fake realities shaped by totalitarian governments controlling information channels, or populist politicians and movements?

The challenge of GDP measurements

Economics is still looking at the effect of structural reforms or policy settings on GDP. But growth as such is just a means and not a goal in itself, even if important, especially for GDP per capita for emerging or developing countries. Final goals are measured better within well-being concepts, which are of course subjective and more difficult to compare. This makes policy advice based on cross-country comparisons of GDP effects rather questionable if it is not put into the right framework.

Even GDP is not a clear-cut concept when it comes to measuring it. A big issue for economics at the moment is the question of how much our current measurements omit a lot of things – for instance, human capital, all sorts of intangible products, and assets like organisational capital or entrepreneurship, from the digital economy to the sharing economy. A more classical challenge is to measure and include external effects of a production process that generates GDP but also produces unaccounted, negative, external side effects, whether positive – such as the encouragement of upskilling or further R&D, or environmental improvement due to better energy balances – or negative – environmental degradation, social dumping, or evaporation of skills. It is probable that, especially in the digital area, our current GDP figures may very much deviate from the 'real' ones we can't measure with our given tools, which may have huge consequences for pro-growth policies and even more for well-being policies.

2   Thaler and Sunstein, p. 145.

The challenge to economics of other structural models

Along with its fundamental rationalist assumptions and its utilitarian economic concepts, mainstream economics takes a market-biased view, without taking into account other structural models based on different traditions, cultures, or states of development. The infamous 'Washington Consensus', for example, clearly assumed that markets require certain structural settings. But when economic policy research occurs within these settings, the issue of unequal market power seldom arises, even though this type of inequality will directly shape the final market outcome on a national or a global level.

There are many 'third ways' that lie outside a strict market economy model. The Nordic countries, for example, enjoy high GDP and well-being while pursuing a market economy model that also features quite a large but very efficient, effective, and empowering state. This model depends on an engaged civil society, where taxes are paid willingly in exchange for the high quality of public goods. Outside the strict market model, there is room for negotiation, regulation, and border control if there is no fair trade due to different market (and political) power, as in the case of developing countries. Again, a very simplistic economic theory, however sophisticated, may not have anything to add to the standard answer: openness is always good. After all, openness is necessary in Ricardo's model of comparative advantages, which brings us to the next argument: economic power.

The challenge to economics of the increasing desire to balance power

Another complicating factor and a looming challenge for our current econometric models is the need for any open civil society to balance economic and political power – of governments but also of multinational enterprises, including effective global and national regulations for competition and against corruption and unfair trade, the quantity and quality of jobs, social security networks, strong trade unions, and effective social partnerships. The 'social market economy' model, as developed in Germany and other Central European economies, for instance, is maintained even when it temporarily delivers worse results compared to neo-liberal economic recipes, as measured by regression analyses. Also how economic results are achieved is important, beyond just maximising growth. But even the more market-oriented Anglo-Saxon approach does not come without normative feedback loops, in regulations arising from institutional design, for example, which override market forces through rule of law. Economists studying non-Western economies with other cultural backgrounds, ethics, political traditions, and social settings will need to look at these complex economic and political interactions, especially because these economies are on the rise, economically and politically.

Standard economics will not be able to deal with the megatrend of digitalisation

Digitalisation is a generic term for a whole class of innovative technologies that use digital communication and digital products, such as big data, e-commerce, e-government, cloud computing, social media, supply-chain management, and less familiar technologies such as radio-frequency identification (RFID). Digitalisation will fundamentally change existing technologies or make them redundant. In combination with other new technologies, such as nano- and biotechnology, robotics, artificial intelligence (AI), and 3D printing, it will change the world we live in, with consequences for communication, the workings of civil society, participation in politics, and social interactions. Some of these innovations are still thought experiments, some are in the research and development stage, and others are nearly market-ready or already available.

Digitalisation is also changing the intensity and quality of globalisation. We have no idea what this really means looking even 20 years ahead. Forty per cent of the world's population in 2017 is digitally connected, compared to 4 per cent in 1995. The digital revolution and transformation will stimulate further innovation, bringing great opportunities for increased productivity in many manufacturing and service industries as well as in the public sector. Information, training, and real-time data are available to all users at little cost. As a result, digitalisation can create growth and quality jobs and also promote social and economic inclusion and general well-being – for example, new forms of mobility can help to reduce CO_2, an ageing population can benefit from health advances, such as services through smartphones, transparency in the public sector can be enhanced, and the delivery of public services can be targeted more accurately.

This is just the upside, however. The downside is the threat to jobs in sectors and regions with a high speed of transition and of once acquired skills. Some data show special risks for an overall loss of jobs or higher transition problems, especially for the middle-skilled group. And inequality is likely to increase because upgrading skills is more difficult for those lower on the income distribution scale.

New digital forms of work are often not covered by the existing social security net. Digitalisation engenders huge cybersecurity problems and new types of cybercrime, as well as restrictions on privacy or the loss of it in the digital sphere. It opens up new possibilities for tax avoidance and the undermining of competition by multinational digital firms. Recent events in the US show that living in a digital (social) media environment is already creating possibilities for different groups to hold such different views of reality as to undermine the fundamental consensus required for an ethical civil society. Designing policy in the usual way in such a 'subjective reality' environment will almost certainly fail. And vice versa – the full use of big data and a 'fake news' digital environment allows politicians and lobbyists to cheat, influence, and manipulate the people more powerfully than ever before.

This increased capacity for manipulation is not only an interesting new campaigning dimension for politics, public entities, and lobbyists, but it is also an increasing practice of big industry, which can manipulate whole governments, their customers, and their employees on a multinational level. So using behavioural aspects to help design better policies and institutions is an important new tool – but one that will also come close to ethical borders that need to be discussed.

As a result of actual or perceived economic and political uncertainty, digitalisation together with other technologies can also undermine state institutions or cast doubt on their legitimacy, with far-reaching political consequences. Conventional government budget financing, management, and control could then be threatened, or at least become more uncertain.

Digitalisation thus poses immense risks. It is already changing policies, business behaviour, and communications in civil society. Employment will face temporary and persistent losses and huge transition issues. Research and development will speed up, simplify manufacturing processes, and generate a multitude of new digital and other business models. Policies must include upfront payment, timely action, proper regulation of the markets, and risk control through democratic processes. One feature will most probably be that exposed groups, for example, workers or other vulnerable groups, must be supported in order to assume a self-defined and responsible role in policymaking. That is a 'whole-of-the-house' task for economic, fiscal, social, education, and employment policy – all in all, creating an empowering state backed up by an open civil society and a strong middle class.

This should, of course, be backed up by economics in a broader connection with other social sciences. Economic evidence should play a role in shaping new policies – but we have already seen that the effects we observe and need to analyse before giving proper policy advice are far ahead of common economic wisdom. The digitalisation megatrend already offers a good indication of what might be missing or overlooked in conventional economics in order to suggest policy adjustments. Economics is light years away from grappling fully with digital issues. Due to its very limited scope, its imperialistic and closed methodological core, and its lack of networking with other sciences, it does not have the capacity to tackle all the digitalisation issues in the necessary holistic way.

Standard economics will not be able to deal with the megatrend of climate change

The challenge of climate change starts with the fundamental economic and still not-yet-solved issue of how to include an economic externality in the market price of a private good in order to avoid free-riding or moral hazard in using a global public good, such as our natural capital and ecological habitat. There are standard economic solutions to this 'tragedy of the commons', like taxing the use of these goods (the Pigovian tax), creating tradeable environmental licenses, and using the economics of regulation. But anyone who has worked with these solutions in practice knows how imperfect and difficult to implement they are. Standard economics alone cannot meet this challenge.

The Paris commitments to combat climate change make it clear that the page must be turned on the 20th-century economic growth model for industrial countries. For emerging and developing countries the issue is not to repeat the failure of the industrialised part of the world. This isn't easy for them. The old industrialised world has already exploited global public goods for more than 150 years, so why shouldn't emerging and developing countries enjoy their own industrial decades now with cheap coal or oil – or, if not, require old advanced industrialised countries to pay the emerging and developing economies to be quicker in the transition to sustainability? This is a difficult problem and hard to sell to old industrialised electorates.

Domestic policy, though important, is not sufficient on its own. Climate-change risk is not local or regional but global. Damage to the environment poses a long-term threat to all countries, albeit initially to a differing extent. Many developing and emerging countries, which are also often under particular threat from rising sea levels, will have a heavy burden to bear. Global solidarity is and will be needed for a long time to phase it in.

Whatever it takes, we are all in it together. But the industrialised nations have an additional responsibility for the others, paying back on a debt they created for all humans in their process of industrialisation. Further, unchecked climate change will cast radical doubt on the ecological basis of our industrial economy, not only in the long term, but even in the medium and short term. Calculations from the global reinsurance industry show that the likelihood of environmental disasters has already increased and that there will be large negative effects on growth and productivity as well as on inclusiveness, since the most vulnerable regions for droughts and rising sea levels coincide with the most vulnerable income groups.

The slower we are to face up to this challenge, which is far beyond just an economic challenge, the harder it will be to adjust in 20 or 30 years. If not enough is done now, conventional growth that neglects the biosphere will ultimately no longer be possible. In the end, the issue is not the survival of the old paradigm of capitalist growth but survival for mankind. But to ensure survival, we will need new paradigms and new thinking – in economics as well as in many other aspects of our current global economic system.

The sheer magnitude of these increasing, non-linear (and hence barely calculable) systemic risks requires the fastest possible global transition to an economic model that is at least greenhouse-gas neutral. There has probably never been a need for transformation like this in economic history, and the transformation process, which we need to steer economically and politically, offers opportunities and risks that go far beyond the purely economic issues. Behind economic models stand not only justified employee and economic interests but also social models and the interest of civil societies that need to preserve their stability and cohesive force under the pressure of adjustment and the emergence of a new economic model.

To fulfil the Paris climate accord goal of keeping global temperature rise to well below 2°C, nearly all countries need to radically transform their economies, investing in clean and renewable energy, for example, as well as insulation, public transport, maritime transport, and many other paradigm-shifting infrastructure transformations and behaviour changes.

But the lack of both public- and private-sector investment is a major problem in nearly all economies. Public-sector investment is lacking, especially in areas such as digital networks, green transport, and the infrastructure for renewable energies, which pave the way for private-sector investment. Net public-sector investment in a lot of countries has been negative in real terms for many years despite full coffers, as, for instance, in Germany. Many billions will have to be spent over the next few years on existing and new public infrastructure.

The lagging climate-change investment is linked to an overall slack in public and private investment, which, in turn, results in low productivity.

This lag in investment also affects many policy areas, especially research, training, labour markets, and social policy. 'Green' fiscal and economic policy should deliver the financial and structural basis for increased investment in order to reach the Paris climate accord goals and also simultaneously maintain and improve private- and public-sector productivity.

As we see again, standard economics is simply not able to build an argument to tackle climate change and other environmental challenges, not even in connection with other important economic arguments for fiscal action and public investment. Building the necessary basis to push the argument by forecasting catastrophic economic events still lies outside the capacity of standard economics.

Standard economics has an in-built tendency to look backwards and not into the longer future

How can we shape the future using just standard economics? Economic forecasting of macroeconomic developments – for example, GDP – for the two years ahead is necessary for policy planning. But we all know the degree of error because every forecast must be based on a baseline scenario, which comes with upside and downside risks that cannot really be measured but need to be judged. You can include some risks in the baseline – in a fan chart, for example, you can show the probability room of possible other outcomes, or you can do scenarios based on other paths. But there are also large tail risks with lower probability that you may have chosen not to include in the baseline. What to include is a forecasting judgement that can be made asymmetrically.

For these and other reasons, macroeconomic projections always come with a high failure rate, resulting in significant consequences for the critical parameters for policies – like cyclical position and potential growth, cyclical or structural partition of fiscal deficits, or surpluses that shape macro-policies driven by fiscal stance and fiscal space and commitment with fiscal rules. Anti-cyclical policies can easily turn out pro-cyclical and vice versa, which may cost jobs and income or result in missing a debt or GDP target of a fiscal regulation.

Projections for 20 to 30 years, or even longer, deal with underlying long-term productivity settings such as technological progress, rule of law, and the development of the production factors of capital and labour, with total-factor productivity as the unexplainable or unmeasurable residuum. The long-term and initially marginal effects of underlying megatrends like climate change or digitalisation are hard to predict over such a long timeline, and a lot may be completely overlooked within the traditional linear thinking of extrapolating trends. Foresight and non-linear concepts or narratives and strategic simulations of the future – or different futures – could be added, but introducing these new methodologies to the rationalistic, closed-shop set-up of economics is not that easy. For standard economics, these things have the stigma of being unscientific and too speculative, with a whiff of metaphysics, like introducing alchemy to a chemistry lab.

Because of the inherent problems of the standard economic tools and the scepticism against using new and more speculative tools, there are only very few and weak economic advisory tools to shape long-term economic policy decisions at a time where these are desperately needed. To integrate foresight work and new technology, it might be possible to create a variety of plausible 'futures' or a constant flow of future scenarios and policy simulations. These 'futures' could even be performed in a structured and real data-based 'game' format by members of the civil society, to add new trajectories and try to shape certain different futures.

The methodological straightjacket and 'closedness' of economics

As we have seen, economists can probably bring light to a corner of a dark room – but even so, the rest of the room remains in the dark. The main challenge for economists is to accept that and then to enrich the economic core of evidence with new approaches to economic challenges. This means looking at new methodologies and subjects from other relevant social sciences (for example, psychology, sociology, political science, and natural sciences, including neuronal networks or contagion schemes) in an interdisciplinary mode that is not forced but sought by economists themselves.

Good policy advice isn't so much based on having a result from the past to shape the present but to see the conditionality for policy perception at a given point in time and space. This point of view could be called 'the reality conditions of policy advice'. As worthwhile as it might be, economics will never deliver the full answer. And a corollary to that is to accept that there will never be a one-size-fits-all solution – we always need a variety of developed policy solutions we can adapt to specific realities.

Problem-solving doesn't require economics to offer the truth as an ultimate goal but to offer evidence-based solutions for economic problems with the understanding that these problems are always embedded in a much broader environment. Such a view of economics may have a rationalist system at the core but will always be entirely instrumentalist in relation to policy advice. The history of economic science contains both rationalist and instrumentalist thinking – Smith, for example, was clearly an instrumentalist, while Ricardo was clearly a rationalist.

When economists acknowledge the inherent limitations of economics and accept that it is only one player in social sciences, without any imperialist prerogative, they will be more humble and more open to add knowledge derived from other sciences or other methodologies to economic evidence.

The 'closedness' of economics poses a mortal threat to capitalism itself

In *Capitalism, Socialism and Democracy*, Schumpeter argued that a capitalist, market-driven economic system, taken to an extreme, will 'eat up' its underlying ethics and normative ties. These ties are fundamental, but nobody is really aware of them, so their loosening and evaporation is overlooked. This neglect, he argues, will finally lead to a collapse of capitalism itself. And it's not just the economic system that will collapse – as we now see, nationalism, populism based on religious and cultural differences, and anti-democracy, or simply dropping out of the 'system', are increasingly common in current capitalistic systems. If we look at a lot of countries around the world, where the rude selfishness of elites, injustice, environmental exploitation, poverty, segregation, greed, inequality, and corruption are growing, a threat to capitalism is not far-fetched.

The need to rethink economics and change the paradigm

To sum up – current standard economics is not able to do the job required by the new global economy and emerging megatrends. Economics and economists must undergo a fundamental paradigm shift, not only leaving the neo-liberal paradigm, but also accepting a completely new and much more modest – although still important – role as an integral part of a problem-solving system.

This new economic paradigm would not only inform economists' attempts to advise policymakers in relation to current economic problems shaped by megatrends, but would also help shape the future, making civil societies and politicians aware of available policy possibilities. These economic policy recommendations need to be made in the context of specific 'reality conditions' in a specific situation in a specific country. As the term 'reality conditions' suggests, economics must take into account all aspects that influence the possible perceptions and reactions to a policy change in a given point in time.

Such a new paradigm in economics starts with a holistic view about problems in which a reframed economic science is just a part of the picture.

Foresight concepts and new approaches to economic challenges will also transform the self-understanding of economists.

If economists cannot make this paradigm shift, it doesn't look good for our future. With no sensible policy concepts and, worse, with not even an understanding of a nucleus of problem-solving methodology, conditions will be ripe for the disavowal of politics and individual and collective withdrawal from civil society, as well as the fostering of xenophobia, populism, protectionism, and nationalism.

Such a breeding ground would be supported by even better digital possibilities for living in a self-chosen reality of selected or fake news. These factors, in turn, are likely to generate political misunderstandings, leading to stereotype-driven decisions and uncertainties, which, in turn, add fuel to the fire, creating a vicious circle. These developments would have consequences for economic judgements or behaviour that would not be in line with the inbuilt economic modelling rationality that currently shapes our policy recommendations.

Also, it's important to remember the challenges for economies and civil societies caused by the shift in the axis of the global economy from the old West to Asia. Later, perhaps, Africa, with its different cultures and traditions, will also add challenges. Political and military power will follow the economic pole position. What does standard economics have on its plate to deal with very different cultural backgrounds in predicting economic behaviour? Close to nothing!

The best way to create a progressive, sustainable, and inclusive approach to policy is to treat climate change, digitalisation, productivity, and inclusion as different aspects of a single overall problem but with no single solution. Once an integrated approach to the future of the economy and society is developed in its principal features, it must be tailored to a country's individual preferences, traditions, and specific circumstances. But dynamic and self-learning solutions starting from the local level will not work without being linked to the regional and global dimension and to an adequate design of institutions on a higher level. For this challenge we need to preserve a cross-cutting global consensus wherever possible, reframe it where necessary, and rebuild it where lost.

What is the new paradigm about? Are there realistic signs of hope?

A new paradigm for economics?

As with all emerging new paradigms bits and pieces are already there. But as we learn from Thomas Kuhn and Paul Feyerabend, the old paradigm will be more successful or convincing in some aspects for quite a while. Even so, the recent and obvious rise of discontent with the solution capacity of the old paradigm will bring the change forward, even if heavily resisted by the bishops of the old paradigm.

There is not much comprehensive economic 'literature' about a new paradigm, but more and more economists, often in contact and interaction with other sciences and civil society, have started to question and rethink the current economic paradigm, including its basic assumptions. These economists recognise the new, far-reaching, and complex problems that need to be solved, but for which no real economic solution exists.

There are important individual and collective initiatives associated with the Institute for New Economic Thinking (INET) and the OECD, such as the latter's New Approaches to Economic Challenges (NAEC) initiative. There are also some nodes of this new economic thinking in think tanks, international organisations, and universities. It is very important that these nodes connect in order to develop the new paradigm and to bring it forward via all channels to policymakers and civil society, and to anchor it step by step in global institutions, such as the G20.

It would also be useful not just to use views derived from data and trajectories from the past, but also to imagine top-down scenarios about what to do, depending on how megatrends evolve this or that way. One aspect of a new paradigm would be an advanced long-term view and long-term policy-planning tools, including games based on real data to do simulations of various scenarios. This means to speculate about a bunch of positive or negative futures amongst a large community or within civil society. Such exercises would very much improve the understanding of how different policies would result in different outcomes.

In addition to this more top-down approach, we also need to see what is happening bottom up. New creative developments that implicitly use these approaches are beginning to happen. For example, many politicians are beginning to campaign on policies based on more holistic views of the global, the regional, and the local. They promote a more realistic pricing of environmental and social costs in products and services. These policies require us to move from a simple GDP goal to a better well-being goal. The sharing economy and other new economic concepts are also beginning to spread at the grass roots.

There are more and more new ways beyond individualistic and solipsistic thinking, including new ways of cooperation among individuals, groups, firms, and public entities that also take into account the healthiness of connections and outcomes.

Technology, the environment, and humanity will change while interacting on the way to the new society of the future. To minimise risks and to create options, 'top-down thinking' and 'bottom-up doing' must get together. A multitude of viable and new options – material and immaterial – are key to designing the future and solving the possible severe problems of the 21st century and beyond. Creating a new economics paradigm most of all needs open-minded institutions and adequate budgets – triggered to the future and not to the past.

Finally, how, exactly, such a new economic paradigm would shape the results in principle and in detail has to be worked out, not just in general but also in each project. But if we stick with our old way of thinking, we will never know what we could have done to make the world a better place for living. Economics as such and alone cannot do it. It is just one piece – although a very important one – of the puzzle.

Works Cited

Feyerabend, Paul. *Against Method: Outline of an Anarchistic Theory of Knowledge*. London: Verso Books, 1975.

Kuhn, Thomas. *The Structure of Scientific Revolutions*. Chicago: University of Chicago Press, 1962.

Lucas, Robert E. Jr. 'Econometric Policy Evaluation: A Critique'. In *Theory, Policy, Institutions: Papers from the Carnegie-Rochester Conference Series on Public Policy*, ed. Karl Bruner and Alan Meltzer. North-Holland: Elsevier Science Publishers B.V., 1976, vol. 1, 257-84.

Schumpeter, Joseph. *Capitalism, Socialism and Democracy*. New York: Harper, 1942.

Thaler, Richard H., and Cass R. Sunstein. *Nudge: Improving Decisions about Health, Wealth, and Happiness*. New York: Penguin, 2008.

About the Author

Christian Kastrop, PhD, is Director of the Bertelsmann Foundation, European Program, former Director of Policy Studies Branch, OECD, and teaches at the Free University and the Hertie School of Governance, both in Berlin. He studied economics, psychology, and philosophy at Cologne and Harvard University.

13   Leadership and the Future of Democratic Societies

Martin Mayer and Verena Ringler

Abstract

Today's government leaders have a hell of a job. Even those who overcome fears and try bold and emphatic action find themselves in the theatre of the past. The toolkits for intervention in international affairs seem hopelessly inadequate. However, new approaches have quietly taken the stage. The art of leadership of the 21st century might be found in lateral – rather than linear – diplomacy: understanding the strengths and complementarities of the top-down and the bottom-up worlds, and fostering the synergies between them.

Keywords: diplomacy innovation, European Union, security, human-centred policymaking, design thinking for peace, leadership, mindfulness

No time to wait

In a famous scene from the film *Lawrence of Arabia*, Lawrence and his companion are sitting in the desert when they see a tiny black spot on the horizon. They can't see what it is, and they don't know what to do – so they simply wait. Slowly, the black spot becomes an animal, then a camel, and then, finally, a camel with a man riding on it. They are caught completely unprepared as the man takes out a gun and shoots Lawrence's companion. Their mistake was to wait and see, while any other move would have been better. In the same way, leaders in government and in large organisations – whether the United Nations or the G20, the International Monetary Fund or the Eurogroup, the human rights community or the German, French, or Italian governments – can no longer sit still, waiting until everything becomes clear, and it's too late to act.

Wilkinson, Angela, and Betty Sue Flowers (eds.), *Realistic Hope: Facing Global Challenges*. Amsterdam, Amsterdam University Press, 2018.
DOI: 10.5117/9789462987241_CH13

Meanwhile, an article published in 2017 that barely caught the public's attention reminds us of the power of empathy to help leaders navigate today's fast-paced global environment of uncertainty and turbulence.[1] Rep. Beto O'Rourke, D-Texas, happened to be at an event in San Antonio with Rep. Will Hurd, R-Texas when a snowstorm resulted in the cancellation of their flights back to Washington. They decided to rent a car together and drive the 600 miles back to Washington while holding an ad hoc citizens' dialogue via social media during their journey.

Over the hours of their trip, thousands of people joined in via Facebook and Twitter and followed their adventure. The two politicians engaged in deep conversation, revealing their different points of view on many issues, but also discovering common ground and shared beliefs and values. Afterwards, one of the congressmen told reporters just how anxious he had been when taking the decision to realise that 'crazy' idea, but that ultimately, the experience opened up new perspectives. The politician said he had come to understand that his fellow traveller was someone he could actually work with in the future.

When did it become so strange for leaders to spend some significant amount of time with opponents outside of the political arenas such as televised debates, senate or parliament sessions, or other live-streamed confrontations? When did we start talking about each other via intermitted (social) media instead of talking to each other to find new solutions to our toughest problems? Something is fundamentally flawed in the way leadership is being incorporated, and it's time to explore the phenomenon and find new ways forward.

The tales of Lawrence and his companion and of the two Congressmen remind us of the realities facing leaders today – they must act not knowing the future, and they must find common ground in the context of deep divides. But leaders feel they do not have enough time for listening, exploring, or consulting because they live within a fast-paced, complex environment where only high-frequency decision-making counts, and where unpredictability has taken over as the main trait of business, institutional, and media landscapes. Even if they move towards action, they find themselves in a theatre of the past, within out-dated frameworks. The toolkits for intervention seem hopelessly inadequate.

In their extensive investigation, starting in 2015 under the Churchill 21st Century Statesmanship Global Leaders Programme, Nik Gowing and Chris Langdon interviewed more than 60 global leaders from corporations, governments, and public institutions and engaged with hundreds more through leadership conferences and seminars to explore why leaders have

---

1   Zorthian.

appeared more unable or unwilling than ever to anticipate the biggest issues of our time.[2] Since 2014 these have included the new assertiveness of President Putin's Russia, the rise of the so-called 'Islamic state', the sudden oil price crash, growing cyber vulnerability, and the exponential growth in mass migration and people movements. In their conversations held even before the votes on Brexit and Trump, many of the top leaders had confided anonymously their apprehension of the future and how scared they had become. Gowing and Langdon conclude that the old assumptions and models on which leaders and their systems relied are broken and discredited. They suggest nine key reasons for missing out on crucial disruptions and changes, including being overwhelmed by multiple, intense pressures, institutional conformity, wilful blindness, groupthink, risk aversion, fear of career-limiting moves, reactionary mind-sets, denial, and cognitive overload and dissonance.

National and international leadership today is a complex affair as global governance proves harder to negotiate. Not only are there more participating state and non-state actors to take into consideration, but the rise of nationalism, populism, and other immediate challenges at home make focusing on global and long-term problems more difficult. Many leaders, however, do connect with their human compass, just like the two Congressmen: they do suspect that empathy, mindfulness, and inclusive governance are necessary for purposeful interventions into messy situations.

The challenge of governance in relation to Western democracies is nothing new, of course. In the 1970s, the powerful Trilateral Commission declared that governability was the central dilemma facing Western democracies: 'The demands on governments grow while the capacity of democratic governments stagnates'.[3] This was understood as a combination of both government overload – the result of citizens asking for too much – and government incapacity – the result of obsolescent institutions seeking to serve the needs of modern states.

Whereas the Trilateral Commission bemoaned overload and incapacity, today's challenges are of a different order. One notices dynamics of disengagement and ossification – citizens vacating the polis or reinventing it elsewhere, and governments that are too stiff-jointed to respond imaginatively to the issues with which they are confronted.[4] Participation in conventional electoral processes in many established democracies is in steady decline, as is public trust in politicians and public institutions.

2   Gowing and Langdon.
3   Benhabib *et al.*
4   *Ibid.*

Many citizens have lost their faith, sometimes abandoning 'normal' politics altogether and sometimes building networks of political participation and discussion outside the boundaries of traditional politics.

Foresight thinkers have coined different terms to describe this new global environment and the new breed of interconnected and global problems we are facing today. Examples include the terms 'VUCA'[5] (volatile, uncertain, complex, ambiguous) or 'TUNA'[6] (turbulent, uncertain, novel, ambiguous). In this era of unpredictable uncertainty, small shifts in social, technological, political, economic, and ecological trends can carry huge and cascading implications for the success or failure of a specific policy design or implementation programme. There is a large consensus among leading global thinkers across the board that the problems we have generated over the course of the 20th century have created a dangerous cocktail of both exogenous threats (such as climate-related global shifts) and endogenous turbulence (driven by increased complexities within many societies with more and more diverse interacting actors). Instead of technical problems, we are now facing complex social challenges.

Two extreme versions of leadership responses to these challenges can be observed. On the one hand, leaders elected based on a programme of radical change, such as the UK Brexit administration or President Trump in the US, try to impose their transformational agenda, arousing emotions and avoiding any form of rational argumentation for their decisions, often hitting institutional barriers of checks and balances along the way. In international relations, this quest for radical change results in transactionalism and the undermining of a rules-based world order. On the other hand, many leaders heavily rely on an 'evidence-based' approach to public policymaking.[7]

---

5   'VUCA' is an acronym used to describe or reflect on the volatility, uncertainty, complexity and ambiguity of general conditions and situations. The notion of VUCA was introduced by the US Army War College to describe the more volatile, uncertain, complex, and ambiguous multilateral world that resulted from the end of the Cold War. The common usage of the term VUCA began in the 1990s and derives from military vocabulary. It has been subsequently used in emerging ideas in strategic leadership that apply in a wide range of organisations, including everything from for-profit corporations to education (Wikipedia).

6   Ramirez and Wilkinson.

7   This is curious because, in fact, awareness of the socially messy, puzzling, or 'wicked' problem nature of today's significant challenges has become more widespread in the futures literature in recent decades. From the 1970s onwards, the need for new approaches to policy and change management has been highlighted both through continuous innovation in futures practices and in the development of other fields of scholarship such as systems thinking or complexity theory. There is also a need for a shift in futures thinking, from adapting to changing environments to continuous learning, redesign, and anticipatory innovation. See, for example, Rittel and Webber, Emery and Trist, and Ackoff *et al.*

The most influential actors on the global stage, including international organisations, national governments, and global think tanks, are still trying to fix their forecasting tools with improved conditional projections and enhanced global data models. With improvements in computational time, big data collection and analysis, and more sophisticated research methods, the story goes, we can avoid forecasting errors in the future and anticipate what's coming. Yet proponents of human-centred policymaking, including Christian Bason (Danish Design Centre), Luca Gatti (CHÔRA), David Puttnam (in his role as founding executive director of Nesta), Catherine Fieschi (Counterpoint), Tim Dixon (Purpose Europe), and Harald Welzer (FuturZwei), have all suggested, through their academic, public, and practical work, that more quantitative research alone will not solve the global leadership and governance questions.

How can global leaders step up, claim power, and reinvent and transform our world in a more sustainable, responsible, and inclusive way? How can cooperation thrive in an era where globalising and nativist tendencies coexist and fuel clashes of value and belief systems? And how can leaders better understand and navigate both the 'hard' factors of globalisation (and its nativist backlash), such as flows and politics of capital, people, and goods, as well as the 'softer' yet equally important aspects like information, principles, values, and narratives?

Opening up to futures thinking and using the future to refresh the present

Complex global systems, such as the ones presented in the different chapters of this book, are difficult to grasp, with lots of feedback loops and unpredictable impacts across scales. In such a constrained context, it becomes increasingly difficult to effect transformation unilaterally. We know that we cannot expect anyone to have all the answers, and yet the political discourse across the world is staged as a competitive platform, expressed through heated debates about who is right or wrong, or who is smarter, or who has moral authority, and who has not.

So where will global leadership come from in a multipolar world of empowered citizens? To answer this question, we need to explore what good leadership looks like. This is particularly difficult since there is no universal theory of leadership or agreement on how good, bad, better, or great leadership can be evaluated or measured. Many different actors, depending on their roles, beliefs, values, experiences, and education, have very different expectations that are not always easy to align. For some it is about defining and communicating an ambitious vision for the future; for others it is about the definition of pathways and strategies to achieve this aspirational future; others again look for the personal traits of honesty and integrity of the exemplary leader.

Betty Sue Flowers has developed a helpful framework that Angela Wilkinson has used to help understand why different stories of leadership coexist. According to Flowers, there are five different myths that shape Western culture.[8]

Mythology	Hero	Religious	Democratic/ Scientific	Economic	Ecological
Ideal	Excellence	Goodness	Truth	Growth	Health (Wholeness)
Behaviour	Competition	Obedience	Reason	Maximising advantage	Communica-tion
Actors	Heroes	Saints Prophets	Philosophers Scientists	Consumers Business	Creators
Communica-tion	Stories	Scripture Prayer	Mathematics Logical arguments	Images Numbers Data	Self-expression

In applying this matrix to leadership, Wilkinson says:

> In the classical Hero myth, a leader was an individual who tried against the odds to achieve the impossible. Success was not guaranteed. It was the competition itself that was important, as it still is in the Olympics – to bring out the best and reward the best, so everyone tries to win. But the loser, too, has honour.
>
> In the Religious Myth, we see the rise of the cult leader as an infallible and unquestionable source of justice and wisdom, who has been chosen by a higher authority to form and nurture the goodness of a whole community. Obedience to the leader's ideology is demanded from all. The penalties for non-compliance can be very harsh and membership of a cult community is not open to all. Examples of modern cult leadership include ISIS and North Korea.
>
> In the Democratic/Scientific myth, a leader is a wise and honest broker of the truth. The quest for knowledge and the truth is the engine of power. Nothing is ever taken for granted, everything needs to be tested and explored.

8   For an explanation of the matrix, see Flowers.

In the Economic myth, a leader is always one step ahead of the competition: winning is everything. A leader who fails, is blamed.

In the Ecological myth, leadership is a whole system capability. Entrepreneurial and generous, individuals play their part in enabling new and shared value.[9]

To be effective and enable large-scale system transformations, leaders will have to figure out according to which myth they are being held accountable and find a relevant and compelling story. To do so, reflection, pausing, focusing, and mindfulness as well as strategic conversations are needed, particularly at the top level of governance systems and institutions.

Combined, these 'softer' approaches lead to a process of interactive and immersive learning, which takes place in imagined future situations, and enable a more open, explicit, shared, and flexible sense of the future. A mix of objectivity, creativity, and empathy is needed to forge common ground and sustain new and more effective collaboration. Empathetic and engaging processes of involvement and caring are keys to create an effective collaborative environment.

To help with these challenges, demand for open foresight approaches to trigger collaborative action has been rising dramatically in the political and public sectors. The profound changes of the international environment due to the Brexit, the US presidency, and state or even constitutional capture in many countries around the world are expected to continue this trend.

The essential driver for any such process has been, and will remain, trust. Yet trust is in decline around the globe. One 2017 survey of more than 33,000 people in 28 countries shows the largest-ever drop in trust in 'the system' (made up of business, government, NGOs, and the media). Globally, 53 per cent of those surveyed felt that the system is not working for them, while another 32 per cent were unsure: 'If we had the ability to step back and view the deterioration of trust dispassionately, I think we'd judge that our system is heading towards significant reorganisation and even possible collapse'.[10]

At the same time, leaders still face the challenge of preparing for the future, and thus of being more open and ready to cope with what the future will bring. To do so, we believe that three key ingredients are needed: competence, trust-building, and emotional intelligence.

Competence in the current world requires a more open and exploratory yet action-oriented foresight approach to drive socio-political transformation.

9   Wilkinson, p. 32.
10   McNulty.

One prerequisite for this quality of competence is the mastery of the modern futures toolkit, which links foresight, innovation, and policy design in an integrated way.[11] The aim of this approach is no longer to better predict the future but to imagine and envision alternative outcomes and prepare for them, provide a space for better strategic conversations, help leaders to engage with a wide range of stakeholders, and stimulate and support the transformation processes.

Just as in the private sector, prototyping of new solutions and iterating through a 'test and learn' approach are ways to success. It's no longer enough to use foresight methods to better understand the contextual environment and build a shared normative vision for the future. Rather, the challenge of our time is to create momentum for transformational change and facilitate collaborative action. To have real impact, foresight needs to be complemented by powerful innovation processes, including service and experience design thinking, agile management (and 'scrum'), SmartMobs, and HackDays.

Building trust requires character and attitude. Recent messy situations in global governance theatres ranging from the US to Turkey, and from climate diplomacy to the G20 summits, have powerfully demonstrated the limits of technocracy and evidence-based policymaking. Empathy and mindfulness, i.e., the ability to pay attention to others' thoughts and feelings without judging them, are essential prerequisites to trust-building and therefore pathways to better solutions. Trust-building can start with simple switches from reading papers to reading minds in an encounter, from briefings to conversations beyond the brief, from presentations to public debates.

Consider one major project that several think tanks have been realising in Europe for the past five years, following the plummeting of trust, especially between South European and German leaders in the context of the Eurozone crisis following the global financial debt crisis in 2008. Once two to three dozen members of national parliaments were given the chance for real-life encounters and exchanges in a safe space (mostly 'firsts' even in long political careers), they attributed high value to these opportunities helping them to 'change perspectives'.[12] In general, particularly when refer-

---

11   Chapter 14 in this book about Slovenia's journey from vision to strategy to action planning is a powerful example of the integrated application of the multi-methods foresight toolbox at the level of the creation of a National Development Plan of a European country.

12   One study among participating members of parliament of several EU member states revealed: 'Learning from others by exchanging perspectives is an important aspect of the programme that was mentioned in almost all the MP interviews' (Schröer and Händel, p. 8). The programme offered 'a platform to discuss mostly European issues in an international European context with your European peers, in a way that you usually don't discuss matters in your own country

ences to 'bubbles', 'echo chambers', and 'government-citizen disconnect' are increasing, leaders as well as their staffers might benefit from getting out of their office buildings and away from choreographed encounters with 'the public' to (re)connect with the world of ordinary citizens through real-life immersion and ethnographic approaches, including expeditions, excursions, and fact-finding missions.[13]

Emotional intelligence, i.e., the capacity to express and manage feelings (our own and those of the people we live, interact, and work with) will hopefully continue to make humans a unique species on earth. Already in today's service economy, most jobs require emotional skills, whether working directly with customers or collaborating with colleagues on a project, and job growth in the US in the last decades was mainly found in areas requiring relatively high degrees of social skills. In a world where robots and algorithms push humans out of cognitive work, there is a big opportunity for societies to shift focus and resources from an efficiency-driven to a people-driven value system. Given that acquiring emotional intelligence is not so much a matter of better formal education as a question of personal commitment and genuine care, this requires a profound change of perception and the willingness to question current paradigms of value creation.

So, the question is can emotional intelligence be trained? So far, the most-studied effort to train people in emotional skills has been to increase empathy in doctors. Over the past decade, medical schools and hospitals have taken note of a broad body of literature showing that when doctors can put themselves in their patients' shoes, it leads to better clinical outcomes, more satisfied patients, and fewer burnt-out physicians. And there's evidence this skill can be taught. A 2014 review found that communication training

or political context. That also means especially in my country where we have a certain way to discuss political matters within your political group, the Mercator European Dialogue offers you a place for an intellectual broader discussion. For me, that helps in your arguments in national politics' (Schröer and Händel, p. 10). Also: 'Participating in those meetings made me meet with colleagues from other parliaments and also other political perspectives, exchanging different opinions is very interesting, because some issues are differently seen in different countries and hearing it from people not only reading in the newspaper, you can hear it from a completely different perspective. It widens your horizon, you can look at the things from a different way, and you might even change your mind on some issues' (p. 8). Learning did not occur only by listening to other MPs' perspectives, but also by sharing methodologies and how each of them takes action in their daily work as an MP. '[W]hen we worked on the refugee crisis, there was a Portuguese MP the last time we were in Barcelona with CIDOB, who was explaining to me what he organised in committee of the Portuguese parliament, like different hearings, using people from the street, citizens just to come to the parliament as well. So I thought this is good, so I suggested doing it here in my own parliament' (p. 12).

13   Schröer and Händel, pp. 22-23.

and role-playing boosted medical students' and doctors' empathy levels in eight of ten high-quality studies.[14] There is also a growing focus on 'social and emotional learning' (SEL) for schoolchildren. While these programmes are still too often marketed as ways to reduce violence, not methods for developing crucial human abilities, the conversations around those issues raise interesting questions.

Whole-systems innovation requires new collaborative formats that build on complex problem-solving competencies, trust-building mechanisms, and emotional intelligence to harness synergies among the relevant stakeholders. Most approaches to address difficult and complex challenges involve the collaboration of different communities of experts, thinkers, doers, makers, and tinkerers applying their skills and energy to accelerate the work of cause-led innovators and change agents. Managed well, these approaches enable diverse groups of people to build on and support each other's ideas, create new solutions, and test and improve them in fast iteration cycles to achieve real measurable impacts on people's lives. The techniques applied are attempts to solve challenges collaboratively – on- and offline – through gigs or sprints (24- to 48-hour creative collaboration events) or permanent communities.

For example, a hackathon is an event, typically lasting several days, in which highly diverse people with complementary skills meet to engage in a process of collaborative innovation, rapid design, and fail-fast prototyping of new products, services, and nowadays also public policies (solutions in the wider sense).[15] In today's public policy arena, using hackathons and variations, such as Open Situation Rooms, is now an emerging practice.

Realising hope: Seeds planted and evidence of new realities already being co-created

So, what about the real world? How can we translate our insights into practice to harness our societies' collective ideas and potential? The following examples highlight just a few of the many innovative approaches linked specifically to breakthrough configurations in governance contexts.

14   Kelm *et al.*

15   The 'hackathon' practice originated in IT project development to improve and debug new software applications by enabling faster feedback between programmer developers, providers, and users. In recent years, this way of collaborative and highly dynamic cooperation of various actors has been adopted as a standard approach to innovation in products, services, business models, processes, and user experience.

1   The Open Government Partnership

The Open Government Partnership (OGP)[16] is a multilateral initiative that aims to secure concrete commitments from governments to promote transparency, empower citizens, fight corruption, and harness new technologies to strengthen governance. In the spirit of multi-stakeholder collaboration, OGP is overseen by a steering committee, including representatives of governments and civil society organisations. To become a member of the OGP, participating countries must endorse a high-level open government declaration, deliver a country action plan developed with public consultation, and commit to independent reporting on their progress going forward. The OGP was formally launched in 2011, when the eight founding governments (Brazil, Indonesia, Mexico, Norway, the Philippines, South Africa, the United Kingdom, and the US) endorsed the Open Government Declaration and announced their action plans. Since 2011, the OGP has welcomed the commitment of 67 additional governments to join the partnership. In total, 75 OGP participating countries and fifteen subnational governments have offered over 2500 commitments to make their governments more open and accountable.

2   Open Situation Rooms

The German foreign ministry conducted more than two-dozen 'Open Situation Rooms'[17] in different cities and at different conferences since 2014. In such a process, an ambassador or a department leader gathers with up to 35 citizens from different walks of life and professional backgrounds, who can join the conversation via a simple application process with the funding organisation Stiftung Mercator. An Open Situation Room begins with the sponsor raising a challenging question, for example, 'How can we improve the situation of refugees in transit countries?' Then, the 35 participants develop many possible answers and ideas in response to the question. They do this in a structured, fast, and facilitated process. Towards the end, the group switches from quantity to quality and focuses on deeper thinking around the best ideas, which are then explored further with the foreign policy decision-maker.

A living prototype of 'design thinking for peace', the Open Situation Room has become a cherished supplemental forum to established crisis response mechanisms and strategic thinking about national and European foreign policy issues. Three aspects create the value of this format to the foreign

---

16   Open Government Partnership.
17   Open Situation Room.

affairs ministry. First, it enables contact and connection between the world of diplomacy and the world of ordinary citizens. Second, it enables wide and deep foreign policy thinking that harnesses the brainpower and collective intelligence of a mixed, ad hoc pool of advisors (the citizen group) whose ideas and considerations enrich the policy formation process. It is crucial to include unconventional, contemporary, and even seemingly paradoxical ideas in the discussion. Third, the voluntary, ad hoc nature of the process and the absence of any mandate or official role for the Open Situation Room keeps it refreshingly unsullied and free from path dependencies or vested interests. Just like other new approaches, the project was first piloted in the 2014 full-fledged 'Review Year' of the Federal Foreign Office, which resulted ultimately in the creation of a new unit in the foreign ministry.[18]

3   *Open State*

Open State is an initiative (located at a Makerspace in Berlin) that aims to harness the potential of open innovation in responding to complex political and societal challenges. The group is 'designing tomorrow's resilient society' by building real-life prototypes trying to prove that alternatives to the seemingly unshakable status quo can be possible. The format enhances the typical product- or service-oriented innovation process by including social tools that tap into the collective intelligence of large participant groups in their work.

For example, the group built an 'international community' and a local crew of supporters to set up Refugee Open Cities. Over nine months the project team settled in a refugee shelter in Berlin and interviewed the inhabitants about their needs and skills. Refugee Open Cities 1.0 ended with a five-day building festival and 150 volunteers who turned an abandoned top floor into a 'village of opportunities'; that team is now developing self-sustaining social business concepts for the new ideas.

In another project, the group organised a five-week innovation camp together with OuiShare (a French company and think tank promoting the sharing economy), inviting more than 300 participants to work on twelve

---

18   In a 2015 address to the Bundestag, German Foreign Minister Steinmeier also announced structural changes in the Federal Foreign Office: 'Crises will tend to be the norm in the next 10 to 15 years. We are responding to this by restructuring our organisation and creating a separate Crisis Prevention, Stabilisation and Postconflict Peacebuilding Directorate-General'. He also said the plan was to 'pool all of the skills that allow us to deal more intensively with the entire spectrum of crises, not only acute conflict phases. We want to learn from the experience of our Crisis Response Centre. However, the aim is that the new directorate-general will be far more active at the policy level' (Steinmeier).

open-source hardware projects. In the context of the 2015 United Nations Climate Change Conference, these projects were the 'proof of concept' (hence the camp name 'POC21') that a climate-safe future can already be built with our own hands. From a $30 wind turbine made of scratch materials to a shower loop that filters and circles its water instantly, the POC21 prototypes inspired more than 25 million media contacts and involved 50 international partners. The open-source product blueprints were downloaded over half a million times.

In September 2017, Open State organised a five-day 'political innovation camp' in Nieklitz, a rural area in Germany's Mecklenburg-Vorpommern region. Convening democracy actors from a wide range of backgrounds and political ideologies, the aim was to test, challenge, improve, and build effective ideas 'for tomorrow's democracy' and a more resilient European future. 'Where are the blind spots in modern-day democratic inventions, which are inhibiting real change? Which strategies are fostering or hindering solutions? How is sustainable transformation possible?' were some of the questions addressed. Several dozen people organised their co-habitation in the camp as well as working alongside on these questions, inspired by a quest for human-centred policymaking and deep introspection into their own assumptions.[19]

4   TechPlomacy

In 2017, Denmark posted the world's first-ever 'tech ambassador' to Silicon Valley who is going to lead a new Danish foreign policy initiative called 'tech diplomacy' (or #TechPlomacy). Foreign Minister Anders Samuelsen said in a press event:

> It is crucial that Denmark positions itself ambitiously in the exponential tech development taking place these years. Technology and digitization is global in its essence, and it has profound impact on all aspects of our society. The tech ambassador will spearhead our efforts to establish a more comprehensive dialogue with a broad spectrum of tech actors – companies, research institutions, countries, cities and organisations. Both in order to plug-in and get a better understanding of the development internationally, and to promote Danish interests and values on this important agenda. We have experienced great interest in this new Danish initiative, also from the tech environment. The perspectives are very promising.[20]

19   Open State.
20   Ministry of Foreign Affairs of Denmark.

5   *Unconventional EU Summitry*

In 2012, a multi-stakeholder process was carried out by several European foundations to decipher pathways out of Europe's crisis that at that point had increased the tensions between many member states. The Network of European Foundations (NEF) hired a team of futures specialists to design and facilitate a three-day 'Unconventional Summit on the Future of Europe', at the core of which were practices of 'collaborative' and 'transformational' foresight.[21] The NEF starting position was that European integration, overall, was too good to fail. Convening seemingly unlikely allies in an era of crisis seemed necessary. Those allies were considered to be people who were already playing or were soon likely to play an important role in bold decision-making, robust social peace, and thriving communal, civic, and economic life in Europe. Fifty participants were scouted and personally invited to a three-day summit. They consisted of two groups, 'EU insiders' (from national and EU public administration and political bodies, think tanks, etc.) and 'EU outsiders' (innovators from a range of disciplines). There was no panel and no PowerPoint. The imperative was not to fix a problem that had been inherited from the past but to clarify and transform future possibilities to overcome inertia and *crises modi*, and to sustain more and more effective collaborative action.

The NEF initiative has proven to be a relevant first step in ongoing attempts to link the parallel fields of foresight, design, strategy, and innovation in Europe's socio-political arena. These have become essential as functional contributions to governance. The NEF prototype presents the advent of a much-needed switch to solve 'wicked' governance questions of the future less through mini-stakeholder multilateralism (e.g., the UN Security Council or the European Council), but rather through multi-stakeholder mini-lateralism (e.g., regional groups, ad hoc civilian intervention groups, or target-oriented, multi-stakeholder groups). The first approach has been necessary in a century where consensus was worth the price of laborious state-to-state diplomacy; the second approach is necessary in a century where regional problem-solving seems worth the trade-offs on universalism and legitimacy as we knew it.

6   *The Slovenia Strategy*[22]

Slovenia is currently working through a unique vision-to-strategy-to action process. Moving from a strategic long-term vision to concrete actions with

---

21   Wilkinson *et al.*

22   See Chapter 14 of this book for a fuller discussion of this project.

transformative potentialities requires significant innovations and a strong commitment to the application of a truly integrated approach and the development of new institutional settings. These innovations include adopting a whole-of-government approach to avoid policy silos, the alignment of various national strategies and fields of expertise (economy, society, environment, security, development, etc.), a strong coordination of multiple stakeholders at different levels (national, regional, local), the application of participatory approaches, various forms of consultations and engagements, support for a long-term planning horizon, openness to resetting strategic direction along the way, and the adoption of multidimensional performance and measurement frameworks to orient and follow up policy actions.

7   *Shop Talk Live*

Shop Talk Live, founded by Chaka Lindsey and Theo Wilson, with chapters in Colorado and Virginia, is an organisation that hosts bi-monthly gatherings in select barbershops and beauty salons, places where people are used to talking about important topics of concern to the local community. According to its founders, Shop Talk Live is an important platform for dialogue and healing. The conversations are open to anyone, and frequently, but not always, focus on issues affecting the African-American community. Two weeks after President Trump issued his controversial 'Muslim ban', Shop Talk Live hosted a conversation between US Army veteran Lacy McDonald and Ari Noorzai, a Muslim American, to discuss the human costs of the US foreign policy and its military interventions in the Middle East. The setting was particularly charged since Lacy McDonald, an African-American soldier, was sent to Ari Noorzai's ancestral home, Afghanistan, to fight a war on behalf of America. The space is designed to favour this kind of courageous conversation, bringing together people with very different roots, experiences, viewpoints, and value systems who are eager to confront them in a respectful conversation. It is empathy in action and the starting point for better mutual understanding. It is trying to keep the tradition of open, engaged dialogue alive by providing a safe space for people to feel comfortable having difficult conversations. Talking to each other might not be enough, but, as Theo Wilson says:

> [O]ne of the best ways to overcome difficult situations is to have courageous conversations with difficult people, people who do not see the world the same way that you see the world. [...] [T]hese conversations may indeed be the key to the upgrade of humanity because remember language was the first form of virtual reality, it is literally a symbolic representation of

the physical world and through this device we changed the physical world, conversations stop violence, conversations start countries, conversations build bridges and when the chips are down, conversations are the last tool that humans use before they pick up the guns![23]

Pathways and pitfalls

Using multiple methods to link foresight, design, and innovation is necessary for co-creating a better future. The mastery of the modern futures toolkit is crucial and depends on an understanding of the strengths and limitations of a variety of methods, an ability to effectively tailor them to the purpose at hand, and the wisdom to avoid conflating or confusing one with another (for example, scenarios are not forecasts or visions).

Building better futures for democratic societies requires a more inclusive approach than the conventional, linear method of speaking truth-to-power across the science-policy interface. Resolving asylum and migration crises, enabling a global energy transition, and progressing global sustainable development are not simple problems but puzzling and messy challenges.

Open innovation, better collaboration, and lasting transformations are overdue in public sector institutions, including in the international public sector as well as in diplomacy. However, to generate acceptance, and ideally to produce a systemic impact, a whole set of challenges needs to be addressed from the very beginning. Buy-in for innovation involving public sector institutions cannot be achieved by technical means or contracting agents alone. Engendering trust and forging new common ground between participants and organisations with different cultures and interests requires attention to constructive conflict and shared learning, rather than a simple push for rapid but shallow consensus building. Thus, caution about fast futures processes is needed. Listening is painful, especially for established experts who are rewarded for knowing the answer rather than asking better questions. Shared, societal learning requires immersion in new and, at first, often uncomfortable ideas.

The full process needs to be designed, understood, and managed

The actual co-creation event is the most energetic, but not the most impactful part of any foresight-to-action process. Possible sponsors or conveners need to be aware that multi-stakeholder settings tend to generate a high level of

---

23 Wilson.

energy and mobilisation just before and during the actual physical (or virtual) collaboration spaces (exploration, ideation, design). For an experienced process design and facilitation team, the main challenge is rarely related to the engagement with the various stakeholders during the strategic dialogues, but rather to the creation of conditions for continued collaboration once the event is over and participants move on with their lives. Only if such events are clearly defined as steps in an overarching process can the intended transformations take form. Change does not happen overnight, and for this reason the collaborative event must be embedded into a continuous and carefully managed (meta)change process. Support and sponsoring measures can range from soft factors, such as branding, convening, liaising, and networking opportunities, to stakeholder engagement strategies or the provision of seed funding for specific initiatives.

Generally, there appears to be a kind of dynamics inherent to public multi-stakeholder agencies (administrations, think tanks, NGOs) that make the funding of closed-loop, project-based initiatives with a clear end much easier to support than open-loop, ongoing, and iterative processes. Also, public agencies and foundations tend to fund research rather than application. Yet learning with futures and collaborative innovation deal with sense-making, experimentation, and execution, all at the same time, through quick iterations and multiple-loop learning processes. Project sponsors should therefore start to think in slightly longer cycles with a 'think-test-learn-adapt' approach, committing to a clearly defined level of support over the entire process chain to move from a single-loop towards a double- or triple-loop learning process.

Conclusions

Empathy – the ability to be aware of the feelings, thoughts, and experiences of another – is key to helping us find common ground to co-create a better future. Good and inclusive governance therefore needs to support the expression and development of basic human traits at work such as empathy, mindfulness, and mutual trust.

Our collective ability to identify with or understand the perspective, experiences, or motivations of others and to comprehend and share another individual's view can be supported by new habits and practices both in corporate and public governance situations and through more courageous face-to-face conversations, field immersions, learning expeditions, and fact-finding missions as well as discussions beyond standardised briefings and business meetings.

Leaders who aim to navigate their organisations, institutions, or branches through unchartered waters might want to focus both on the top-down, grand-scale solutions and on the bottom-up, emerging solution spaces, becoming the bridge builders between these two approaches, and thereby harnessing the strengths and power of both. The art of leadership of the 21st century might therefore be found in lateral – rather than linear – diplomacy: understanding the strengths and complementarities of the two approaches, and fostering the synergies between them.

Works Cited

Ackoff, Russell L., Jason Magidson, and Herbert J. Addison. *Idealized Design: Creating an Organization's Future*. Upper Saddle River: Prentice Hall, 2006.

Benhabib, Seyla, *et al.* 'The Democratic Disconnect: Citizenship and Accountability in the Transatlantic Community'. In *Transatlantic Academy 2012-2013 Collaborative Report*. Washington, DC: Transatlantic Academy, 2013, pp. 3-4.

Emery, F.E., and E.L. Trist. 'The Causal Texture of Organisational Environments'. *Human Relations* 18.1, 1 Feb. 1965, pp. 21-32.

Flowers, Betty Sue. 'The American Dream and the Economic Myth'. Fetzer Institute, 2007. Reprinted in *Huffington Post*, 10 July 2013, http://www.huffingtonpost.com/betty-sue-flowers/the-american-dream-and-th_b_3575951.html. Accessed 17 Mar. 2018.

Gowing, Nik and Chris Langdon. 'Thinking the Unthinkable: A New Imperative for Leadership in the Digital Age'. 16 Jan. 2017. https://www.cimaglobal.com/Documents/Thought_leadership_docs/Enterprise_governance/Thinking-the-Unthinkable-cima-report.pdf. Accessed 5 July 2018.

Kelm, Zak, James Womer, Jennifer K. Walter, and Chris Feudtner. 'Interventions to Cultivate Physician Empathy: A Systematic Review'. *BMC Medical Education* 14.219, 14 Oct. 2014. https://bmcmededuc.biomedcentral.com/articles/10.1186/1472-6920-14-219. Accessed 2 Nov. 2017.

McNulty, Eric. 'How to Lead When Global Trust Is Plummeting'. *Strategy+Business*, 5 June 2017. https://www.strategy-business.com/blog/How-to-Lead-When-Global-Trust-Is-Plummeting?gko=d18b3. Accessed 2 Nov. 2017.

Ministry of Foreign Affairs of Denmark. 'Denmark names first ever tech ambassador'. 25 May 2017. http://um.dk/en/news/newsdisplaypage/?newsid=60eaf005-9f87-46f8-922a-1cf20c5b527a. Accessed 31 Jan. 2018.

Open Government Partnership. https://www.opengovpartnership.org/. Accessed 31 Jan. 2018.

Open Situation Room. https://www.open-situation-room.de/en/. Accessed 5 July 2018.

Open State. http://openstate.cc. Accessed 17 Mar. 2018.

Ramirez, Rafael, and Angela Wilkinson. *Strategic Reframing: The Oxford Scenario Planning Approach.* Oxford: Oxford University Press, 2016.

Rittel, H., and M. Webber. 'Dilemmas in a General Theory of Planning'. *Policy Sciences* 4 (1973), pp. 155-69.

Schröer, Andreas, and Richard Händel. 'Evaluation Report on Mercator European Dialogue'. Internal report for Mercator Foundation, Darmstadt: University of Applied Sciences EH Darmstadt and IZGS, Institut für Zukunftsfragen der Gesundheits- und Sozialwirtschaft der EHD, July 2016.

Steinmeier, Frank-Walter. 'Conclusions from Review 2014 – Crisis, Order, Europe'. Press release, 25 Feb. 2015. https://www.auswaertiges-amt.de/blob/692042/cef1f6308ebdb0d2d7c62725089c4198/review-2014-data.pdf. Accessed 5 July 2018.

Wikipedia. 'Vuca' *Wikipedia.* https://en.wikipedia.org/wiki/Volatility,_uncertainty,_complexity_and_ambiguity. Accessed 2 Nov. 2017.

Wilkinson, Angela. 'The Future of Leadership in Europe'. In *Shaping the Future: Thoughts on the Future of Society and Governance.* European Policy and Analysis System, 2016.

Wilkinson, Angela, Martin Mayer, and Verena Ringler. 'Collaborative Futures: Integrating Foresight with Design in Large Scale Innovation Processes – Seeing and Seeding the Futures of Europe'. *Journal of Futures Studies* 18.4 (2014), pp. 1-26. http://jfsdigital.org/wp-content/uploads/2014/06/Articles1-Wilkinson.pdf. Accessed 2 Nov. 2017.

Wilson, Theo E.J. Ted Talk posted 14 Aug. 2017. https://www.youtube.com/watch?v=FdHJwoveVNY. Accessed 3 Dec. 2017.

Zorthian, Julia. 'The Future of Bipartisanship in Congress Might Be Roadtrips'. *Time*, 16 March 2017. http://time.com/4703631/beto-o-rourke-will-hurd-road-trip-congress/. Accessed 2 Nov. 2017.

About the Authors

Martin Mayer is Co-founder of YouMeO, a strategic foresight, design, and innovation lab based in Paris. He works on different initiatives across various sectors, building leadership capacity through catalysing better strategic conversations.

Verena Ringler is Director of European Commons and former International Affairs Director of Stiftung Mercator. With previous stints as associate editor of *Foreign Policy* and as deputy head of press with a diplomatic team of the EU Council to Kosovo (2006-2009), Ringler specialises in diplomacy and democracy innovation in Europe.

14 Prototyping the Future: A New Approach to Whole-of-Society Visioning

Alenka Smerkolj and Timotej Šooš

Abstract

Slovenia made a commitment to a comprehensive new vision and development strategy that would meet the shifting needs of society and service new international commitments on sustainable, inclusive, and responsible development and growth. Rather than moving faster and alone through the usual, expert-led review process, the Slovenian government courageously embarked on an ambitious, whole-of-society, participatory foresight initiative. The Vision of Slovenia is a 'provotype' – a provocative prototype introduced in the early exploratory phases of the design development process to cause a reaction. It has caused a reaction, it has provoked and engaged many, and, most importantly, it has opened up a path of imagining possible futures of a nation and a country.

Keywords: vision, democracy, social contract, trust, provotype, strategy, Slovenia

> *The future is only scary if we try to avoid it.*
> – Simon Sinek

The global trust deficit

Democracies around the world – even the richest and oldest – are struggling with an ironic and growing challenge. Even though democracies are designed to reflect 'the will of the people', citizens in these countries are growing increasingly distrustful of their governments. Many feel their governments are dysfunctional in their ability to make and implement policies and that

Wilkinson, Angela, and Betty Sue Flowers (eds.), *Realistic Hope: Facing Global Challenges*. Amsterdam, Amsterdam University Press, 2018.
DOI: 10.5117/9789462987241_CH14

their governments do not create policies with their best interests in mind. Some are even turning to populist politicians who promise more effective, even if more authoritarian, governance. The leader of China is trusted more than the leader of the US.[1]

In this context, it's worth looking at an experiment undertaken by a democracy with a long history of distrust – an experiment that offers some realistic hope that steps can be taken to strengthen the bonds of trust between governments and citizens.

A small country adrift in a global ocean of changes

Slovenia is a small country, linguistically defined and with a unique history. It is well endowed with natural resources – water, forests, good soils – and has a favourable geo-strategic location at the crossroads of East and West and between the Mediterranean and Central and South-eastern Europe.

Since its independence in 1991, the country has made steady progress in economic and social development. It has achieved its initial independence ambitions: joining the European Union in 2004, introducing the euro as the national currency in 2007, and joining the OECD in 2010. Living up to its inherent societal value of peaceful coexistence – which is enshrined in the seventh stanza of the national anthem – Slovenia is an active international partner in global efforts for peace and security and respect for human rights and the rule of law.

Despite its natural endowments and development successes, however, Slovenian society is not in great shape. It is characterised by low levels of trust and life satisfaction, and disruptions caused by new technologies. An ageing society and an increase in inequality are impeding further productivity gains. The most talented people are leaving the country.

While Slovenia remains strongly committed to the European project, Europe's uneven and slow recovery from the financial crisis of 2007-2008 within Europe, an expected European migration crisis, the Brexit process, and a re-emergence of tensions between Russia and the West have all contributed to a European identity crisis. EU institutions do not currently serve as an anchor of regional alliance and stability.

Beyond the region, a global context of faster and more fundamental changes impacts Slovenia. A 'TUNA' world – turbulent, uncertain, novel, and ambiguous – is unfolding, characterised by sudden shifts caused by globally

1   Wike *et al.*

cascading and connected economic and environmental changes and crises and political volatility resulting from rising populism and extremism.[2]

Countries across the world, including Slovenia, are grappling with the accelerating, uneven, and uncertain pace of technological innovation under globalisation. Within this context, Slovenia, with its vibrant community of entrepreneurial coders, is on the forefront of the digital revolution in Europe.

The combination of increasing inequality under growth, intergenerational unevenness, regional insecurity, and accelerating technological globalisation adds new pressures on any national government that is committed to delivering prosperity and well-being while meeting an array of international commitments, including the global goal of *no one left behind*, embodied by the UN Sustainable Development Goals and the Paris climate accord of the UN Framework Convention on Climate Change (UNFCCC).

All these changes are particularly challenging to a small country with a big heart. Slovenia has an open-minded culture and inherent shared values of peaceful coexistence and love of nature. But as a new era of digitally enabled governance and flexible cooperation becomes possible, governing also becomes more challenging. Slovenian society and its government are faced with the uncomfortable challenge of renegotiating their expectations of one another and finding more effective ways to come together to co-create the future they want for themselves and their children.

Realising a new future path for the whole of Slovenia in a shifting world requires agile, adaptive, and inclusive policymaking and governance. Achieving this is hard, especially given the emphasis on stability and the presentism bias and incrementalism that characterise best practices in evidence-based policymaking.

In spite of these tendencies, it is possible to prototype new models of society. In Slovenia we have attempted this through introducing an inclusive whole-of-society strategic conversation that directs attention to uncomfortable societal realities. This conversation avoids top-down prescription while enabling bottom-up prototyping of integrated policy solutions. In this process there is a need to invest in addressing the deficit of trust and to develop more coherent polices, both of which are achieved through deep, immersive, and interactive social learning processes. We have had to learn how to walk forward with one foot in the dominant policy paradigm of economic growth and the other in the emerging paradigm of well-living.

---

2   For a discussion of TUNA, see Ramirez and Wilkinson, pp. 6-9.

Opening up the future: Confronting uncomfortable realities in realistic visioning

Our starting point for the exploration of a new future for Slovenia is not rooted in the politics of 'sugar-coating the pill' but instead starts with reflection on four already emerging and less comfortable realities – a rapidly ageing population; a low-trust society; the inability of states to control technology under globalisation; and the paradox of progress.

1   A rapidly ageing population

The Slovenian population is rapidly ageing. Fewer births and increasing longevity, combined with outward migration of talent, mean that 140,000 fewer workers and 130,000 more pensioners are projected by 2030. The growing proportion of the population aged over 65 is expected to exert a significant upward effect on public expenditure on pensions, healthcare, long-term care, and other costs related to ageing. This demographic move to the old will also require changes in social care and employment, as well as appropriate policy responses in many other areas, such as adjusting the environment and services to the needs of older people. The ageing of Slovenia also raises questions about whether this demographic shift could be adequately addressed using an unconventional combination of innovation through new technologies, user-centred policy design, imported talent, and a shift in social norms and behaviours towards new paradigms, such as active ageing policies.[3]

2   Low trust

The Eurobarometer survey comparing trust in national institutions with trust in EU institutions shows that Slovenes have considerably more trust in EU institutions than in national institutions – although in general, they don't really trust any institutions. In addition to distrusting their public institutions, Slovenes also do not have much trust in their fellow citizens.

This 'habit of distrust' has multiple drivers, including an undiscussable and painful history associated with the end of communism. Both trust in the political system and trust in the legal system are decidedly lower in Slovenia than in the other EU and OECD countries. Trust in the legal system in Slovenia is the lowest among the group of European OECD countries.[4] Trust in institutions, in turn, is closely linked to the active participation of the

---

3   Bednas and Kajzer.
4   Eurostat.

population in the drafting of regulations, in elections, etc. Voter turnout in Slovenia, for example, is one of the lowest amongst OECD countries. Between the 2008 and the 2014 parliamentary elections, voter turnout fell by 11.4 per cent to 51.7 per cent.[5] With regard to trust in the political system, Slovenia belongs to a group of very low-trusting countries, including Portugal, Spain, and Greece. Slovenia also performs worse than some of its geographically close peers, such as Hungary, Austria, and the Czech Republic.

The effective functioning of the country and its institutions is crucial for establishing the population's trust and improving the competitiveness of the economy. Economic assessments of the main barriers to doing business in Slovenia are the restrictive labour laws, bureaucracy, and high tax rates.

3   *Inability of states to control technology under globalisation*

The accelerating, uneven, and uncertain pace of technological convergence and innovation in a new digital era comes with the great potential to solve some of our biggest challenges. However, this new era also raises new questions and unprecedented threats. In many ways, the Fourth Industrial Revolution is very similar to the three revolutions (industrial, electrical, digital) that came before.[6] Its effects cannot be predicted, and in itself, it is neither good nor bad.

Choices matter. The shift to a digital economy, virtual forms of community, and the prospect of artificial intelligence is happening on a global scale and at a very rapid pace, and carries implications for the future of the entire species, not just individuals within it. Who decides which technological choices matter – and how they should be made – is more important than before. Big questions about the future of humanity and the meaning of a good life – what it means to be alive, natural, human, or happy – are fuelling polarised political debates on new and difficult choices about where and what alternative futures of society exist beyond demographic or technological determinism.

If we want to steer towards the best and avoid the worst, it is necessary to revisit deeper beliefs and assumptions about the nature and role of technology in society and to bridge the institutional, social, and policy specialisms – or 'silos' – that emerged in parallel with the maturing of the industrial revolution. Importantly, we will need to develop a wider and more shared and systemic understanding of the co-evolution of socio-technological-ecological

5   OECD.
6   Schwab.

systems, learn how to make our way into a new future for society, and improve the quality of our forward-looking judgement.

Learning across the whole of society is more important today and different from the system of education that supported learning in schools in the industrial era.[7] With global digitalisation and rapid social ageing, the mismatch between skills and opportunities within societies is intensifying. On average, adults in Slovenia score below the OECD average in literacy, numeracy, and problem-solving in technology-rich environments. This calls for a different approach to public education to include continuous lifelong learning across all ages and for the establishment of a completely new skills management system for the whole population.

It will also require new approaches to governance and government. Some countries – such as India, Finland, UAE, Singapore, and Estonia – are actively exploring how digital technologies can enhance the role of government and enable more effective and efficient systems of governance, including more voices and scales of society from local to global. According to a 2017 report by the US National Intelligence Council, 'technology will expand the range of players who can block or circumvent political action'.[8] Cybercrime and the rising costs and frequency of cyberattacks provide clear signals of how uncivil elements of society can move faster than large, bureaucratic, high reliability organisations, such as national governments.

The speed of technological innovation also increases the need for governments to learn faster than – or at least to keep pace with – criminal and terrorist organisations. Governments must become even more agile, adaptive, and capable in anticipating change and prototyping solutions, rather than waiting to react until crisis arrives.

In the spring of 2017, the government of Slovenia conducted the review of its strategic and sustainable development policies. The analysis showed that policy implementation is faster in cases when just one actor, department, or stakeholder is responsible for it. It also showed that the policy outcome or impact was least successful when horizontal cooperation was needed.[9]

---

7   Friedman.
8   National Intelligence Council.
9   In response to the UN Agenda 2030 for sustainable development, Slovenia conducted its Voluntary National Review of the Implementation of Sustainable Development Goals. The report was presented at the 2017 High Level Political Forum at the UNHQ (see Government of Slovenia, 'Slovenia').

4   The paradox of progress

The OECD analysis of measurable, multidimensional well-being indicates that quality of life in Slovenia has improved substantially over the past two decades and relative to other OECD countries. In fact, it has been improving since the Second World War. For example, educational attainment is high: 87 per cent of the adult working-age population in Slovenia has completed at least upper secondary education, which is much higher than the OECD average. The sense of personal security also one of the highest in OECD countries: 85 per cent of Slovenians feel safe walking alone at night, and the homicide rate is among the lowest in the OECD.[10]

However, and despite continued slight improvement in recent years, people in Slovenia feel that their quality of life is worse than in the past. We suggest that this apparent mismatch of perception and reality can be explained by the rising inequalities within Slovenian society, which have occurred under global economic growth.

Even though income inequality (measured by the Gini index) and the average household net adjusted disposable income show Slovenia to be a relatively equal society, there are enormous inequalities – real and perceived – in opportunities for education, jobs, and housing, which have been further exacerbated by recent financial and economic crises that led to higher youth unemployment and an increase in the numbers of working poor.

Increasing the dissatisfaction is the difficulty young people have in affording adequate housing. Meanwhile, the ageing population has put additional pressures on the healthcare system, and the degree to which older people remain healthy as they age remains relatively low (75 per cent of total expected life for men, and 69 per cent for women in 2015), with mental health issues on the rise.

The rise in inequality mirrors patterns observed in other OECD countries and is best explained by the theory of scarcity developed by Robbins *et al.*[11] While economic globalisation has brought many benefits and improved the quality of many people's lives, concentrated wealth and the global communications village means that people everywhere can more easily compare their lives with those of elites and others living in different countries. This sense of relative deprivation, rather than absolute poverty, has strengthened the scarcity mind-set prevalent in Slovenian society – and when people operate with a scarcity mind-set, their decision-making abilities are greatly impaired. So although living standards are still improving, and

10   Adapted from OECD.
11   In addition to Robbins, see Mani *et al.* and Shah *et al.*

high levels of educational attainment enable younger generations to be more self-confident, the widening gap of intergenerational inequality of opportunity is perceived by the young as a state of scarcity, which, in turn, 'imposes a cognitive load that saps attention and reduces effort'.[12]

Despite the quality of life improvements and increasing technological connectivity, some segments of Slovenian society have never been so unequal, trust levels have never been so low, and Slovenians have never felt such a sense of disconnection.

Since 1991, Slovenes have shown in a number of ways that they know how to assume responsibility for shaping their future. They demanded independence, and since then they have successfully integrated into the EU, the European monetary union, NATO, and the OECD. Until the financial crisis of 2007-2008, from which Slovenia has largely recovered, Slovenians enjoyed remarkable economic success. And individual Slovenes all over the world are to be found at the top of global lists of experts, researchers, and inventors.[13] But the challenge of developing a shared and realistic vision in the context of a more critical and less equal society requires an approach that differs from past practices of expert-led, top-down visioning and prescriptive strategies.

Co-creating a realistic whole-of-society vision, not just the government's vision for society

1   A courageous commitment to moving together
Slovenia's previous national development strategy ended in 2013. Since then, successive governments have been subject to public criticism for the lack of a clear strategic vision and direction on the overall national development path. A proliferation and failure to fully implement numerous (over 140) sectorial strategies was associated with this lack of clear direction and ambition, as well as creating, in some cases, conflicting objectives. The implementation deficit remains one of the main elements contributing to the general public's mistrust of the government and the public sector in general.

In the autumn of 2014, recognising the fragile state of Slovenia society in a shifting world, the incoming Slovenian government made a clear commitment to a comprehensive new vision and development strategy that would meet the shifting needs of society and service new international

12   Mani *et al.*, pp. 976-80.
13   See, for example, Cain. Also see Government of Slovenia, 'Slovene Contribution to World Civilisation'.

commitments on sustainable, inclusive, and responsible development and growth. Rather than moving faster and alone through the usual, expert-led review process, the Slovenian government courageously embarked on an ambitious, whole-of-society, participatory foresight initiative. The new approach was not without its ups and downs, but with persistence it resulted in the successful co-creation of a new, nationally shared Vision of Slovenia. This vision, which was first drafted in November 2015, was finally launched in February 2017.[14]

The Vision of Slovenia is defined by five core elements:

1   Learning for and through life;
2   Innovative society;
3   Trust;
4   Quality of life;
5   Identity.

These elements fit together through the narrative that quality of life in Slovenia strongly depends on a high degree of trust and social innovation. This is possible in a society driven by learning for and through life, based on our Slovenian identity with its distinctive language and culture.

Through a sustained effort and a large-scale process of strategic conversations, the draft vision statement galvanised wider commitment – the new shared vision has been translated into action. This was not an easy nor a linear learning process but involved a new, interactive approach to strategising that involved whole-of-government, cross-ministry workshops, engagement with diverse regional communities, and galvanising the support of wider policy shapers and stakeholders. The relevant strategic priorities and goals are embodied in the Slovenian Development Strategy 2030, which was adopted by the Slovenian government in December 2017.[15]

The basic principle was to ensure that the process remained as open and inclusive as possible, and that the future of Slovenia reflected the shared vision of all its inhabitants. A multidisciplinary approach was adopted to ensure effective engagement and to support the drafting – and redrafting – of documents. The approach included a combination of conventional policy tools and strategic foresight methods (for example, disruptors analysis, megatrends, and scenarios). Economic analysis was supplemented with a new well-being framework, and analysis and attention were also directed

---

14   Government of Slovenia, 'The Vision of Slovenia'.
15   Government of Slovenia, 'Slovenian Development Strategy 2030 Is the New National Development Framework'.

to the need to monitor and track policy impacts through a more integrated whole-of-government budgeting cycle and performance measurement framework.

The purpose of the new vision was to provide a shared framework and direction that could be used to exercise a better quality of forward-looking judgement – for example, clarifying new strategic choices and priorities for action. The vision was developed through multiple engagements with a large number of Slovenes from different demographics. In this process, the government recognised that it is not enough for a society to be told where it is headed. The challenge, instead, is to grapple with the futures already emerging beyond the direct control and influence of Slovenes and to co-create meaningful words describing the kind of society Slovenes want to create in the future.

2   *A strategic engagement process with many interacting parts*
The process of drafting long-term development documents began in July 2015. The Organisation for Economic Co-operation and Development (OECD), one of the rare international organisations with the knowledge and tools required to help countries draft complex development policies, including the formulation of a national vision and strategy, also participated in the process of drafting development documents. The creation of a vision and strategy was based on inclusive integration and the collection of ideas.

A series of structured discussions were held in August and September 2015 with representatives of civil society, the government sector, and the business world. During these discussions, we identified different views and notions about Slovenia shared by its citizens. These discussions uncovered areas that Slovenia would have to consider in the future and led to the identification of strengths that encourage us, weaknesses that limit us, and opportunities that inspire us. The participants also discussed the priorities which the vision should address; what the vision should contain; and what kind of role this vision could play in the development of Slovenia. Fundamental values and policies were also discussed.

Since each individual sees the future and imagines it in their own way, before beginning any discussions about the future of Slovenia, a comprehensive assessment of the current situation, future outlook, and cultural and historical elements was made available as a neutral starting point for discussing the elements of a new shared vision.

The initial in-depth discussions were held in November 2015 when an interactive workshop, 'The Future Is Not Far – Slovenia 2050', was attended by about 50 representatives of Slovenian society. The careful selection of participants ensured a voice for different parts of society as well as a balance of gender and age groups. Building on an initial synthesis of interviews with leaders of government, business, and civil society and a supporting analysis, the workshop participants initially became frustrated and expressed their criticism about various aspects of the process: for example, event pace (too quick for that stage), use by some experts of buzzwords, the OECD's growth-based ideology, and key missing vision content elements (e.g., respect and empathy).

3   Creating a safe space for constructive conflict

The facilitators responded by creating a safe space for a more 'courageous conversation' about what was really missing in the debate thus far. What emerged was powerful – the group identified an unexplored space of 'constructive inter-actions' – and went on to fill the 'void' by discussion of issues relating to workshop participation, societal values, mind-set, reconciliation with the past, and culture.

In the discussion of the 'void' it became clear that all parts of Slovenian society are burdened with significant mistrust, within and among various stakeholder groups, which hampers the country's efforts to move ahead with joined forces. After this point, the continued 'shaping up' of the vision elements gained a completely new momentum in the workshop. Participants became fully engaged and self-organised their work in 'seeding the void'. They focused on new solutions spaces, including: a new education system; the meaning and galvanisation of 'active society'; a paradigm shift from economic growth to society-centric well-being; the implications for labour markets of mastering time choices; moral responsibility; and a vibrant entrepreneurial mind-set.

Through the workshop process, the new vision was represented in the form of a systems map rather than a wish list. The new systems map highlighted the fundamental importance of finding systemic intervention points and managing linkages by filling the 'void'. It also revealed a new interaction space enabled by developing new capabilities across the whole of society in active citizenship and mastering time. And it emphasised the importance of managing three reinforcing loops: *trust, well-being*, and *social innovation*.

The workshop resulted in the first draft of the Vision of Slovenia. The process was then continued through discussions within the state administration to identify parallels between the content that was singled out by citizens and the work areas of the various government departments.

4   *Coming down from the vision mountain to cultivate seeds in the*
         rich soil in regional valleys

Following these discussions, the *general public* and *key stakeholders* were
given the opportunity to participate in five regional workshops organised
throughout Slovenia in the first quarter of 2015 and in two additional
workshops in which the representatives of the youth and main stakeholder
groups were able to voice their opinions. They were all given the opportunity
to discuss the elements of the draft Vision for Slovenia and to indicate
possible areas where concrete steps should be made in the coming years for
the vision to materialise. Furthermore, an opinion survey was conducted
in which citizens were asked about their life satisfaction, about the areas
most important for their personal satisfaction, and about what they wished
Slovenia to be like in the future. Through these workshops, and several
smaller events and engagements, including the opinion survey, the elements
of the vision were thoroughly tested and refined.

The whole-of-society Vision of Slovenia, released to the public on 9 February 2017, was taken note of by the government of Slovenia. The Vision
provides a symbol of unity and offers a new platform for flexible cooperation
towards a realistic, yet desirable new future. It also provides a mirror that
can be used to hold successive governments to account. The social and
policy learning enabled in producing and using a realistic, actionable,
whole-of-society vision is neither instantaneous nor quickly exhausted. The
Vision provides an essential normative starting point – both shared and
meaningful – for developing new rational principles about integrated policies
and for prioritising, designing, and implementing new strategic initiatives.

The Vision also provides an answer to the question of why we need to
think about the future now. It offers reassurance that whilst the future
cannot be predicted, societies can still make choices that shape their future.
As such, it is an antidote to the habit of distrust that is still an undiscussable
aspect of Slovenia society.

What followed next, in the move from vision to action, was a rollercoaster
ride that fluctuated between periods of inertia and acceleration with reverse
and fast-forward gearing. A year on, progress in implementing the vision is
both unsteady and exponential.

Realising hope: Prototyping a new model of society

When *The Economist* chose France as country of the year in 2017, it noted
that 'The struggle between the open and closed visions of society may well

be the most important political contest in the world right now'.[16] Trying to transform society in an open way raises many kinds of challenges. Arthur Schopenhauer said, 'All truth passes through three stages. First, it is ridiculed. Second, it is violently opposed. Third, it is accepted as being self-evident'.

After the launch of the Vision of Slovenia, many journalists wondered why on earth someone would use one year of discussions to produce a one-page vision of the future of a country. Further comments by mostly self-proclaimed commentators, Twitter activists, and many group-thinkers showed an enormous lack of understanding of the concept of 'vision'. Many people confused a 'vision' with a 'strategy', looking for an action plan for a specific policy field. It almost seemed as if the vision of a country – whatever that may be – should be defined by a small group of enlightened individuals. But we wanted something quite the opposite – a society-wide discussion on our common future that we would co-create together.

Many also questioned why the government would be focusing on the future when there were so many challenges that needed to be solved here and now. These comments reflected the lack of trust in the government by Slovenian society in general. They also expressed the disappointments many experienced as they faced the consequences of the economic and financial crisis during a time when Slovenia faced a profound lack of political leadership. As we knew from interviews, Slovenians suffered low levels of life satisfaction. This, along with the habit of distrust and negative effects of the financial crisis, resulted in a strong presentism bias.

Sceptical about our true intentions, some commentators even came up with various conspiracy theories, speculation that the project was a marketing tool of political parties or simply a way for some people to make money. And many single-subject experts offered perspectives that relied only on their own narrow lenses.

While negative comments in public focused mostly on various conspiracy theories about the reasoning behind such an undertaking and the cost of the project, very little was debated about the actual content of the Vision. There was, however, one exception to this. The fifth paragraph of the vision starts with the sentence: 'In 2050, Slovenians are a happy people.' This sentence was discussed and commented on time and time again in the weeks after the release of the vision. Mainstream media, trivial and serious journalists, academics, and many others debated questions such as 'Who is responsible for people's happiness?' 'Why would Slovenia be happy only in 2050?' 'Why aren't Slovenians already happy in 2017?' In a way, the vision was already

16 *The Economist.*

sparking a national conversation that went right to the heart of what had been uncovered during the arduous vision-building process.

Sprouting seeds of the vision

As commercial mainstream media and ideologically biased commentators had their own 'party' ridiculing the Vision of Slovenia, we also began to receive a massive amount of smart yet very quiet support. People would call or write private messages, even though they wanted to avoid investing their energy in confronting obnoxious Twitter commentators. Many who contacted us right after the announcement of the vision would quickly add that they consider themselves above the level of discussion that was happening on social media. Others said that it was more important to focus on implementing the vision rather than on wandering around. Significantly, none of the political parties (even from the opposition) voiced disagreement with the vision, and leaders didn't make negative comments about it. It was as if party leaders were simply waiting to see what would happen with this daring articulation of a nation's desired future.

After the initial daily, weekly, and monthly news cycles were over, invitations and proposals for cooperation started to fill our inboxes. And they were diverse – from the national scouts' association to the local office of a multinational company, and from professional associations, networks, schools, and some of the most successful companies in Slovenia. To our satisfaction, they did not want to focus on the project itself, but rather on the content of the Vision of Slovenia, and on how it could drive social change for the betterment of the whole nation. We tried to respond to every invitation and request to present the Vision of Slovenia, and soon we began to notice elements of the vision appearing in various conferences, forums, government documents, political programmes, and private institutions' discussions.

The main benefit of the exercise was the process itself. In the past, in Slovenia, there were not many, if at all, governance processes which would be designed to be participatory from their very beginning and then through every step until the end. The idea to include all stakeholders in the initial phase and at the workshop where the elements of the vision were sketched, proved to be a very courageous one as well as the only right decision. The engagement of stakeholders mobilised an enormous energy and uncovered the main 'blockages' in the society that prevent Slovenia from moving forward and grasping the opportunities it has.

The need to open up the visioning-to-new-strategy process even further became evident as lack of trust among various societal actors was identified as one of the most important bottlenecks. As a consequence, instead of narrowing down the possibilities for public participation, a participatory snowball effect started, leading to several different workshops with various stakeholders across Slovenia. This open and transparent public participation gave the process of the vision preparation much stronger legitimacy and also reduced the possibility of potential 'hijacking' of the process, a fear expressed by the participants of the initial workshop.

It also became evident that we needed to create a platform that would enable us to capitalise on the ideas, energy, and motivation of those who were already involved in the process and to attract newcomers to the task of 'sowing the seeds of the future' in Slovenia. Such a platform could also make up one of the cornerstones of building citizens' trust in the government and its institutions, provided that relevant input via the platform was reflected and acted upon. By the end of 2017, specific actions were not yet visible – but several of the political parties were campaigning for the 2018 elections on programmes that pointed to all five elements of the Vision of Slovenia.

From vision to action

The Vision of Slovenia is an idea consisting of three connected, reinforcing loops that support a dynamic of deepening of trust, progressive enhancement of quality of life, and a widening skill base for social innovation. Pursuing this holistic and systemic vision requires the mobilisation of diverse financial and human resources and a portfolio of policies that span different policy domains. The new social value-creation system represented by the vision cannot be built in one go.

For a nation of gardeners, the image of growing the future rather than engineering solutions provides a powerful metaphor. 'Seeding' and 'transplanting' new ideas better characterises the agile and adaptive approach to national development strategy that will be needed as Slovenians continue to establish and understand the new value creation system. This new approach also implies a shift in policy from control, based on predict-and-decide, to learning through trial-and-error using new, integrated policy frameworks and cross-cutting solutions.

Policymakers will need to pay attention to the potential for new feedback loops created by positive synergies among policies. The discovery of transformation intervention points within the 'system' can be enabled through active monitoring of success and by developing a tolerance for learning with failure within the policy system. This approach to systemic learning will help guide new investments and enable a new set of performance measures relevant to progressing the whole vision to be identified.

In Slovenia, the so-called 'implementation gap' is rather significant when it comes to implementing adopted strategic documents, even when the level of their complexity is relatively low. It soon became clear that the current tools used to monitor budget spending and their impact on policies would not be sufficient to encompass the complex landscape of interventions, actors, and resources needed to pursue the Vision of Slovenia.

In the months that followed the release of the Vision of Slovenia, the second phase began with the drafting and adoption of the Slovenian Development Strategy 2030. This strategy builds on the Vision of Slovenia and the current state of the economy, the society, and the environment; it takes into account global challenges and trends; and it is designed to incorporate the UN Sustainable Development Goals. While the document is intended for policymakers, who are responsible for delivering on it, the outcomes are oriented to Slovenian citizens, who are at the centre of the agenda.

The strategy serves as a roadmap and identifies the key intervention areas where action should be taken to achieve a better quality of life for all. This means that future sector-specific development policies, programmes, and actions will be designed to be in coherence with the strategy. Each of the development goals combines different sector-specific policy priorities under the responsibility of different ministries, which dictates the need for strengthening the effectiveness of inter-ministerial coordination and cooperation in order to successfully deliver the strategy. The policies and actions of each government department will be designed to facilitate and support the achievement of the goals of the Slovenian Development Strategy 2030, which will be monitored and followed up by a set of 30 performance indicators with associated target values assigned to each of the twelve development goals.

The strategy's delivery will be built on medium-term planning. To this end, a Four-Year National Development Programme and a Medium-Term Fiscal Strategy will be prepared. Additionally, a special advisory body – the Government Council for Development – will be set up to oversee the delivery and potential revision of the strategy. The council will include a range of stakeholders representing social partners (management and labour), the private sector, civil society, professional institutions, regional and local communities, and the government.

Vision as a 'provotype'

The Vision of Slovenia is a 'provotype' – a provocative prototype introduced in the early exploratory phases of the design development process to cause a reaction.[17] This is exactly how the Vision of Slovenia has functioned in Slovenian society. It has caused a reaction, it has provoked and engaged many, and most importantly, it has opened up a path of imagining possible futures of a nation and a country.

Today, almost a year after the release of the Vision of Slovenia, it feels almost as if we were in a spaceflight business. Just as the expendable launch rocket separates from its payload, disintegrating during atmospheric re-entry, the technical project of creating and launching the Vision of Slovenia has burned out. The content of the Vision, however, has been safely embedded in public discourse in Slovenian society. Trust, quality of life, learning, innovation, and our identity are being emphasised, debated, and put on centre stage everywhere. This provides a real source of realistic hope and an important signal that the Vision of Slovenia already plays the role it was intended to play: to help society escape quarrelling about the past and succumbing to presentism bias, and instead, to give it wings to fly and co-create its own future. The Vision of Slovenia has become an enabler of realistic hope for Slovenia.

Works Cited

Bednas, Marijana, and Alenka Kajzer. *Strategija dolgožive družbe*. Ljubljana: Urad RS za makroekonomske analize in razvoj, 2017.

Cain, Phil. 'Peter Florjancic: Slovenian Inventor Extraordinaire'. *BBC News*, 13 April 2011. http://www.bbc.com/news/13048155. Accessed 8 Jan. 2018.

The Economist. '*The Economist* Reveals Its Country of the Year – Formidable Nation'. *The Economist*, 19 Dec. 2017. https://www.economist.com/news/leaders/21732811-it-sober-argentina-plucky-south-korea-or-revolutionary-france-economist-reveals-its. Accessed 27 Dec. 2017.

Eurostat. '2013 EU-SILC Module on Wellbeing: Assessment of the Implementation'. EC Directorate for Social Statistics (Eurostat), 2013. http://ec.europa.eu/eurostat/documents/1012329/1012401/2013+Module+assessment.pdf. Accessed 5 Nov. 2017.

Friedman, Tom L. *Thank You for Being Late: An Optimist's Guide to Thriving in the Age of Accelerations*. London: Allen Lane, 2016.

---

17   Weiler and McKenzie.

Government of Slovenia. 'Slovene Contribution to World Civilisation'. 2001. http://
    www.slovenija2001.gov.si/10years/contribution/. Accessed 8 Jan. 2018.

Government of Slovenia. 'Slovenian Development Strategy 2030 Is the New National
    Development Framework'. http://www.vlada.si/en/projects/slovenian_develop-
    ment_strategy_2030/. N.d. Accessed 8 Jan. 2018.

Government of Slovenia. 'Slovenia: Voluntary National Review of the Implementa-
    tion of Sustainable Development Goals: Contribution to Eradicating Poverty
    and Promoting Prosperity in a Changing World'. UN Sustainable Development
    Knowledge Platform, 2017. https://sustainabledevelopment.un.org/memberstates/
    slovenia. Accessed 8 Sep. 2017.

Government of Slovenia. 'The Vision of Slovenia'. https://slovenija2050.si/vision.
    N.d. Accessed 10 Jan. 2018.

National Intelligence Council. 'Global Trends: Paradox of Progress'. US National
    Intelligence Council, Jan. 2017. https://www.dni.gov/files/documents/nic/GT-
    Full-Report.pdf. Accessed 8 Sep. 2017.

OECD. 'How's Life? 2017: Measuring Well-being'. Paris: Organisation for Economic
    Co-operation and Development, 2017. http://dx.doi.org/10.1787/how_life-2017-en.
    Accessed 10 Dec. 2017.

Mani, A., S. Mullainathan, E. Shafir, and J. Zhai. 'Poverty Impedes Cognitive
    Function'. *Science* 351.6149 (2013), 976-80.

Ramirez, R., and A. Wilkinson. *Strategic Reframing: The Oxford Scenario Planning
    Approach*. Oxford: Oxford University Press, 2016.

Robbins, L. *An Essay on the Nature and Significance of Economic Science*. London:
    Macmillan, 1932.

Schwab, K. *The Fourth Industrial Revolution*. Geneva: World Economic Forum, 2015.

Shah, A.K., S. Mullainathan, and E. Shafir. 'Some Consequences of Having Too
    Little'. *Science* 338.6107 (2012), pp. 682-85.

Weiler, A., and D. McKenzie. 'Moving from Prototyping to "Provotyping"'. Medium
    website, 2016. https://medium.com/@thestratosgroup/moving-from-prototyping-
    to-provotyping-cedf42a48e90. Accessed 8 Sept. 2017.

Wike, Richard, Bruce Stokes, Jacob Poushter, and Janell Fetterolf. 'US Image Suffers
    as Publics around World Question Trump's Leadership'. Pew Research Center
    website, 26 June 2017. http://www.pewglobal.org/2017/06/26/u-s-image-suffers-
    as-publics-around-world-question-trumps-leadership/. Accessed 8 Jan. 2018.

About the Authors

Alenka Smerkolj is government minister responsible for strategic planning and development of the Republic of Slovenia. She leads Slovenia's government efforts to define and implement Slovenia's long-term vision and development strategy. Smerkolj has over 25 years of work experience in the field of international business and financial markets.

Timotej Šooš is a career diplomat and currently serves as a National Coordinator for the 2030 Agenda for Sustainable Development and as a Slovenian Development Strategy Lead. Before that he was a Special Adviser to the Minister of Foreign Affairs, Digital Diplomacy and Young Bled Strategic Forum Director at the Ministry of Foreign Affairs of Slovenia. He also worked at the Slovenian Mission to the UN in New York and the OECD in Paris. Recently, he was awarded the Marshall Memorial Fellowship by the German Marshall Fund of the United States.

Five Principles of Realistic Hope

Angela Wilkinson and Betty Sue Flowers

While editing *Realistic Hope*, we were sometimes asked what we had learned. Of course, our authors offer insightful analyses of specific problems and illuminating examples of solutions to these problems. But we knew we were being asked something different: in addition to specific insights, what *general principles of realistic hope* do you see? In short, we saw five interconnected principles: diversity, dialogue, experimentation, systems thinking, and futures framing.

Diversity has to do with the power of *who's* in the room; dialogue describes *how* they interact with each other; experimentation is *what* they do; systems thinking is the *context* in which they approach problems; futures framing relates to the *purpose* of co-creating a future that's different from the past.

1 Diversity

Incremental improvement from a familiar and accepted starting point is relatively fast because it relies on quick and easy consensus. But *transformation* requires moving beyond familiar solutions. Welcoming diversity and embracing difference lead to more options. And optionality is the key to avoiding 'lock in' – a situation in which successful organisations using habitual perspectives and routine practices become overwhelmed by wider changes beyond their control.

Sometimes our digital connectivity leads us to assume we are including diverse perspectives just as a result of the total number of participants involved. But we often choose to connect with people like us – people in our tribe, even if there are many of them, who think the way we do.

Diversity requires us to be alert to different ways of knowing and learning not just from disciplinary experts but also from experiments in other parts of the globe. The richest societies or most developed nations don't always have the answers. Inclusiveness is not a task of melding difference into one undifferentiated whole, but of rendering and working with a number of genuinely different yet logical perspectives on any messy, connected challenge.

Wilkinson, Angela, and Betty Sue Flowers (eds.), *Realistic Hope: Facing Global Challenges*. Amsterdam, Amsterdam University Press, 2018.
DOI: 10.5117/9789462987241_FIVE

2   *Dialogue*

It's striking that so many of the sources of hope in this book arise from what diverse people and groups are doing together. While we need high-level leadership to offer perspectives on the bigger picture, especially in meeting challenges like climate change, new solutions are coming bottom up from a more diverse mix of state and non-state actors, including cities, NGOs, and other groups.

None of the socially complex, connected challenges discussed in this book can be addressed by any one person, community, company, or country working alone. The search for solutions requires collaboration among diverse groups of actors with different interests and needs.

Flexible cooperation is sustained through a process of social learning involving many-to-many, rather than one-to-many, or many-to-one, interactions, which, in turn, are catalysed by the quality of strategic conversation. Effective multi-stakeholder dialogues require a safe space for conflict to enable constructive engagement with uncertainty and disagreement to become a learning asset. A good quality strategic conversation can enable attention not just to what others are saying but also to the common ground from which a new, shared future can emerge. Using conversation as a form of interactive, social learning process that enables messy and connected global challenges to be seen and reseen from a diversity of perspectives enables deeper understanding of the underlying situation. It provides a platform for discovering new insights, generating new options, and catalysing the flexible collaboration necessary to work with seemingly intractable problems.

3   *Experimentation*

If solving large problems is not a 'one-and-done' proposition but an ongoing flexible collaboration, continual learning is absolutely necessary. In this context, uncertainty is a source of hope – a friend, not a foe, because it reminds us of the possibilities to shape the unpredictable future.

But uncertainty in the face of large global problems must not be a barrier to action. As in the case of climate change, there is no time to wait until we know the future for sure. We must engage with uncertainty in order to act. And we must act in the spirit of experimentation, with a willingness to observe results, accept and learn from failures, and change.

Even collaboration itself must be open to experimentation, with new forms of social organisation and the creation of temporary, platform-based groups and robust public-private partnerships.

4   *Systems thinking*

For centuries, our most successful approach to problems has been incremental and mechanistic: take apart the whole, divide it into manageable smaller pieces, and solve in relation to each piece. But this approach does not work in dealing with the complex, multifaceted, and connected challenges we are now facing.

Flexible and holistic thinking is essential. Every challenge explored in *Realistic Hope* is a living system or is embedded within a living system – a complex, adaptive, dynamic whole in which many different parts interact and co-evolve. That means that while we must act with experimental openness and humility, we must also take care to avoid forced and premature consensus. Systems thinking helps us to clarify a more effective place – or places – to start to intervene in the current situation but does not claim full knowledge of the *whole system* or its future. There is no single, right perspective, since all perspectives are developed from a specific situation in the system.

To address any of these messy and connected global challenges, we must work with an awareness of the relation of parts to each other and of parts to the whole. Relationship is a key dynamic, because at the most fundamental level, every living system is interrelated.

Leading holistically within and across living systems is not the same as exercising authority over a hierarchy. At present, there is no such thing as global society or global government. Neither may ever materialise. In this world of messy, connected challenges, we need to avoid prescriptive and detailed top-down blueprints that focus on one part or claim full knowledge of the whole. Instead, we can achieve shared goals through iterative, action-learning processes that remain alert to the evolving big picture and include opportunities to rehearse new options using immersive storytelling.

5   *Futures framing*

We can't think a better future into existence, but without learning *with* the future and reflecting on what a better future might be, we risk overlooking important choices. In an era of real-time big data analytics, we can use virtual reality to enable better-quality futures learning experiences, and we still cannot rely on numbers alone to speak the truth about the future. We can, however, use virtual reality to simulate future learning experiences, and we can use serious gaming to explore the implications of new interactions on the emergent behavior and 'health' of the whole system.

The future is neither empty nor neutral. Whether or not they are made explicit, assumptions about the future are always shaping our understanding of the present. While the future itself cannot be predicted or controlled, it can be imagined, especially through scenarios – sets of two to four stories of alternative, equally plausible futures designed to offer a platform for dialogue and learning. Because scenarios are about what *might* happen rather than what *should* happen, they lead us into the practice of saying not *why* something *can't* happen, but *how* something *could* happen. In itself, futures thinking can nurture realistic hope – but only if we move from this process of disciplined imagination to action.

Scenario building enables deeply held assumptions about the future to be made explicit through the process of storytelling. The world is in the midst of a contested paradigm shift, from a dominant story frame of the economic myth (and its ideal of growth and efficiency) to new conceptions of well-living which are rooted in an emerging ecological myth (and its ideal of the interconnected health of individuals, societies, and the planet). The key actors in shaping these new futures are dreamers, experimenters, builders, and connectors.

Principles of realistic hope

Realistic hope is open to diversity – it doesn't assume that all the answers will come from a single perspective or in one go. It practices deep listening, social learning, and collaborative leadership. It engages with uncertainty as an opportunity and acknowledges failure in order to learn from it. It recognises we are each part of a whole, not the main or only one. And it doesn't assume the future will be like the past.

These principles, which we see emerging more and more, are *sources* of realistic hope. We need to use these principles in a spirit that is positive, humble, and persistent.

Why positive? – because imagining a better future is energising, whereas fear of the future is paralysing. We also need to remain humble in order to learn – and at the same time recognise we must act to create new and different future possibilities. And, as all the examples in this book show, the significant challenges facing us all cannot be solved in one go – we have to be persistent.

Epilogue: From the Eclipse of Utopia to the Restoration of Hope[1]

Jay Ogilvy

The financial crisis of 2007-2008 cast a pall of pessimism over many forecasters' views of the future. As familiar as the mass psychology of economic cycles may be, there seems to be something different going on: Are we witnessing some sort of transition in attitudes towards the future?

The history of utopian thinking has passed through four stages.

Stage one: The cyclical time of tradition

Once upon a time there was the time of no history, the time of the ancients and the traditionalists, in which the basic features of reality were understood to be unchanging and eternal. Yes, there was a distinction between better and worse, and there were aspirations to gain access to the idea of the good. But those aspirations were not so much towards the good yet to come. The love of wisdom, philosophy, was an upward quest towards eternal ideals, towards a kind of great blueprint in the sky that did not change.

Stage two: Modernity and progress

Following the first stage, when time was regarded as 'the moving image of eternity', there came the time of progressive history and evolution. Christian eschatology pointed towards a future salvation. In the 19th century, a sense of progressive history came to define the very spine of modernity. From getting better every day in every way, to DuPont's advertising slogan from 1935 to 1982, 'Better living through chemistry', the march of progress through advances in science gained a firm foothold in Western culture.

During this long second stage in the history of utopia, the quest for the good no longer followed an upward path towards eternal truths. Instead, a more worldly path lay in the direction of a better future. Invention flourished.

[1]   This epilogue has been adapted from a much longer article published. See Ogilvy.

Wilkinson, Angela, and Betty Sue Flowers (eds.), *Realistic Hope: Facing Global Challenges*. Amsterdam, Amsterdam University Press, 2018.
DOI: 10.5117/9789462987241_EPILO

But just as people were inventing better technologies, so they invented better utopias. The very nature of utopian thinking underwent its own form of progress. In the 19th century utopian thinking evolved away from the physical particulars of cities and towards the more ethereal aspects of the human spirit. Utopian thinking passed through a period during which it shifted from architecture, city planning, and drainage systems to psychology, philosophy, and states of mind. During what might be called the *sublimation of utopia*, the terms 'utopia' and 'utopian' came to connote more about minds than about bricks and mortar. Delusions of utopia fed the kind of totalising metanarratives that can send millions to their deaths.

Stage three: Postmodernism and the eclipse of utopia

The march of progress met with reversals in the 20th century: senseless deaths in the muddy trenches of the First World War, the Holocaust, the advent of nuclear weaponry, and humanity's ability to extinguish itself by our own technologically enhanced hands.

Socio-political utopianism in the 20th century also foundered on the shoals of failed revolutions. The improvers of mankind had their chances, and each, one after the other, ended in their own respective versions of a reign of terror. The American experiment succeeded, but it was based not on some grand vision of a social order that would improve the souls of men and women. For all the faith in individual progress that the American Dream allowed, there was very little by way of collective dreaming – for the race, for the species, for the human condition. But here lies the rub: after the sublimation of utopia from physical arrangements to mental aspirations, the eclipse of utopia flushed out the baby of a better humanity with the bathwater of utopian living arrangements.

The fourth stage: A tragicomic future

Now time itself is taking yet another turn. We no longer live in the ahistorical or circular time of the ancients. Nor do we enjoy the optimistic, progressive time of the moderns. Nor, hopefully, the apocalyptic closing time of the postmodernists. Now we live – or could live if we choose to – in the tragicomic time of multiple scenarios. Now the future is flying at us both faster and less predictably than ever. Surprise is its middle name. There's promise to be sure, but risk just as surely. Our research labs are churning out discoveries at an unprecedented rate.[2] The life expectancy of individuals is increasing even as the life expectancy of the species is not.[3]

---

2   Kurzweil, *The Singularity Is Near.*
3   According to Sir Martin Rees.

This fourth form of lived time – the first being the traditional, the second progressive, the third apocalyptic, and the fourth tragic-comic – has about it a certain intensity. The stakes are high. Choices matter.

The scenaric stance

We are now facing a landscape described by the ways that nature *branches* from time to time, and often in ways that a calculus of continuity has difficulty describing.

We need some tools to handle the uncertainty and complexity of an unpredictable future, and scenario planners have begun to provide those tools. But even among scenario planners there is often a tilt towards modern optimism or a tendency towards postmodern pessimism. It is the burden of this epilogue to advocate for a more disciplined balance between both the high road and the low road. Both have their gifts and those gifts are even more generous when held in mind together.

In adopting the scenaric stance by holding multiple futures simultaneously and constantly in view, one achieves a kind of emotional and intellectual maturity that is not available to either the simple optimist or the simple pessimist. Yes, things could turn out badly. But, no, that is not in itself reason for inaction. Yes, things could turn out very well, but, no, that is not in itself reason for foolish bravado. By holding in mind several different futures at once, one is able to proceed deliberately yet flexibly; resolutely yet cautiously.

The scenaric stance isn't simply a tool to solve a problem, like a calculator, or double-entry bookkeeping. It's a frame of mind. Its framework can be measured in three dimensions. First, you find a relentless curiosity, a willingness to learn, an eagerness to experience new frames of reference. The scenaric stance is curious not just for facts, though certainly you want plenty of those. A good scenario shows you a way of looking at the world that you hadn't seen before. This is its outside-in or afferent dimension. Second, you gain a capacity for commitment, a resoluteness towards action, and once having acted, a clarity of follow-through. This is its inside-out, effective, or efferent dimension. Third, you achieve a capacity to balance these in-coming and out-going flows.

The restoration of hope

How, then, does a scenaric stance restore the hope that the utopian tradition held out? And what does that utopian tradition have to tell us about how we might craft more optimistic scenarios together with their dystopian counterparts?

To embrace the digital optimists' computational metaphor for consciousness is to claim that the brain is a biological computer and that our ideas are so much software running on the hardware, or 'wetware', of the brain. Some have objected that the brain, if it is in any sense a computing machine, must be an analogue machine and not a digital machine. But this objection is not that serious. Mathematician and computer scientist John von Neumann proved some time ago the logical equivalence of analogue and digital approaches to computation. No, the real problem has to do with entropy – the Second Law of Thermodynamics that tells us how, due to the thermodynamic hum at the heart of reality, things tend towards disorder, not greater order. Left at room temperature, your cup of coffee gets cooler, not warmer. Put cream in your coffee, and it does not stay on one side of the cup in a neat order, white on one side, black on the other. The initial order of white and black, even if it is a swirl rather than a straight line, quickly gives way to the disorder of the mixed white and black.

In computation, creators of both hardware and software go to great lengths to eliminate entropy. Unlike natural language, which contains all kinds of ambiguities, computer code is unambiguous. A properly built, properly programmed computer will produce the same output every time it receives a given input. Computers don't prevaricate. They are utterly predictable. Not so the human brain. And where entropy and disorder are threats to orderly computation, introducing 'bugs' that need to be removed, for human thinking, entropy is a feature rather than a bug. As with the random variation of genetic mixes produced by sexual reproduction, in human thought, so-called 'noise' can be the source of innovation – a feature, not a bug.

Computers run on unambiguous algorithms – rules specifying that *every* time there's a given input, a specified output will be generated without fail. Computers are thus deterministic. In protecting against the deterministic inevitability of technology's agenda, or the economic means of production, or genetic heritage, we are holding out for free will as opposed to determinism. But this freedom cannot be the negative freedom of indeterminacy or randomness. The kind of freedom that makes for purposeful autonomy depends on the setting of goals and intentions – reasons rather than causes. But this kind of information processing is fundamentally different from the sort of information processing that goes on in a computer.

Intentional action requires semantics and pragmatics. Semantics relate signs to the things they represent. Pragmatics relate purposive intentions to their ends or goals. Computers don't have goals. My laptop doesn't give a damn. It has no desires. Computation is purely syntactical, relating signs to other signs in purely predictable ways, never reaching out to refer to things in the world semantically. *We* make those interpretations once we see the output. Much less does a computer exhibit purposive, pragmatic autonomy by setting its own goals and then achieving them. A computer just shuffles bits and bytes, ones and zeros, never knowing (semantically) what they refer to, much less (pragmatically) why.

Realistic hope – and human will

Whether we witness the promise of digital utopianism, as Ray Kurzweil sees it, or instead we experience 'an atrophy of the very vocabularies of citizenship, moral responsibility, and political community' is not something we can determine by seeing into a future that is inevitable. It's not a matter of trying to catch a glimpse of some predetermined reality, as distinct in its outlines as the far side of the moon prior to our first circumnavigation. Instead the issue is very much one of the choices we make – of human will.

In his important book, *You Are Not a Gadget*, Jaron Lanier makes a strong case for not giving in to computationalism, even as he sees that low road as a distinct possibility. 'Human beings are free', he writes. 'We can commit suicide for the benefit of a Singularity. We can engineer our genes to better support an imaginary hive mind. We can make culture and journalism into second-rate activities and spend centuries remixing the detritus of the 1960s and other eras from before individual creativity went out of fashion. Or we can believe in ourselves. By chance, it might turn out we are real'.[4]

We need a new approach to the future, a new attitude towards time. Neither ahistorical like the ancients, nor optimistic like progressive modernity, nor pessimistic like the postmodernists, this new approach would hold in mind at once both the high road and the low road, acknowledging the possibility of either, and giving full weight to human will in determining which path we actually take. We have it in our power to choose the high road. But it will take more than an epistemology based on computer code. It will take human will.

Works Cited

Kurzweil, Ray. *The Age of Spiritual Machines*. New York: Viking, 1999.
Kurzweil, Ray. *The Singularity Is Near*. New York: Viking, 2005.

4   Lanier, p. 44.

Lanier, Jaron. *You Are Not a Gadget: A Manifesto*. New York: Knopf, 2010.
Ogilvy, Jay. 'Facing the Fold: From the Eclipse of Utopia to the Restoration of Hope'.
    Foresight 13.1 (2011), 7-23.
Rees, Sir Martin. *Our Final Hour*. New York: Basic Books, 2003.

About the Author

Jay Ogilvy co-founded Global Business Network together with Peter Schwartz and Stewart Brand and is the author of nine books, including *Facing the Fold: Essays on Scenario Planning* and *Creating Better Futures*.

Acknowledgements

We owe our deepest gratitude to our authors, who were open to thinking and sharing their expertise within our realistic hope frame, and who responded to our queries, requests, edits, and cuts with unfailing good humor. What a pleasure to work with you!

Our publishers have been extremely helpful: Saskia Gieling, our supportive Senior Editor; Mike Sanders, our eagle-eyed gatekeeper; Jaap Wagenaar, our patient project manager; and Ed Hatton, our very understanding copyeditor, who answered questions even on a Sunday. Thank you!

Throughout the process of creating *Realistic Hope* we had the most extraordinary support from Minister Alenka Smerkolj and diplomat Timotej Šooš of Slovenia. Not only did they write the final chapter, they hosted an authors' workshop at Lake Bled in Slovenia and featured *Realistic Hope* through a panel at the Bled Strategic Forum. Our thanks to Dr. Danica Purg, who provided the workshop space at the IEDC Bled School of Management and Mr. Žiga Vavpotič, Chairman of the board, Outfit7, who provided our workshop lunch, including the famous Bled cake. We owe additional thanks to Tim and Alenka for introducing us to David Fartek, our wonderful cover designer, and to Tim, for helping us with thorny technical software issues. To our Slovenian friends: we can never repay the debt we owe to your support and hospitality, but we hope you know how deeply grateful we feel.

All errors and omissions are ours. This book is itself an example of realistic hope – an achievement enabled by collaborative, voluntary effort. We hope it starts a new social movement.

Name Index

Subject Index

Endorsements for *Realistic Hope*

Building and sustaining hope about the future is important for many reasons, but it's not really about sleeping better at night – it's about moving forward to do the work we need to do. Wilkinson and Flowers leave us off exactly where we need to be: clear-eyed about the challenges we face, from climate change to job creation, to democratic leadership, but also equipped to make a real difference. What is possible when people committed to a better future engage with the principles of diversity, dialogue, experimentation, systems thinking, and futures framing to solve tough problems?
– *Judy Samuelson, VP Aspen Institute and Executive Director, Aspen Business and Society Program*

Pressing global issues, from climate change and rising inequality to resurgent nationalism and the threat of war, require global solutions. But, as we see in this important collection, global solutions are built on a foundation of national actions. From the Sustainable Development Goals and rebuilding trust in vital institutions to the harnessing the benefits of the technological revolution as widely as possible, we need to think globally and act locally. And we must not give up hope.
– *Doug Frantz, Former Deputy Secretary General OECD and Former US Assistant Secretary of State*

The numerous challenges facing humanity seem daunting and hopeless to many. This book brings together stories of hope and offers creative solutions to issues that weigh heavily on our minds. Thanks to the group of distinguished authors for bringing us a book which should be required reading in schools and in public policy fora everywhere to help us prepare for a future that is possible and truly sustainable.
– *Julia Marton-Lefèvre, former Director General of the International Union for Conservation of Nature (IUCN)*

The future is so uncertain these days, that even having a framework to creatively inspect those uncertainties is a huge help, and the function of this text. Chapters like 'The Future of Work' don't make predictions, but do make perspectives so the leading edges can be seen.
– *Kevin Kelly, Senior Maverick for* Wired *Magazine*

It's great to see discussion of how the global challenges are being turned from 'unnecessary despair into realistic hope'. This is particularly important for young researchers and other professionals who are starting out on a career in almost any walk of life.
– *Dr. John Ingram, Food Systems Programme Leader, Environmental Change Institute, University of Oxford*

The public square is not short of sober analyses and qualitative research about many of the multitude of challenges that we are facing on a global scale, but Angela Wilkinson's and Betty Sue Flowers' *Realistic Hope: Facing Global Challenges* offers a different perspective: what if we were to look at problems in relation to climate change, food and water shortages, digitalization, technology, poverty, political leadership and others with a more optimistic mindset? What if we were to develop realistic hope that we can actually tackle some of the biggest global challenges successfully? The authors of the various book chapters invite the reader to approach some of the most serious global challenges not through pessimistic but optimistic eyes. Yes, the eradication of poverty will certainly not happen overnight, but there may be concrete and realistic ways to reduce it. It is true, too, that at first glance the intersect between climate change, water shortages, and the global food system seems almost hopeless, but then again, the authors offer some compelling ideas how this huge challenge could be tackled. This is a highly refreshing approach. I enjoyed reading this thought-provoking and stimulating book, and I am confident that I will read some of the chapters more often!
– *Dr. Stephanie Babst, Head, Strategic Analysis Capability, NATO ESC*

'Transcending Boundaries – the Realistic Hope for Water' offers a penetrating, yet crisp and highly readable analysis of the growing water emergency and its dangers. Although, in history, nations did not go to wars exclusively because of water, the future may not look as merely continuation of the past. Major challenges of water quantity and quality are likely to feed internal tensions and disputes within states, leading to the danger of armed conflicts with serious international repercussions. At the same time, water conflicts are not a matter of historic inevitability. Alejandro Litovsky discusses the problems of water governance today and makes valid proposals of solutions for the future. He offers a number of possible policy models to be followed both nationally and internationally. I am particularly intrigued by his comments on the circular economy and considering the water cycle as an integral part of a circular economy, a general approach that has already given rise to new technological solutions to improve water management

and to redesign business models. This is an important path to preventing water-related tensions and disputes and to securing peace.
– *Danilo Türk, Chairman of the Global High Level Panel on Water and Peace and Former President of the Republic of Slovenia*

Realistic Hope: Facing Global Challenges is an insightful, timely, and much needed tool. The complexities in this interconnected, fast-paced world cannot be denied: multilateralism and the internationally rules-based trading system are under threat; climate change and water scarcity are recognized by science worldwide; innovation and digitalisation pose questions about the future of work; health, food, and nutrition are still denied in a large part of the world. The future is often seen as a threat, generating fear and a sense of hopelessness. While people's concerns are real and must be addressed, leaders should stop nourishing fears and should focus on providing hope and concrete answers instead. This requires a new model of responsible leadership, including investing in and giving voice to the cities. As the authors say, there is no time to wait.
– *Emma Bonino, Senator of the Italian Republic and a former Member, European Parliament*

Realistic Hope is truly a rare book because, from the title onwards, it balances noble aspirations with practical solutions. As a guide to navigating the policy challenges of the 21st century it does not just help us understand where we are going, but how we can get there. We are, as Alenka Smerkolj and Timotej Šooš explain, in a 'TUNA' world – turbulent, uncertain, novel, and ambiguous. But we can restore trust and confidence in our communities by putting people at the heart of policy-making, giving them a greater sense of agency not just to understand the world around them, but to shape it. From the 'provotypes' that challenge traditional thinking to the concept of growing rather than engineering solutions, this is a must-read for policy makers and citizens who believe that wellbeing can be the defining purpose for society and government.
– *Her Excellency, Ohood Bint Khalfan Al Roumi, Minister of State for Happiness and Wellbeing, Director General of the Prime Minister's Office, United Arab Emirates*

We can only face the global challenges when we go in the same direction with realistic hope, and this book is an important step in the right direction.
– *Ambassador Pio Wennubst, Vice Director General, Swiss Agency for Cooperation and Development, Federal Department of Foreign Affairs*

This is a powerful read. The essays in this book pull us out of our increasing focus on the short-term and convincingly make the case that we will only be able to effectively address global challenges and opportunities if we learn to harness the rich potential of systems thinking and scenario thinking. This approach can shift us from a sense of hopelessness and helplessness to a growing sense of optimism about our ability to make a difference.
– *John Hagel, Founder and Co-Chairman, Center for the Edge*

It is time to be very loud about the good in this world. It is time to smoothly transition into a new global eco-civilisation based on cooperation, inclusion, and mutual sustainable engagement. It is time to join the global actions for planet Earth to thrive. It is our duty to show to all segments of our society and to all portfolios that there is an alternative to fear, hunger, poverty, exploitation, chrematism, and war and that we have knowledge, experiences, and manifestation capacity to rethink our economics, to strengthen democracy, and to build trust that nobody will be left behind. *Realistic Hope* is exactly that – a tool and voice to develop strength and to believe again in good.
– *Violeta Bulc, EU Commissioner for Transport*

This is an important book that anyone interested in politics, economics, and business should read with utmost attention. Angela Wilkinson and Betty Sue Flowers have managed to put together a team of renowned experts and practitioners to help us get a deeper understanding of the toughest global and connected challenges of our time. But more than knowledge about these challenges, this book gives Realistic Hope by uncovering new and actionable solutions that are already contributing somewhere to creating a better future for all.
– *Mohamed Mezghani, | Secretary General, International Association of Public Transport (UITP)*

In times of rapid change and complex challenges, both thinkers and policy-makers need to look beyond the crises of today and into the possibilities of tomorrow. This book invites us to do that. Institutions such as the OECD were built on the hope that a better society could rise from the ashes of a difficult past. As our world once again faces difficult times, we must envision realistic and achievable ways to not just withstand the storm and survive, but to take the future into our hands and thrive. This book is a clear expression of the belief that vision, foresight, and multilateralism can deliver on our realistic hopes for a peaceful and prosperous future.
– *Angel Gurría, Secretary-General, OECD*